A Love Of Nature
Writings Of Roy Bamford

A Love Of Nature
Roy Bamford

Illustrations are often contemporary with the articles.
Illustrations by Victor, Alan, Duncan and Roy Bamford.

Thanks are due to the Cambrian News, where many of these articles were first published.

Front cover photograph: Ynyslas, Ceredigion, September 2006.
Rear cover photograph: Yr Rhinogydd, Eryri.

Printed in the United Kingdom by Gwyllt a Rhydd.

Cover design and typesetting by Duncan Bamford at Insight Illustration Ltd.
Typeface: Garamond Premier Pro.

ISBN 978-1-3999-6666-5

Gwyllt a Rhydd
Hengwrt
Newtown Road
Machynlleth
Powys
SY20 8HE

gwyllt a rhydd

Writing for Roy was a way to communicate his love and care for the natural world to a readership outside of conservation, and a useful way of getting some thoughts and worries out of his head. Most of these articles are from Roy's weekly *Country Diary* written for the Cambrian News between 1984 and 2017.

Acknowledgements and gratitude to all Roy's friends, family and colleagues.

Un peth y gallwn fod yn sicr ohono, waeth faint o lanast rydan ni'n ei greu dros y degawdau nesaf, o leiaf y bydd byd natur yn dal i droi. Falle wir y caiff ecosystemau eu trawsnewid, ond yn y tymor hir, dyna beth mae ecosystemau yn eu gwneud, esblygu dros filiynau o flynyddoedd, byth yn aros yr un fath.

Ar hyn o bryd, mae fel petaem yn benderfynol o ecsploitio, manipiwleiddio a siapio popeth er ein budd ein hunain heb fawr o ystyriaeth o'r dyfodol.

Os allwch chi, ewch allan i'r awyr agored a rhyfeddwch at y cymhlethdod sy'n ein hamgylchynu. Mae'n rhad ac am ddim, fel arfer, ac ar gael pob awr o'r dydd a nos.

Yn ddiweddar, fe dreuliais bron i bum awr yn gwneud arolwg adar yn yr ucheldiroedd i'r de o Lanelwedd. Bron imi anghofio am y niwl a'r glaw mân wrth wrando ar yr ehedyddion yn canu gerllaw, a sawl pâr o gylfinirod.

Yn anffodus, ni welais dim un gylfinir yn ystod yr arolwg, ond roedden nhw'n ymwybodol iawn ohonof i. Yr hyn sy'n bwysig ydi eu bod yno.

Rhyw ddiwrnod, wrth ddychwelyd, dwi'n siwr y caf gyfle i'w gweld - gyda'u cywion bach, gobeithio. Dyna'r her nesaf, magu'r genhedlaeth nesaf a gadael rhywbeth iddyn nhw allu gweithio hefo fo. Dim ond gobeithio na fyddwn yn gwneud llanast llwyr o bethau.

Extract from Planetary Kickback (page 199).
Translated by Angharad Penrhyn Jones.

Contents

Origins and Influences

The Place Where I Grew Up

I WAS BORN in Heanor in 1949, the fifth of six children, and did not leave until in my late twenties. Three children were born before the 2nd World War and three afterwards. For a short time, five brothers and a next to eldest sister shared a brick terrace house with our parents in John Street but it was not long before the three eldest were married and living elsewhere. For a terraced house it was quite spacious with three large bedrooms and one smaller, a large pantry (we never had a fridge), large front-room (hardly used) and its own private entry, ie the way through to the back door. However I do remember, at least for a short while, we three youngest boys sharing a bed. Of course we had an outside loo but it wasn't quite at the bottom of the garden. There we had a coal shed on the right, what we called the bike shed on the left and a small tool shed in the middle. All built of brick, slate roofed and with much of the outer wall covered in a very prolific pink rose.

The back garden was inevitably small but well kept and we even had a paved area where we played cricket, football, marbles and other games. A small lean-to beside the loo wall sometimes served as an aviary for various finches and the occasional young magpie that one or other of my elder brothers might rear, Kes-like.

My father also kept an allotment, about half a mile wheelbarrow ride away. When we were small it was great to be wheeled up in the barrow though as we got older we might sometimes balk at the labour and time spent on the allotment.

Heanor was a mining and textiles town with a number of pits in the neighbourhood providing much of the male employment. I. & R. Morleys clothing and Fletchers Lace factory were other major employers. Morleys being a tall and sprawling, red brick factory straddling the main road on the hill up the north side of town towards Red Lion Square and, what was then, a busy market place.

Mining in the area ceased in 1970 with the closing of Ormonde Colliery at nearby

Loscoe. Morleys and Fletchers closed in the 90s. Most of the surrounding countryside has at some time been opencast (outcropped) for near-surface coal, the first site having been worked in the Shipley area during the early 1940s. Even now (when Roy wrote this) there are working opencast sites and others to be potentially reworked or on the drawing board. The Morleys site now boasts a 24 hour Tesco and filling station with numerous other retail outlets nearby across the main road to Ripley. A lot of the corner shops have disappeared and the town and market seems to have been in a steady state of decline since the demise of the coal and textile industries. There appears to have been little long-term stability in the jobs market since, although the Heanor Gate Industrial Estate has slowly expanded and there are proposals for more manufacturing units on the old site of the American Adventure theme park. Shipley Country Park has been developed from a large opencast site that transformed a huge area previously under several collieries and their associated spoil tips and other infrastructure. There can be no doubt that coal mining and clothing/materials were the two industries that for long periods were main threads that held together the fabric of this and many other communities in the immediate area.

The mountainous spoil heaps that threatened to surround Heanor are now long gone, as are the larger factory units such as I & R Morley's.

John Street has changed remarkably little, though all the houses have now been spruced up and where once it was an important playground, now it is part of a one-way system with cars parked all the way down both sides. Nowhere for the kids to play, even if they were interested or their parents would allow them out. We were often out until well into the night, playing under the streetlights. The single light halfway along the school lane, connecting the top end of John St/Holmes St to the top of Milward Road, barely took away the gloom and if alone I always found it a nervy section to be negotiated quickly in the dark.

It seems incredible that double-decker buses once used these streets to carry children to and from Smalley and Horsley Woodhouse to Howitt Secondary Modern school. The allotments by the school and our own allotment are long gone and one of my saddest memories is of our magnificent pear tree, bulldozed over to make way for more housing.

We loved climbing this tree and some years picked barrowloads of pears, even from the very top where there was a panoramic view. The pears were carefully lowered in a strong, black canvas bag attached to a rope. Some were carefully stored (wrapped in newspaper) in drawers at home, along with various types of apple. But most were eaten while quite fresh or if there was a glut they would very often be distributed amongst various neighbours.

Colliers, pitmen and factory workers and everyone else that contributed to this varied community, all seemed to get on without too much hassle though there was sometimes a complaint about football on the street and potential damage to a wall or window somewhere. Now it seems to be much more hustle and bustle and there is (if anything) a disconnect between individuals and families on the streets. They do not need to meet so much, are less reliant upon one another and therefore less community orientated. Whereas in the past someone might call round for a chat or even to watch the telly, the entry doors are, more often than not, now kept locked!

March 1994
Coiled Spring

SPRING is just around the corner. Snowdrops have been up for a long time and soon the daffodils will be opening. However it is the birdsong that tells me (over and over again) that we are well on the way. Since late December there only has to be a glimmer of sun and the birds are at it!

The mistle thrush has a song that carries far and his delightful calls have been reverberating about the valley for weeks now. An early nesting species, they will be hoping for a mild spring to help them raise two or even three broods in the season. Also echoing across the valley each night are the haunting calls of the tawny owls. Calls that emanate from the darkest depths of a spruce forest. In the daytime, buzzards and ravens spectacularly display in the thermals overhead and spring again is undoubtedly in the air.

We can see in the hedgerow that the sap is rising and things are beginning to awaken, female flowers have already opened whilst elder and honeysuckle are well into leaf.

Blackthorn remains stubbornly dormant but when the buds do burst it will be the flowers not the leaves which will bring a brilliant splash of white to what is an otherwise bleak landscape. Already, the earliest hawthorns are breaking into leaf. An important 'early bite' to a population starved of fresh greenery in the past, hence its alternative name of Bread and Cheese Tree, not that the leaves taste anything like bread and cheese. Also known as quickthorn, hagthorn, May tree or moonflower, it is often locally referred to as whitethorn. Presumably to differentiate from its hedgerow companion the blackthorn. Two trees that could hardly differ more in their strategies.

Both are regularly used by the chaffinch and other species, birds which find their near-impregnable, thorny depths ideal for nest sites. I look forward to the first halting notes of the chaffinches' complicated song. They seem to have to re-learn it each Spring but at those first faltering attempts, I will know Spring is sprung!

A spell of dry weather should bring Spring on at last and a trickle of migrants soon to be a flood, weather permitting.

I saw my first sand martins over the Afon Teifi at the Welsh Wildlife Centre early in March but the weather deteriorated to such an extent thereafter that it was approaching mid-April before I saw any more, a small group battling against a fresh N. Westerly over Cors Fochno near Borth.

Chiff chaffs have been around even longer and they have now been joined by the much more musically accomplished willow warbler and blackcaps. Along the coast wheatears have been passing through and I am sure the waders are on the move too. Dunlin, sanderling, godwit and whimbrel will all be conspicuous on the Dyfi, Dysynni and Mawddach estuaries as they stop over to feed and rest on their way north to their breeding grounds in Scandinavia, Iceland, Russia and Greenland.

Quite amazing really, some of the warblers weigh less or little more than half an ounce, yet they travel such immense distances. And what a feat of navigational skill to return (as many do) to their natal area over a period of years! Contending as they must with the vagaries of the weather and all manner of other hazards, from shooting and trapping to other avian predators, is it any wonder that upon arrival they almost immediately burst into song? Perhaps singing with relief at having made it back again, but more importantly, singing to establish a territory and attract a mate to rear a family.

It's all go from now on in a bird's life until the young leave the nest. Hectic in the extreme no doubt, but in so many ways infinitely preferable to our own hectic, human way of life.

Which would you prefer, dropping into the Dyfi or Mawddach service area for a couple of days rest and refreshment or a quick snack in Julie's Pantry on the M6? Given that I could acquire a whimbrel's taste in food, I would much prefer the lugworms to the reconstructed chipsticks and cotton wool buns of the motorway. Much more healthy and quite frankly I do envy the independence and freedom that our long-distance migrants enjoy.

CHAFFINCH

May 1995
Plant Hunting with Bill

I HAVE just read Willam Condry's latest book; 'Wildlife, My Life'. It charts a full life and details the many influences that led to an abiding interest in natural history in all its aspects. Famous names associated with Welsh botany and conservation (including Mary Richards, Price Evans, Col Morrey Salmon) regularly cross paths with the Condrys as they flit about mid and north Wales. Many are deliberately sought out as like-minded people and not infrequently quite momentous achievements result. For example, the establishment of Ynys Enlli (Bardsey Island) trust and bird observatory and Ynys Hir, RSPB reserve. Bill Condry was instrumental in both developments.

More often than not it was plants and plant hunting that held sway. I can vouch for the fact that even a non-botanist can be infected by this bug.

Scrambling about the rocks and gullies of Yr Wyddfa, Aran Fawddwy, Cadair or some remote part of north Wales is not the arduous task you might imagine. It is always interesting (especially with Bill Condry) and can be exciting if not downright dangerous! Sometimes it is the thrill of finding a rare or long-lost plant but often it is the excitement of climbing out of the predicament you have absentmindedly got into. Quite likely, the only practical exit is out over the top!

A Country Diarist of note (The Guardian) Bill Condry has a long memory ably assisted by his daily jottings. The account of a night on Ynys Enlli as shearwaters come home to their nesting burrows is typical. Detailed reminiscences of plant hunting, alone and with famous botanists will take the reader over most of Wales, to Ireland, Scotland and briefly as far as the African bush and the USA. But it is Wales and its wildlife that draws this book and the Condrys' life together. Wonder at the variety and the tenacity of nature comes through all the time. Speculation as to why a plant should thrive here but not there! The book is also a natural history 'Who's Who' of Welsh conservation, from the 20's onwards and refers often to the inspirational pioneers, travellers and botanists of previous centuries.

A threatened species, the true naturalist is not to be come across often nowadays. If you are curious as to how one is made, then this is your reference book. William Condry is notable in that his abiding interests have found their way into eminently readable print.

Readers familiar with his other work will recollect the easy flowing style of a true lover of nature in every paragraph. As usual, an excellent read and illustrated with his own photographs, Wildlife, My Life'. by W M Condry is published by Gomer Press of Llandysul and is available now from all good bookshops.

April 1994
A Bird's Eye View of Football

FOOTBALL and ornithology have been major, lifelong pastimes with me and here in Wales (over the past 16 years) it is surprising how often I have been able to combine the two. A bright Saturday afternoon at Penrhyncoch, Bryncrug or Machynlleth and almost inevitably a buzzard would put in an appearance, quite often a red kite too! Distracting perhaps whilst playing, but not quite such a problem for me now as a spectator.

Park Avenue, Aberystwyth is on the evening flight-line of large flocks of starlings heading for the roost beneath the pier. A fine sight on a cold winter's afternoon but not as fine as the mute swan which rose gracefully and powerfully from the Afon Rheidol (behind the stand) during a recent match.

On this occasion it hardly compensated for a poor Aber performance against a moderate Inter Cardiff outfit but they have since put this result to rest with a much better performance in the cup.

Newtown, and a cold N Easterly brought rain and sleet to an already sodden playing field. Watching younger football players is more the norm now and this particular day was memorable for the weather. The kids were freezing, I was freezing but in a brief respite a merlin caught my eye as it dashed across a leaden sky in pursuit of a quick meal.

Blaendolau, Aberystwyth just before Christmas and we had some beautiful, crisp, clear days - remember them? And red kites low over the playing fields almost bringing the games to a halt! Then there is the Plas Crug sparrow hawk and the ducks in the ditch, although we all hope the ditch will be piped and in-filled soon for health and safety reasons.

Further afield, I still try to see a game or two at the City Ground, home of Nottingham Forest. Here cormorants flying high over the River Trent are a common sight as they commute to and from the extensive gravel pits just outside the city limits. Back here in

Wales the games may not be quite so big but the views are certainly much more panoramic and none more so than at Cae Glas, Machynlleth. Huge beeches in the parkland with a backdrop of wooded slopes can hardly be beaten for a setting and although the football may not quite reach the standards set at the City Ground, Mach play with flair, serving up good quality, entertaining football.

On my most recent visit to Cae Glas we watched as buzzards and a red kite (harassed by a pair of crows) put in a brief appearance. Machynlleth won (on a glue-pot of a pitch) quite convincingly with incidents aplenty, the views were marvellous and the birds had appeared despite a steady downpour, but when, oh when is the rain ever going to cease?

June 1992
Rio Summit

HAS IT REALLY been a bit of a scorcher this last May? Is it just my imagination or thoughts of a hole in the ozone layer? A 20% reduction in the ozone layer over the Northern hemisphere, and its possible effects, is certainly something for the Rio Summit* and all of us in the 'Rich North' to ponder.

Here I am afraid I fail to come up with figures on ozone or any other layer in the atmosphere for that matter. What I can lay hands on, however, is basic weather data for May in North Ceredigion over the last nine years. For days without rain, May 1990 comes out just ahead with 25 remaining dry. In each of the years 1984, 1989 and 1991 we had 24 dry days in May. This May had 15 dry days, including 10 consecutively.

The thunderstorm late in the afternoon of the 28th brought to a dramatic end the mini-drought, with almost an inch of rain falling in not much more than an hour. Unfortunately most of this disappeared rapidly as surface run-off, straight into watercourses, the ground was so hard and impervious. However a series of overcast, showery days since has certainly softened the ground and brought soils back into condition. The wettest May recently was in 1988 when a total of 90.3 millimetres fell over the month. May 1992 comes a surprisingly close second with 81.9mm thanks mainly to 17.7 mm on the first, 19.9mm on the 12th and that thunderstorm on the 28th.

May temperatures have been high and it does seem to me that there is more power in the sun. It has been glaringly bright on occasions and I do wonder and worry that this is a result of something amiss up there!

On 23 May the monthly maximum of 26.2°C was recorded, however we have had one hotter day in May over the past nine years, the 5th in 1990 when the temperature soared to 28.5°C. This was one of twelve days in 1990 when the temperature climbed above 20°C but 1992 actually comes out on top with 15 days at 20°C and above. So we can say it has been hot and wet, hence the humidity!

Thanks to plentiful rain in April and during the first half of May the water table hereabouts seems more or less normal. But it was brought home to me how things may be changing, even locally, on a recent visit to Ynys Las National Nature Reserve. I was involved in leading one of the many 'Festival of the Countryside' walks from the visitor centre. Picking a bank holiday weekend I expected a few people to be about and interested in birdwatching. I also expected the weather to be awful, it usually is on bank holidays, isn't it? The wind was blowing strongly from the north-east but a hazy (glaring) sun kept the temperature up and the sands were heaving with holidaymakers. Not much chance of seeing a great deal of birdlife, at least with feathers that is! However in the dune slacks where the water table is usually close to the surface, we did have excellent views of a whimbrel striding the short turf and probing successfully for worms and invertebrate larvae.

I do not get down to Ynys Las half as often as I would like but to my recollection this last winter is the first to go by without my seeing the slacks flooded. This will have an effect on the flora, and the orchid spikes in the main slack certainly seem few and far between, the dykes are dry and so too is the small pond.

However in the slack areas where the water is, as yet, not far beneath the surface the sphagnum moss in the damp lowest points and the rather odd adders tongue fern seem to be thriving. The whimbrel too, seemed to be getting along fine. It will be interesting to see how things develop as we go deeper into the summer.

*The 'Earth Summit' to address urgent problems of environmental protection and socio-economic development, concluded that the concept of 'sustainable development' was an attainable goal for all the people of the world, regardless of whether they were at the local, national, regional or international level. Most of the documents that came out of it were not binding and as such did not achieve their objectives.

November 2005
A Bit of a Pessimist

AS WE SLIP into the longer nights and darker winter period I feel I ought to at least try and brighten up the prospect somewhat, disperse a little of the gloom that will inevitably settle given half a chance.

Difficult for me, as I am all for hibernation and a bit of a pessimist at the best of times and we have floods and other disasters occurring with frightening regularity all over the world and flooding already in several parts of Wales. Hopefully the Met Office with its premature warnings of the possibility of a particularly cold winter are proved wrong.

The trees are turning and it looks like being quite a spectacular autumn for colours, and they can certainly brighten even the dullest day. One thing about north Ceredigion, there is such a wide variety of trees and they all add so much to the landscape with such subtle colour variations.

The Allt y Crib plantation, alongside the Afon Leri near Talybont, is always attractive with its blocks of red oak and beech often outstanding. Further south you have Coed Craigyrogof and Coed Maenarthur flanking the Afon Ystwyth and of course, the Hafod estate woods just a little further upriver. Hafod is well worth a visit at any time of year, if only to see the cascade and spectacular waterfall at the 'Robbers Cave' Ogof y Lladron. But really, we are exceptionally lucky and never have to travel far to be impressed by the landscape and autumn colours in Ceredigion.

Despite some periods of heavy and prolonged rain we have had a few butterflies enjoying the unseasonally warm southerly winds we have been getting occasionally. Red admirals, small tortoiseshell and even a very late speckled wood have put in an appearance in the garden, never in any great numbers and I suppose 2005 must still go down as one of the worst years for butterflies, ever. Still it was nice to see some of these late fliers in mid-October and I look forward to seeing more next spring.

And some good news of the nightjars that I mentioned way back in December 2004. I am pleased to say that the statisticians have had a look at the figures and the preliminary results indicate a significant increase in the UK population since the last major survey of 1992. Up from 3,400 territories in '92 to something like 4,020 territories in 2004, and in Wales up by 24% to something like 230 territories by my calculation. Since this mammoth survey and an upsurge in interest amongst us ornithologists, a few more sites have been found in Ceredigion during 2005. Virtually all the larger forestry blocks now have suitable habitat for nightjars but it remains to be seen if this increase can be sustained and how much of that suitable habitat is ultimately occupied.

Another small but bright note has been the sighting of water vole in the ditch alongside Plascrug Avenue, almost in the heart of Aberystwyth. On being told of recent sightings I wandered along there one evening quite recently and saw a water vole myself. I have tried a few times since but so far I have not been so lucky again. The neatly strimmed, grassy bank and verges beside the ditch look to be quite poor habitat for water voles. They are vegetarians and usually prefer quite rank watersides often dominated by tall, uncut grasses and rushes. Dense vegetation in which they can make extensive pathways and under which they can feed in relative safety. What they are feeding on here I would be interested to know. However at least one is surviving so perhaps there is hope for them in Aberystwyth yet?

Interestingly, while looking for the water voles I have seen a few brown rats, (horror of horrors) sometimes feeding on the few blackberries in the hedge along the north bank of the ditch, at other times swimming the ditch. Quite tame, or at least quite bold, these urban rats are interesting to observe, but not nearly so nice as the harmless water vole which is under severe pressure and a cause of great concern. In the UK as a whole, it is estimated that there has been something like an 85% decline in the water vole population over the past ten to fifteen years.

Quite serious issues also surround Avian Flu and an expected or imminent pandemic creeping in from the east and north. Migratory birds are thought to be likely carriers. However the wintering flock of white-fronted geese at Ynys Hir are of the Greenland race and they will have come in from the north-west. The first of these apparently turned up right on schedule on the 12th of October. Occasionally we do get a flock of Russian white-fronts but as far as I am aware it has been a few years since the last visit.

Anyway I suspect the main route of transmission, if it does mutate and jump species, will be via we humans flying about the place in aeroplanes, but that is beside the point. Eat healthily, get plenty of fruit and veg down you, take some exercise in the open air and get some regular sunlight into the system if you can, and do keep warm.

Oh, and do let the authorities know if you come across any unexplained, mass bird deaths!

April 2006
Keeping Notes

IT IS that time of year, the time when I delve into my last year's pocket diary to extract snippets of information which may or may not be of use in the County Bird Report.

My notes tend to be somewhat on the skimpy side, but throughout 12 months it usually amounts to a fair few records, and without my diary I would be lost!

For some species, you can never be absolutely certain what might constitute a notable record for any particular year. It could be an early arrival or a late departure date for some quite common migrant.

Overwintering warblers such as blackcap and chiffchaff, or perhaps a common sandpiper on the estuary, are certainly worthy of note. Flocks of thrushes, finches, wildfowl and waders are always likely to be of interest to the Bird Recorder, and depending upon numbers will likely get a mention in the report. Some species such as dipper, kingfisher and almost any breeding waterfowl (bar mallard, Canada goose and moorhen) will also usually merit some mention, and be of interest to local and visiting ornithologists alike.

My diary reminds me that excursions onto Cors Caron in October brought to light a bittern on one occasion, a species that definitely merits a special note. This particular bird was flushed from dense vegetation beside the Afon Teifi and being such a secretive species and on such a large site, who is to say it is not still around?

Despite one or two cold snaps there has not been a real freeze-up nor any significant snow for any length of time. This is the weather that is known to be problematic to the bittern, and to several other species that are water-edge specialists.

Bitterns are almost always associated with extensive and dense, phragmites reedbeds. That is common or Norfolk reed, the stuff that is typically used for thatching. Such reedbeds are scarce in Wales, but moves are afoot to see them increase in number and in size.

At Ynys Hir the area of reedbed has increased considerably over recent years, and much work has gone into reedbeds on Ynys Mon, on the Teifi Marshes reserve and down in south Wales on the Gwent levels. This benefits a wide range of species, but one of the main aims is to re-establish the bittern as a breeding species in Wales.

It is impossible to say where this Cors Caron bird came from. It could quite possibly have been an east-coast, British bird, but equally it could have come down from the north or over from the Continent.

Interestingly I also found noted in my diary some dates for the last butterflies I saw flying. There were several red admirals on 16 November! Has anyone any later record? Equally noteworthy was the record I made of the first frog spawn I found. In 2005 that was on 29 January.

We certainly have had more easterly and northerly winds than normal since January 2005. My diary also reminds me that it was particularly cold through much of April and even in to May last year.

November 2015
Failed Dropout

BEFORE I FLED to NW Scotland to embark on a new career as a 'Failed Dropout' I worked in the aero engine industry for a well known firm based in the East Midlands. Inspection was just one of several jobs I had as I worked my way through a long apprenticeship, and it was amazing to experience the care, craft and ingenuity that went into the making and putting together of those complex engine parts.

An engine cowling could have literally thousands of rivets and spotwelds and numerous nuts and bolts holding it together, all inspected to the nth degree. If one or a few failed it probably was not a disaster as within aero engine manufacture there is a high, (built-in) safety factor. If a whole load should fail then we could be into a different ball-game with who knows what consequences. As you can imagine, on the few times I have flown (bar falling off a ladder- not to be recommended) I have taken more than a passing interest in the wing and engine cowlings visible from a window seat!

Sometimes I consider the similarities of aircraft manufacture to our status on this planet and our apparent disregard for its well being. We have plenty of information and know what we are doing but I do get the impression that we may be losing more than a few of those rivets and those nuts and bolts that hold the structure together. There can be no doubt that the environment is being put under stress, resources are becoming scarcer, energy poverty more commonplace, climate change is a huge issue, conflicts, pests and diseases are spread at a rapid rate and the human race, on the whole and despite all the modern distractions, is apparently not a happy bunch. In the developed world most of us could manage on less but there seems to be no serious appetite for that. Contraction and Convergence was the title of a talk I went to (at least 25 years ago) in the Old College in Aberystwyth. This postulated simply that one way out of our predicament was for the developed nations to contract (ie reduce consumption) in order that Third World Nations might converge, ie approach our position.

Well, it hasn't happened, it's a fact that the rich get richer and the gap between rich and poor has increased over those 25 years and more, both within the UK and globally.

Competition driven growth and exploitation are the signposts most often followed and it seems unlikely to me that anything major will happen through political or policy decisions. As another analogy, maybe we are on another Titanic, heading full steam ahead through the fog for that iceberg?

We only have this one planet and so far we have not found anything else like it, anywhere near enough to be colonised, and (despite my love of Science Fiction) we are never likely to. It is a great place to live if you have food, shelter, peace and employment and a whole lot of other stuff. It would be the greatest shame on us all to absolutely mess this up, but we seem to be well on the way to doing it.

Recently I was down at Ynys Las witnessing a feeding frenzy of gannets as there was an abundance of sprats and mackerel close inshore, auks and red throated divers were about too and a flock of golden plover overhead in a cloudless sky. Later that same day, (from the Glandyfi layby) there were at least fifteen little egret visible, a peregrine on the saltings, thirty pintail on the river with lots of teal and wigeon, and even more interesting there was a red breasted goose grazing on the saltings with a party of barnacle geese. This is a really stunning bird that may be an escape/ feral bird, but equally, may well have been blown off course on its migration down from Arctic Siberia where they breed, pushed over to west Wales courtesy of some strong easterly winds. They normally winter around the Bulgaria, Romania and west Turkish, Black Sea coast and it will be intriguing to see if this stray sticks around on the estuary over the winter.

Here in west Wales I have always felt relaxed and appreciative of the landscape, the people and the environment. It is a stunning area and deserving of the greatest care. A great place for a 'failed dropout' to hang out and do things.

October 2008
Learning From The Master
A letter to the Editor of The Guardian (Northern Edition)

I RECENTLY attended the William Condry Country Writers evening at the Tabernacle, Machynlleth. I thought it was a very successful event and different. It doesn't seem like 10 years since Bill died but then time travels faster as we get older it seems.

Many coincidences and connections between ourselves and the Condry's have occurred over the past 30 odd years. On first working in Wales (1977) I was assistant to Bill at Ynys Hir, RSPB reserve and asked to return the following season. This was allowed by the RSPB hierarchy, much to our surprise. During those two seasons and over many years thereafter he pointed me in the direction of many special places and many special plants in Snowdonia. Apart from some company he was grateful (I think) for my better map reading skills, as some of his grid references for plant locations were way out.

In subsequent years he handed over honorary wardenship of a local nature reserve to me, and even his bees and bee keeping equipment. I always thought he was less than frank about the time that bee keeping to any good standard might require. He also handed over the red kite monitoring in this area. Obviously he was clearing his desk and responsibilities to concentrate on his writing and the associated research.

When Bill and Penny came to live in this Parish they lived at Felin y Cwm and we have now been here for very near 30 years. Many of the plants/trees that my wife now tends were planted by Penny, with Bill's labour I suspect. Bill was a teacher at the crammer (Lapley Grange) in the village. I worked there for 12 years when it was known as The Plas and was a well-established outdoor pursuits/rural studies centre for children, mainly from the East End of London.

Another coincidence is the writing, it must be something to do with the place, the pace of life and some of the people that settle here I suppose. For more years than I care to remember (over 10) I did a regular piece for the Cambrian News and when the urge takes me I might submit the occasional longer piece with illustrations even now.

Bill did much the same but I have never looked at any of his Cambrian News pieces, I must make a point of seeking some out. Bill was apparently dropped for a religious article and I was eventually dropped as a regular, for a children's piece. We had a laugh about that coincidence not long before his illness.

I now still get out and about on various contracts for Environment Agency Wales, Forestry Commission Wales, Countryside Council for Wales and the RSPB amongst others. Lots of survey work gives time to wonder at what is going off in the environmental field and occasionally it helps if I can offload it onto paper.

My wife and myself have very fond memories of Bill- thanks for rekindling them on a very enjoyable evening and thank Jim Perrin especially for that clip of Ogof Owain Glyndwr. Moel Hebog was one of Bill's favourite places.

Fieldwork

October 2015
Map and Compass

OCCASIONALLY in my travels about Wales, I am left wondering, where exactly am I? Sometimes it can become more philosophical and I begin to wonder, what am I doing here, or even, what have I been doing for the past several decades? But getting back to practicalities usually resolves into how to get out of the situation safely and with the least amount of effort - not dwelling on the past 20 years (or more!).

Ever been lost on a wet, Welsh mountainside? It can certainly concentrate the mind, but with a good map (preferably a 1 :25,000 OS) and a compass it is usually possible to sort yourself out. Having said that, in some of the more featureless areas it is a great lifter of spirits to find that sheep fold by the wall, that stream confluence, cairn, fence line or ruin. All manner of features take on great significance if they are marked on the map and the weather has closed in, and you just happen to be temporarily lost.

A GPS (Global Positioning System) is another invaluable piece of kit if you need to ID exactly where you might be, (to within a few metres anyway). This satellite-aided technology is invaluable where there are no streams, fence lines or ruins as guides, but you will still have to consult the map and possibly use a compass to sort out the best way forward. In the past, I have also found GPS useful to accurately locate curlew nests and other points of interest on the map, locations that in some featureless landscapes would otherwise be much more of a guess-timate. Recently, I was in a part of upland Wales where looking at the map and reading the contours and comparing it to the terrain was simply not enough. There simply were no features in sight from which I could triangulate a position and the GPS came to the rescue on numerous occasions.

On this featureless hillside and valley bog, there were no curlew, but I did find stags-head clubmoss to be quite common and some patches of sphagnum with butterwort (an insectivorous plant) in flower were a bit of a bonus. On other visits, there had been a hatch of small pearl-bordered fritillary butterflies and I even caught a very brief glimpse of a male hen harrier. On the very last visit, a curlew heard passing high overhead was likely a failed breeder from elsewhere, en-route to the coast. However, the females of this species often leave the later stages of looking after any young to the male, so it may have been a female knocking-off early.

I tend to use a map, compass and GPS in combination when sorting out transects in these most featureless of landscapes. All three are indispensable in some situations and, depending on the weather, with a bit of luck the job gets done. There are probably moves towards getting everything on-screen/at the push of a button, but when push comes to shove you have to rely on the map and a compass and sometimes on instinct.

I would caution against instinct overriding what a map and compass might be telling you though. Always recheck your bearings from a known location (GPS if you need to and if you have one) and trust the compass. It is the safest thing to do and can save a lot of wasted effort.

Trigonometry points are great vantage points, as they needed to be when the mapping first took place. You can be fairly safe in assuming these are located accurately on the map but always beware that the occasional wall may be marked as a stream and vice-versa (I have found a few) and that forest boundaries and standing timber can change landscapes over time. I am fairly certain that the curlew didn't have a map or a compass(except in its head), or a GPS for that matter. But relying on some instinct or knowledge, it would hopefully get to the coast and find its preferred place until next breeding season.

They are relatively long-lived birds and will return to favoured wintering areas as they are known to return faithfully to preferred breeding areas. Sadly, ever fewer are breeding in Wales and it is surely going to take some effort and a lot of time before we might begin to see any recovery.

March 2006
Squacco Heron

Tuesday the 3rd of June started as just another day of fieldwork. Having spent several seasons working on lapwings for the RSPB it was nothing out of the ordinary to be searching for lapwing chicks and missing radio signals, particularly at this stage of the season.

Aber Leri, near Borth we knew to have fox problems and we had already found several radio tags at nearby fox earths. Having driven the Landrover on to the site it remained so quiet that co-research worker, Joe Lee and myself decided there was no alternative but to explore some of the area on foot. Still no sign of any radio signals but as we walked alongside one of the main ditches towards the hide we had a surprise.

I must admit that my very first thought was, what is a barn owl doing out here at this time of day? A rear view, rather buoyant flight and the general colouration could have applied to barn owl. These thoughts were quickly displaced as I realised the size of the bird and that we had something quite different here. Then the bird turned and flew past giving us a much better, side-on view. Although neither of us had seen a squacco heron before, I had no doubts now as to what we had stumbled upon.

Seen in striking profile, the pure white wings contrast with a beautiful buff on the body and there is no mistaking it. Flushed from dense sedges and rush at the waters edge, the bird seemed to favour this spot (30m or so to the front and to the left of the hide) throughout its stay at Aber Leri.

Having retreated to the hide we subsequently had excellent views through the telescope as it perched for some time on one of the nearby gates. Very few of the numerous twitchers who came from far afield, were rewarded with such clear views as it kept very much to the denser marginal vegetation. We had few subsequent sightings as ranks of birders and a lack of lapwing chicks meant that we kept quite a low profile ourselves.

December 2015
Spider Webs at Dawn

It seems to me that we had more frosts in October than we had in the entirety of the past two winters, but that could be my memory playing tricks. However, it has definitely been a tonic to have had another Indian summer, some sun (albeit weakened and intermittent) and those autumn colours- fantastic. In October, in the midst of that dry spell, Cors Caron was at its most atmospheric. The weather was set fair over the whole of west Wales and a widespread, if slight frost was expected in most rural areas.

There was an icy glaze on the board walk and the rank vegetation alongside was saturated but there was no sign of what might be called a typical ground or air frost and with not a breath of wind the day certainly held promise as a weak sun struggled to disperse the mist.

This low angled light combined with the moisture laden air to help pick out the spider webs in their hundreds and thousands. It is amazing how many spiders there must be in a few cubic metres of marshland such as can be found at Cors Caron. Usually, you don't see them, but in some situations, there is no way to avoid them.

Occasionally, I would detour around a particularly big web but in so doing inevitably break and disturb a multitude of others. A basic lesson in fieldwork. It is impossible to be out there and just be looking at stuff and not have an effect on the environment and at least some of the wildlife.

Apparently there are something over 600 species of spider in the UK and clearly Cors Caron has quite a few represented. Approximately 250 of those 600 belong to the money-spider family and as all of these are quite small, barely a couple of millimetres across, generally they are tolerated, even by most arachnophobes. The bigger bodied and longer legged species are a different matter altogether and I have to admit, some of the larger, speedy, house-spiders can be a bit nerve racking to catch in the hand! It is that wriggling before release, much less stressful to use an empty upturned glass and a sliver of paper or card to get them out of the way. The Arachnid class to which all spiders, scorpions, mites and ticks belong is one of the oldest and stretches back well over 300 million years.

It was a mistake not to put on waterproof trousers as within a few minutes of wading through some waist hjgh vegetation (looking for signs of water voles) I was almost as super saturated as that air.

During the morning we heard at least four water rails and even caught a brief glimpse of one. A close relative of the moorhen, these are difficult birds to see as they only rarely emerge from dense vegetation. Water rails breed at many wetland sites throughout Wales and many more arrive here about now (from the north and east) to spend the winter months in the relatively mild climate of the west. By early afternoon the sun was at its most effective and the mists had long gone. It still wasn't enough to begin drying me out, but at least it was warm and as most fieldworkers do, I carry a complete change of clothes, so I was again comfortable.

The high pressure/anticyclonic weather had its effect in the record of the day - a clouded yellow butterfly that was feeding on red clover at the north end of the course of the old railway. A butterfly more associated with southern Europe and North Africa it only occasionally makes it as far as west Wales as successive generations move northwards during suitable weather.

This was the first I had seen in Wales in well over a decade, but I am sure there have been more recent records. It was a pity to find a continuing decline in water voles, but the spiders webs, the mist, the fantastic autumnal colours of the bog and that clouded yellow compensated somewhat.

July 2012
Field Poppies

Well, it has been another wet week, which I suppose does allow for catching up on some paperwork, but what an absolutely diabolical summer it has been so far. There was unprecedented rainfall in June and disastrous floods when all we wanted to see was a glimpse of the sun on a more frequent basis.

Sunshine and blue sky can lift the spirits and we certainly don't want to be going into autumn and winter lacking in vitamin D.

Anyone who suffers from SAD (Seasonally Affected Disorder) is probably struggling a bit, but I also seem to suffer from my own syndrome - GLAD, at this time of year, that is Green Leaf Affected Disorder. I find the amount of green leaf and the lack of colour and contrast quite lowering, and it is definitely worse when the leaves are wet!

Recently I managed some fieldwork without getting wet but on several occasions it has involved a soaking and even some wading to get the job done. For a time towards the end of 'flaming' June it was so bad that you could have been forgiven for thinking it was November and that all we had to look forward to was Christmas!

Light levels were poor, it was cold and if it was not raining it was overcast and threatening to rain. Adult and fledgling birds were decidedly hungry, and we even had a family of dormice visiting the bird table in broad daylight, a very risky business that!

Since that low point, we have had some respite and the odd day when it has warmed up, the sun has shone and things have appeared to be beginning to get back to something near normal? Of course, those households who suffered in the floods will likely be many more months getting anything like back to normal and sympathy goes out to all of them.

On Cors Caron (Tregaron bog), I came across a predated snipe egg on one of the boardwalks. Snipe nests are usually well hidden in taller vegetation and I suspect this egg had been washed out of a nest by the floods before being scavenged by a crow, although having seen Cors Caron crows at work on waders in the past I would never put it past them to have actually found the nest.

On a brighter note and as an example of natural resilience, snipe were display-flight drumming overhead, so at least one bird still thought there might be time to get a brood off! Also on a brighter note and despite the Teifi being bankfull, it was a warm and sunny morning such that there were a few butterflies about. A handful of large heaths, a species that overwinters as a larvae/caterpillar, pupates in May and emerges as an adult butterfly in mid to late June. But there was very little else. It has definitely been a poor year for Lepidoptera and insects in general.

Cors Caron is the most southerly location in Britain for large heaths and on a good day you might also see them on Cors Fochno, (Borth bog) where they are known to occur.

Trying to keep on the brighter side, the flowers were also quite stunning and few in my estimation can beat the ox-eye daisies that proliferate alongside the old railway at Cors Caron. A swathe of ox-eye daisies can brighten up even the dullest of days and the simpler the flower the better as far as I am concerned. The dog rose and buttercups are other good examples but if pushed I have to go for the red field poppy as the absolute, none better stunner.

I have been travelling further than normal for some fieldwork this year and came to pass by a field of barley with that incredible splash of red that could mean only one thing. Poppies.

Unusually for me, I actually turned around and pulled in for a closer look as it is such a rare sight now and extremely rare in Ceredigion and mid/west Wales generally. These were just over the border in Shropshire, not exactly thousands or spread throughout the crop but several hundred at the field entrance and spread around the field margins.

They flower over such a long period and their significance through the Great War and Remembrance Day can only add to their attraction. Though I doubt this particular farmer thought much of their presence in his crop.

Occasionally I have seen poppies and other wildflowers used on roadside verges and even on traffic roundabouts, on the A5 out of Telford for example, offering a splash of varied colour and texture, and low on maintenance as most are annuals and readily reseed themselves for the following year.

Morrisons' roundabout in Aberystwyth and many uncut verges all the way from Penparcau to Aberaeron are beginning to look interesting with their flowers and grass seed heads. I expect it helps SAD sufferers and it definitely gives sufferers like me a break from GLAD as well.

September 1993
Bird in the Hand

As usual this spring, and during part of the summer I was involved in bird ringing. This year has been particularly difficult, what with the weather being so wet and generally unpredictable.

Clearly there is no sense in catching birds, ringing and releasing them if their routines or survival are in any way threatened. Recaptures, often year after year, testify to the survival of ringed birds and their ability to cope with occasional careful handling.

The rings used are made of an extremely light alloy, and compared to the normal daily fluctuation in a small bird's bodyweight the weight of the ring is insignificant.

Inclement weather will rule out mist-netting and most other forms of trapping. On many occasions this year it has been impossible to even consider a ringing session due to rain or the threat of rain. However, on the few occasions this year when conditions were favourable there was a modicum of success. My last session actually produced, perhaps the 'best' bird of many years effort here in North Ceredigion.

In fact it was the very last bird caught on this particular morning - a bearded tit, or if you like bearded reedling. A denizen of extensive beds of common or Norfolk reed, this most attractive bird is found mainly in East Anglia, with smaller colonies in Lancashire and elsewhere.

Apart from the possibility of a few birds in Flintshire, it is quite possible that this bird was the only bearded tit in Wales - certainly there have been no other reports from within the county.

Having a bird 'in the hand' obviously allows for very close examination, which is one of the attractions of bird ringing!

The soft browns and greys and the beautiful long tail of this bird were a sight to behold.

It has quite a stout, yellowish beak, and the bright orange/yellow iris of its eye is another mark of distinction. Another point of interest, which can only ever be seen with birds in the hand, was the "brood patch". Females (and some males in species which share incubation) have a featherless lower breast and under-belly known as a brood patch during the breeding season. This allows the bird to incubate its eggs without any feathers getting in the way of the birds' own body heat. This female had a very pronounced brood patch, and I would like to think there was a mate somewhere nearby and that they had bred, but quite honestly I don't know.

Bearded tits are known to be very faithful to their mates, and a male would have stayed at least within sight of its mate. I can only assume this female had experienced something akin to a 'phantom pregnancy'. Perhaps she even built a nest and in the absence of a mate, laid infertile eggs, and attempted to hatch them. She has been about since early spring and has been seen quite recently.

Hopefully there may soon be another eruption of birds from one or other of their breeding strongholds. It's a long shot I know, but if she survives the winter and if a mate does arrive perhaps we could have the beginnings of a new bearded tit colony here in west Wales.

June 1991
Catching Birds and Dodging Midges

ANY BIRDWATCHING that I do is usually on a casual (in passing) basis. Very rarely do I actually set out in pursuit with binoculars around my neck. Birding, for me, more than likely entails either a bird ringing session or perhaps checking some nestboxes to see how the season is progressing. Over a few days recently I did manage to spend time 'birding' and on the nestbox front I am happy to report that the season has gone well. From the 18 boxes I checked it is apparent that pied flycatchers and both blue and great tits have had a successful season. Only one abandoned nest amongst the 15 boxes that were used, most of which were crammed with almost fully fledged young.

On the ringing front, another visit was planned with some trepidation as the midges have been diabolical of late. Hoping for a cold morning, and insect inactivity, a very early start was called for. By 4.30 a.m. I was out and by the house it was warm, 'muggy' and still, ideal midge conditions! However we live in the shelter of Foel Fawr and down beside the Dyfi estuary, much to my relief, a stiff easterly breeze was blowing. I managed to get through the whole morning without a single midge bite! Sedge warblers were everywhere, though C003668, an old friend from past years, failed to put in another appearance. The female sedges were off the nest looking for a bite and food for their just-hatched young, and they were in immaculate condition, contrasting with the plumage of the already washed out males. The males will have been foraging that much longer, feeding the females while they incubated.

Bird of the day was a song thrush, although a fine male redpoll added a startling splash of colour: dark red on the crown, hence redpoll, but more, brighter red splashed liberally on the breast and a pinkish flush on the upper tail coverts. They really do look as if they have been through a recent, nasty accident.

Barn owls have faithfully returned for many years to a box erected in an open barn nearby. Armed with my licence (barn owls are amongst several specially protected, rare species), ringing pliers, ladder and rings I found them doing exceptionally well. Five downy young, very smelly and quite aggressive, hissing a lot! The nest, a scrape in the old pellets, had long since been flattened. Four of the young were ringable, the baby of the bunch being way behind the rest. Owls and other large predators begin incubation on the first egg being laid. Therefore there is a spread to the hatching which allows for the strongest (oldest) to survive and fledge should the food supply dwindle during the season. The oldest here would be at least 10 days ahead of the youngest and it would surprise me if the youngest survived to fledge.

To round off the birding weekend I checked the dippers on the Afon Einion. In previous pieces I mentioned a suspicion that they might be back after something like a seven years absence. Well, we did find a nest this year and from a distance watched the parents, buzzing up and down river, returning to feed the young. No sign of activity this day and on closer inspection the nest was obviously empty, the birds had flown! But which way, up or downstream? Actually when I come to think of it there was only one possibility. Upstream there are two waterfalls, each about 15ft in height, no way for newly-fledged dippers! It had to be downstream and I did actually hear them and catch sight of one of the adults just below the bridleway bridge. Since then I have heard and seen nothing but I live in hope (and expectation) that they may return to raise a second brood, which is common practice amongst dippers.

C003668 is the unique number stamped on a light alloy ring attached to the leg of a very well travelled sedge warbler. Having wintered in tropical and South Africa, sedge warblers return to Europe for our summer. This particular one happens to like north Ceredigion!

Sedge warblers are relatively easy to identify if you can get a good view. They are basically a pale straw colour, yellowish, and boldly striped about the head. Their skulking habits amongst dense beds of phragmites (common or Norfolk reed) make them difficult to see but their harsh, scolding song will always give them away.

Redpoll: They look as if they have been through a recent, nasty accident

June 1992
C003668

C003668 was ringed in north Ceredigion sometime before June 1984. On the 13th of May this year I caught him again at the same ringing site where he has turned up for seven out of the past nine years. He was missing in 85 and again in 91.

My guess is that we have here a serious contender in the longevity stakes. Nine years is some age for such a small bird and a long-distance migrant to boot.

1991 was a poor year for sedge warblers in the parish of Ysgubor y Coed. Early in July, when the adults should have been joined by juveniles leaving the nest, only four were caught at this particular site.

This year it looks much more promising, the reedbeds are alive with sedge warblers and given a reasonable breeding season the July catch, I am sure, will be greater. To some extent Bird Ringing or Banding as the Americans call it, satisfies the hunting instinct. The information derived from a Constant Effort Site (CES), such as this one, is infinitely more useful than any random, casual ringing effort could be.

At a CES site the ringing effort each year is consistent and as well as establishing a birds 'site fidelity' and age it will give some idea of the breeding season's productivity.

At 5.00 a.m. on the 13th of May it was overcast and humid, we had been promised a heatwave! Six 'mist nets' totalling 290 feet in length, held between seven bamboo poles take a while to put up but by 5.45 a.m the first birds had been caught; a willow warbler and a reed bunting held in the 'slack' pockets of the net.

Midges are the most frightening prospect on a warm, overcast day. The 13th proved no exception and at times it was uncomfortable extracting birds from the nets whilst face and arms crawled with these little, biting monsters. However by 9.00 a.m. the cloud was beginning to lift and the summits of Tarren Hendre and Tarren y Gesail were revealed in the distance above Pennal and the Dyfi Forest.

At 9.30 the sun broke through and I began believing in the heat-wave. Midges do not like bright sunlight so I was able to breathe a sigh of relief and relax a little.

Now I could flick through the log book at leisure and establish just how old C003668 actually was. I knew he was an old friend and regular customer but until I began searching the records I had no idea exactly how old. Caught as an adult in June 1984 he went missing in 85. Retrapped no less than five times in '86, once in '87 and once again in '88. Caught on three occasions in '89 and four times in '90 he was A.W.O.L. in '91. Assuming he was born in 1983 that makes him nine years old, absolutely the grandfather of sedge warblers I would have thought.

By the way, if you do find a 'ringed' bird (racing pigeons excepted) the address to send the details to is: British Trust for Ornithology (B.T.O.), The Nunnery, Nunnery Place, Thetford, Norfolk. They will be most grateful if you include the ring and the details of where and when the bird was found. In return you should receive details of where and when the bird was ringed, and the species if you did not already know.

December 2014
Nightjars

NIGHTJARS can be found on the bird list between the owls and the swifts, and share at least some of the characteristics and habits of both. Like the owls, they are active at night, nocturnal but more often described as crepuscular, which merely means particularly active at twilight, be it at dusk or just before dawn.

It is a fact that nightjars are most likely to be noticed in the evening twilight as this is when we are more likely to be about and their rather eerie, churring song and strange calls are most likely to be heard. Nightjars are significantly larger than the more familiar swift but have a somewhat similar if less streamlined body and head shape. Both have very small beaks that open to reveal a surprisingly wide gape with which to snap up the insects they exclusively feed upon. The tail of a nightjar is long and more akin to that of the kestrel, great for manoeuvrability as are the more rounded wings. Not designed for swift speed the nightjar will display frequent twists, turns and glides with quite exceptional lightness and a general buoyancy of flight.

Having wintered in Africa our birds sensibly delay arrival in Britain until May and will have left by August or at the latest during September. My guess is that they left early this year, I certainly would have!

In 1992 there were thought to be around 3,400 pairs in Britain, 188 of these being in Wales. The most recent survey (2004) has just been completed and at least here in Wales we should expect them to be holding their own as many of those dark, blanketing spruce forests are being broken up and many providing sanctuary for the nightjar.

You might say that clear-felling leaves ugly scars, but the economics and practicalities of extraction make this the preferred method in most situations. On a typical clear-felled area, dead stems, surviving broadleaves and areas of check (poor crop growth) are all likely to be left as the crop is harvested. And remember it is a crop! Together with a more accepting attitude to invading scrub and a wider age range of crop trees the biodiversity within your average plantation is going to increase enormously. It can take up to ten years for a cleared area to become completely revegetated and dominated by either scrub or replanted conifers and most foresters will accept a mixture.

Clearings and clearfell areas are ideal habitat for nightjar, often sheltered by surrounding crops, with any native broadleaves given a new lease of life on release from the high conifer crop recently removed. Recent clearfells also have lots of bare and disturbed ground on which the incredibly well camouflaged nightjar likes to nest. What more might they require? A little less wet weather might be high on the list.

In Ceredigion (not renowned as a nightjar hotspot) there were at least 10 pairs on the sample, surveyed areas. Considering the suitable habitat in the county, not a great total but it was only a sample and birds were found on forested areas from just above sea level in the north, to 350m above sea level further inland, and to the south.

There is something special about being out late at night, alone (apart from a co-worker not too far away in a vehicle hopefully) in a quiet, isolated forest plantation.

As the light fades you certainly have to rely on senses other than sight a whole lot more. Of course there are owls, the wind through the trees, strange scrabblings and rustlings in the undergrowth. In the half-light imagination can run riot and it is important to be realistic. Werewolves have been extinct for quite a while now, have they not? The piercing whistles emanating from the bracken beneath the young larch trees turned out to be the calls of young long-eared owls. The rustling and snorting just off the track, merely a group of three badgers breakfasting at dusk on a super-abundance of bilberries. One by one they appeared on the track, the boldest coming right up to my feet to investigate before scurrying off to join its pals who were waiting 20 metres or so down the road.

It is important to get to know sites in daylight. We had to preview sites to record habitat features anyway but it is essential you know your way around before it gets dark. Also bear in mind that in poor light the human eye will often lose birds temporarily and it is sometimes surprising where they next reappear. On one particularly calm and clear night, not far from Lampeter, I had been watching a male nightjar for 10 to 15 minutes when things went quiet. Was that it for the night? Beginning to really relax as there was no other suitable habitat in my grid square, I was leaning on a Forestry Commission sign admiring the twinkling lights far below and wondering how long my co-worker was going to be. Until a slight sound behind me had the hairs on my neck prickling, just a bit.

Slowly turning I was confronted by a pair of nightjars barely six feet away hovering in a tail-down attitude just above my head. They are one of the most inquisitive of birds and will almost invariably take a look at any human intruder on their patch. This was a bit different and easily the closest I was to get all summer. It will be a good few months before anything remotely conclusive is drawn from the 2004 survey. Has there been an increase since the1992 survey? It would be a sad day and cause for some concern if this ornithological oddity was again to fall into decline.

October 2001
Keeping Track of Britain's Birds

SITTING out more wet weather, I decided to do a cursory analysis of a few of my own bird survey field maps, the result of several visits to a small area of woodland over the past two breeding seasons. In doing so I soon came to the conclusion that it pays to take a bit of care when recording in the field, care to keep things as tidy and clear as is possible. Though on occasions the wind and rain do have an effect on how clear the records might be, I have no excuse this time as I was able to choose my days, time and weather. Fortunately the BTO (British Trust for Ornithology) and others use a system of abbreviations for each and every bird species likely to occur in the UK, (a list can be found on the BTO website). These are generally common sense abbreviations such as WR (wren), CH (chaffinch), BT (blue tit), but there are a few weird ones. Greylag goose for some reason is GJ.

This was ingrained in my memory for ever during a winter month spent in Ireland, seeking out GJs. Many are feral, but most are winter visitors, mainly from Iceland. Here in west Wales they are generally of the feral type and breed somewhat sparingly at a few sites. The BTO are always on the lookout for volunteers and occasionally for paid field workers to carry out various surveys, usually (but not always) in the spring and summer breeding season. Therefore it is important that the common conventions are followed by fieldworkers wherever they might be working- it makes any analysis so much easier and accurate. I find it can also pay to use the codes/list for your own records, after all it takes up space to record red-breasted merganser and lesser spotted woodpecker when RM and LS will do the job perfectly adequately.

Be aware that there are species that at first might be confusing, for instance mistle thrush and marsh tit and, amongst the summer visitors, grasshopper warbler, garden warbler. The first two are coded M and MT respectively and the latter are designated GH and GW. And there are a few others that might sometimes require thinking about and a half decent memory. So I always have a laminated sheet-cum-list with all the abbreviations on it for reference, attached to the clipboard and beneath any map of a site that I might be surveying. Over nearly 40 years it has been a delight to explore, visit, record/monitor, see and hear so much bird, mammal, plant and other wildlife in such a wide range of habitats as can be found in north, mid and west Wales.

Without a shadow of doubt the Cambrian area, Snowdonia and the associated coast has more than its fair share of what remains of our native wildlife and semi-natural landscapes. Inevitably some birds have been lost as breeding species and more seem likely to follow. However, on the up side we have gained others such as LE (little egret), RW (reed warbler) and CW (cettis warbler) and there are programmes and initiatives aimed at saving some of those near to being lost.

Birds are invaluable indicators of the state of the countryside. We have changed things irrevocably and through industrialization and advances in agriculture we are changing things still, after all it wasn't so very long ago that horsepower meant exactly what it said. It seems to me we may well have changed the climate. Anyone who thinks the last few winters and summers are merely a blip, has to be quite a wishful thinker in my opinion and where we go from here could be anyone's guess.

Over the two seasons of surveys and that wet afternoon of analysis I calculated there were 37 breeding species using the eight acres of woodland, not a bad total at all. WR was most common and LS and SF were amongst the scarcest. SF stands for spotted flycatcher, a summer visitor that is sometimes not easy to locate in woodland as its weak song and contact calls can be drowned out by the much louder species.

Late in August I heard a (GC) goldcrest singing. Apparently you are lucky if you can still hear its high notes after 50 years of age, so here's looking forward to next spring and another dawn chorus!

January 2010
Nest Box Surprise

AS THE NEW YEAR comes in I have at last got around to emptying some of those nestboxes that the Forestry Commission obligingly allows me to put up in their plantations here in North Ceredigion.

Apart from soggy nest material, the occasional smelly, infertile egg, and the skeletons of those fledgings that did not quite make it, we have other things to look out for.

Bats regularly use the boxes for roosting and on a cold or wet day it is not unusual to find a small colony of long-eared bats clustered about the top inside edges. Of course the lid is then carefully replaced and disturbance kept to a minimum.

Quite apart from it being illegal to handle or disturb them unnecessarily, they will need all their energy to see them through without being forced into flight from out of a torpid state.

Dormice have long vacated the boxes, preferring, I assume, a more stable environment (temperature?) for hibernation than can be found in a nestbox, a hole in a tree, or in the ground perhaps, where any fluctuations in conditions can be slight.

That picture book illustration of the dormouse asleep with its long furry tail curled over its head is exactly what you will see should you be lucky enough to find one in hibernation. A beautiful orange-brown coat and enormous black eyes when awake is unmistakably the dormouse, a rare creature indeed and seen even more rarely as it is for the most part nocturnal in its habits.

Other small mammals occasionally turn up, the wood or long-tailed field mouse being one. Wood mouse perhaps best describes this very active mouse, although in the country it often finds its way into your house. Its close relative the yellow-necked mouse is much less common, but worth looking out for. Brown above, white below, long-tailed, big-eared with big, black beady eyes describes both these mice, the yellow-necked having a yellowish collar across the white of its chest.

A very different small mammal that surprisingly turned up last year was the pygmy shrew. Incredibly minute, weighing only a few grams, how and why on earth do they climb five feet or so of tree trunks to get into a nestbox? Certainly a dry, perhaps unused nest from summer would make lovely winter quarters and I suppose there is every possibility of finding some insects in the boxes. Shrews are insectivorous or more correctly, invertivorous. They must consume vast quantities of insect, worms, and other invertebrates if they are to keep their hectic life going.

Of course, the vast majority of small mammals will die during the winter. Many fall prey to the owls, then there are the stoats and weasels not to meantion the fox and don't forget the domestic cat and the humble mouse trap.

Species

January 1992
Raven

EARLY CHRISTMAS EVE found me in the garden tidying up some of those leaves that had escaped previous rakings. A relatively bright, brisk morning had not only tempted me out, it had also brought out the playful acrobatic instincts of the ravens.

Here I was privileged to watch an amazing display as four ravens twisted, tumbled and turned overhead, all within a matter of 20 to 30 metres away.

Perhaps there was some courtship taking place, whatever, they seemed oblivious to me as their hoarse, distinctive croaking calls echoed up the valley.

21st December marks the turn of the year and it was no surprise to me to see such antics so soon after the longest night. As the days begin lengthening the songbirds and in particular the mistle thrush, will need little encouragement to get in some practice. The exuberance of the ravens was just another sign that the year had turned the corner.

Ravens dwarf any other member of the crow family and for sheer character they take some beating.Their antics include rolls and flips that come into their more leisurely flights, just for the fun of it. And those powerful wings can be audible from a distance as they pass on more powerful missions.

An enormous beak, large head with shaggy throat feathers and a distinctive wedge-shaped tail help in identification, as with all the 'black' crows you are often relying on size, silhouette or the call for identification.

They are amongst the earliest of nesting species and from now on will be visiting their favourite haunts occasionally or when weather permits. Staking a claim to the nestsite and perhaps adding to what eventually becomes an enormous pile of sticks.

Ravens are thought to pair for life, as do others of the crow family. A few months ago I recall watching eight ravens fooling about in the thermals around Snowdon's summit, (Copa'r Wyddfa); it was quite apparent that some of them were paired! They like to nest on some overhung, inaccessible cliff or in the uppermost boughs of a tall tree, often a conifer. Here in a massive stick nest, lined with wool, will be laid the four to six eggs. Lowland pairs may begin laying in February but most of the upland nests will have their first eggs in March.

Near to home, the jackdaw is perhaps the most well-known crow, a pest with a penchant for chimneys!

Virtually every village has its flock of jackdaws. Look out for them as they pass in a loose flock to feed or roost and it is quite easy to pick out the 'pairs'.

Amazingly resourceful, incredibly successful, some of the crows may be despised by the farmer, gamekeeper or householder, but undeniably they add immeasurably to the rural landscape.

February 1992
Frogs and Toads

THERE MAY NOT BE FAIRIES at the bottom of your garden, but if you are lucky enough to have a pond, there is a fair chance, that about now, you will have frogs!

Frogs, toads and newts are the British representatives in the world of amphibians. Equally at home on land and in water, they all need to return each year to water to breed.

Just recently I picked up a large frog, which I am sure was a male, on its way back to the breeding pond from whence it had emerged, perhaps three or more years ago. Apparently, it takes three years for a frog to mature, with the longest-lived surviving for eight years or so, although 'captive' frogs have been known to live for 12 years.

Frogs can be very faithful to their particular pond. How they find their way back to it from their summer wanderings remains a mystery, but given the chance, this is what they will do.

Toads, too, are famous for being faithful to a particular puddle. The 'Toads Crossing' roadsign is not such a rare sight nowadays and the local papers like to have their annual toad article.

The frog I picked up proved to be quite a handful. They are very powerful for their size and amazingly slippery. On a beeline for the pond it was faced with a problem; namely, a five foot high stone wall. I am sure that eventually it would have found a hole or the door, but my deed for the day was to take it just past this barrier.

Since the beginning of February, this particular pond had been well populated with frogs and lately, when the frogs have been startled, the water boils with activity. Lots of spawn has already been laid and with each batch containing 2-3,000 eggs, soon there ought to be plenty of tadpoles. Spawning will be later in the uplands. The few traditional sites known to me, around Nant y Moch and Pumlumon will be several weeks behind, I expect.

At breeding ponds I have often found spawn at the bankside where some unfortunate female has fallen prey to a predator which has eaten the frog, rejecting the spawn. Tadpoles live a precarious life and suffer heavy losses to the larger aquatic predators such as the dragonfly nymph and water boatman.

The tiny frogs that crawl and hop into the grass then become prey for a whole range of birds and mammals. Larger frogs will be taken by herons, foxes, snakes, otters and frequently by owls. The long, hollow, fluted bones of frogs are regularly found in owl pellets.

I suppose we ought to be grateful for all this mortality. Were more than a few to survive from those thousands of eggs, the whole place would be heaving with frogs. Garden ponds have taken on greater importance as farm ponds have been lost.

Although there is now a resurgence in farm ponds, these are mainly for fish, which is not so good for invertebrates or the tadpoles!

I have been told of one small garden pond, within a stone's throw of the famous Machynlleth town clock! Last year it was host to a mass of frogs at spawning time. I expect with such mild weather it is again heaving with frogs and chock-a-block with spawn. It is certainly a feature lacking in our garden at the moment. A small pond, lots of frogs – what more could one ask for?

May 1986
Sponsored Bird Watch & Chernobyl's Radioactive Rains

THE EARLY HOURS of the 10th May saw the 4 team members of the West Wales Trust for Nature Conservation assembling in north Ceredigion to begin the sponsored birdwatch.

The aim? To raise funds for the British Wildlife Appeal. The means? Sponsorship of team members in their efforts to identify as many bird species as possible during the day, and night if necessary. The rules? All 4 team members must see or hear each bird, and be able to identify it.

Before a grey dawn broke a few birds had already been logged, identified by their song or calls and it was not until 05.40 that the first sight record went into the book.

The first, by no means the last, and probably the longest detour of the day had taken us into the hills amidst cloud and rain to catch sight of a male black grouse displaying at a long established lek (meeting place). The weird bubbling and screeching calls fitted in well with the dank, misty surroundings. On such a dismal day, more suited to mid March than mid-May, few other birds cared to show themselves in the uplands and after a good soaking with radioactive rain driven by winds approaching gale force we descended to the relative calm of the RSPB reserve, Ynys Hir.

By now, 06.50, our total stood at a mere 17, not very impressive, but soon to be bolstered by reserve residents, we hoped. Continuing strong winds, and the occasional shower made for difficulties in locating some of the smaller species, however a pair of noisy jays put us on to an elusive tawny owl, the most briefly glimpsed bird of the day as it swooped silently away.

Continuing through the woodland to the West Marsh the species total now had to be added to and amended almost constantly as birds previously only heard were sighted and other new birds joined the lengthening list. A disappointment on the marsh was the total lack of grasshopper warblers, not a sound never mind a sighting. Nevertheless after a few failed attempts due to other avian distractions all four team members did get a sighting of a sedge warbler.

A male kestrel brought up the half century by 08.30 hours, then out to the estuary to pick up curlew, whimbrel and the first surprise, a female goldeneye.

A brief visit to the Marian Mawr hide yielded coot and moorhen, but no bonus birds. On a tight schedule to catch the tide, hopefully high at Ynys Las, it was back to the car park. Over 5 hours gone and the first welcome tea break during which starling and sparrow-hawk raised the total to 66. We departed the reserve fairly well pleased to have picked up from a slowish start.

With the tide falling fast at Ynys Las we fortunately quickly found the wader roost. Dunlin, ringed plover and a few sanderling were expected, a solitary turnstone was a bonus. Reluctance to leave without a grey plover in the book ultimately paid off but entailed almost an hour without a new species. Side-tracked in pursuance of a distant godwit (bar-tailed) the elusive grey plover finally came to book. One of many species this day to be represented by a single sighting of a single bird. Even buzzard and raven were to prove difficult as the day progressed.

The cliffs below the monument at Borth provided a brief sit and watch interlude and another seven species, including the trust emblem, the manx shearwater, a small group skimming low over the waves not far offshore. A whooper swan, probably the oldest bird of the day, was added to the list as we continued on into Aberystwyth and Tan-y-Bwlch beach.

Wheatear seen in the background of a clay-pigeon shoot saved a trip back into the uplands but we missed out on a red kite over Pen Dinas. Not to worry, a considerate kite, 90, put in a brief appearance as we made our way south to New Quay head. Here we added another eight species, bringing the days total close to the 100. The day's only brief glimpse of a raven perfoming wonders in the air currents off the cliff-face hardly made up for missing out on the choughs.

Back northwards for stonechat and at last, one hundred with a dipper on the Afon Arth. Gone 5pm and birds, at least 'new' ones, very difficult to come by. Peter Davis managed to pull a lesser-spotted woodpecker out of the hat and visits to Falcondale, Tregaron and Nanteos inched the total up to 107 by nine o'clock.

Bleary-eyed and leg weary it was back to Aberystwyth for the finale.

Here we hoped to get purple sandpiper at their regular high tide roost. Sure enough three faithfuls were there, huddled tightly to the rockface in a gathering gloom above a heavy swell.

That closed the book at a respectable 108, not bad for such a day, hardly spring-like. On a fine day in a normal spring, a total of 120 ought to be within reach in a county with such varied habitat as Ceredigion.

Most of the species identified were bread and butter to the average twitcher and the miles covered, (100 by car and 6 to 7 on foot) minimal, as twitchers go. Nevertheless, with the wind and rain it was plenty enough. The day had begun with black grouse on the tops and ended with purple sandpiper at sea level, two species few other teams could hope for.

On behalf of the team members and the British Bird Wildlife Appeal I would like to thank all sponsors and particularly those individuals who took on the onerous task of touting sponsor forms, far and wide. Over £380 was raised by the team members themselves and hopefully some of it will go towards ensuring that our children's children can see and hear blackcocks in the flesh at their leks. That is, if they can be persuaded to get up at 04.30 in the morning!

December 2004/March 2008
Dormice

WHEN TORPID and tightly curled up the dormouse might amount to the size, but nowhere near the weight, of a snooker ball. Big black eyes, amazingly long whiskers, light gingery in colour and with a long furry tail, it has a lot in its favour. Not least its reluctance to bite when handled. Possibly this lack of aggression was a major factor in the dormouse being prized as a pet in the past.

Its range in England and Wales has contracted considerably over the past 60 or so years and it seems more than likely that this contraction is related to habitat loss. Where have we heard that one before? Some of this will be directly related to the removal and neglect of hedges and a decline in traditional woodland crafts involving coppicing.

Here in west Wales the dormouse is now most frequently found in and around forestry plantations, often associated with Planted Ancient Woodland Sites or PAWS to the forester and woodland owner, woodlands where coppicing would have been a common practice in the not too distant past.

Despite a range of woodland and agricultural initiatives, a worrying proportion of the surviving native woodland is still heavily grazed and thus absolutely hopeless for your average dormouse and a wide variety of other species too. Unmanaged and grazed woodlands will have a sparse field layer and next to no shrub layer. To be really healthy and sustainable a woodland needs all its components, from canopy to a thriving and dynamic shrub, field and ground layer. Importantly, a heavily grazed wood will also often lack any great accumulation of leaf litter as it is all free to be blown about and often out of the wood by those autumn and winter winds. Little or no leaf litter means fewer ground invertebrates and fewer fungi and as there is no build up of leaf mould, moisture retention is affected and there is no recyling of nutrients. The soil can become impoverished and eventually even the mature trees may struggle to survive.

Managed woodlands will often benefit from coppicing/felling to an established timetable that can invigorate the system by letting in light that allows the field and shrub layers to flourish and encourages the natural regeneration of tree species.

In the past, hazel has been the favourite coppice species and hazel coppice has long been associated with dormice. But you might need more than hazel if a population of dormice is to thrive.

Dormice have to be much more adaptable and they will survive in a wide range of scrubby, brambly habitats and even among overgrown and scruffy hedges, ideally with some connection to woodland. Broadleaved scrub at a forest plantation edge or the remnants of hedges/ hazel coppice within a plantation might equally well suffice. Being true hibernators they will sleep through the winter from November to perhaps sometime in April. An adult might tip the scales at 18 to 20 grammes throughout the summer. Come autumn and a glut of fruits, nuts, berries, insects and nectar they may weigh in at 40 grammes and be absolutely rolling in fat that keeps them supplied during hibernation through those dark winter months.

Hibernation nests are usually constructed on the ground and consist of a tightly woven ball of fine grasses. The dormouse in the photograph (used in the article) roused itself from the torpid state on 23rd April last year. Interestingly it was discovered in a small flower bed in a garden in north Ceredigion, surrounded by a tightly mown lawn. The books tell you that dormice do not like travelling over the ground and they are certainly arboreal by preference.

Unless this dormouse parachuted in, I can't see any other way than over the considerable distance of open ground that this one could have got to where it was found.

More puzzling for me is how do they manage to weave such a complex and tightly woven hibernation nest and end up inside it?

If they complete the outer walls first what do they use for material for the very fine inner lining and if they complete the inner lining first how do they finish off the outer layers without totally wrecking what they've already constructed? There must be some quite easy answer.

May 1993
Butterflies

THE LAST DAYS OF MAY saw the summer off to a blistering start. A fresh and chilly north easterly wind ushered in a prolonged dry spell with clear skies and lots of sun.

Exactly how healthy it is to take large 'doses' of this sun still causes me some anxiety, particularly on behalf of the children. Depleted ozone layers over Europe and unfiltered UV rays bombarding us do nothing for my peace of mind.

Much more relaxing are the butterflies. A small tortoiseshell (which we had watched as it hibernated through the winter in an upstairs room) finally came back to life on 28 April – a day when the temperature soared over the 20 degrees mark and we enjoyed 12 sunny days thereafter.

Peacock butterflies appeared in good numbers at about the same time, far outnumbering small tortoiseshells which remain relatively scarce. I also heard reports of commas in early May and saw a solitary holly blue myself. As we progressed into May more orange tips appeared and also the speckled woods, unusual butterflies in preferring dappled shade to full sunlight.

The male orange tip is well named and easy to identify but the females look very similar to other 'white' butterflies. They also have similar habits when it comes to larval food plant preferences. Unfortunately most whites prefer cruciferae, which might include your cabbage plants. However, the orange tip favours 'wild' cruciferae such as the hedge mustard and cuckoo flower or lady's smock which is now in flower.

The speckled wood has much more acceptable habits, its caterpillars concentrate on various grasses, being particularly fond of couch grass of all things!

Away from lowland woods and fields an excursion recently took me to the vicinity of Llyn Craig y Pistyll, source of Aberystwyth's water supply. The unimproved hillsides around Craig y Pistyll still support a (rather poor it must be said) dwarf heath community, i.e. heather and bilberry. Ideal habitat for one of our smallest and most unusually coloured butterflies, the green hairstreak. The hairstreaks (of which there are five British species) are closely related to the blues and coppers, the best distinguishing characteristics for most are usually to be found on the underside of the hindwing.

In the case of the green hairstreak there is no problem, the underside of both fore and hind wing is bright, almost emerald, green. Absolutely unmistakable and, as it invariably settles with its wings held vertically above its back, quite noticeable.

Its flight is very fast and erratic, it is so small and its brown upperwing so unremarkable that you often wonder, have you actually seen anything flutter past and away or have your eyes deceived you?

Concentrate and stealthily approach one once settled, and you will be rewarded with a glimpse of that amazing green underwing.

July 1992
Snakes

REPTILES AND AMPHIBIANS, a topic to produce many a 'shudder' with frog, toad and snake phobia being as common a complaint as 'arachnaphobia', a fear of spiders. At least in Britain, the reptiles can be distinguished from the amphibians by the nature of the skin. Dry and scaly in reptiles -snakes and lizards, moist and soft in the amphibia - newts, frogs and toads.

Here in Wales we have a representative sample of the reptilia with the grass snake relatively widespread and quite common whilst the adder (our only venomous snake) is locally common. We also have the common lizard and the slow worm (a legless lizard), perhaps the two most abundant reptiles in the area.

In Wales and elsewhere in Britain there are always tales of enormous serpents, tales that have been passed down through the years. In the telling and passage of time I am sure some of these serpents have continued to grow, although there is no doubt in my mind that years ago snakes were likely to be bigger. More people, more roads and loss of habitat equals fewer snakes, i.e. less likehood of any large snake surviving!

Now it is unusual to see even a snake of more than three feet in length, though they can exceptionally reach twice this size. The grass snake is very slender, olive grey/green with black spots on the upper surface and usually has a prominent collar of white or yellow followed by a black band behind the head. It is a superb swimmer and a delight to watch gliding across a pool. It is also a very competant climber and I can testify to this also, as I was fortunate to have one pointed out to me by someone more observant, a few years ago. Entwined in the shrubbery this snake approached three feet in length and was superbly camouflaged, remaining perfectly motionless apart from the occcasional flickering of the tongue.

Grass snakes are quite easy to handle and in captivity will become quite tame. If, however, they are alarmed then unpleasant things can happen. They may discharge the contents of their anal gland from their vent and I can vouch for the fact that this creates the most appalling smell imaginable, difficult to get rid of and very attractive to flies! This is done to 'disconcert' the molester (it did) and allow the snake's escape (grass snakes never bite).

Adder on the other hand must never be handled, they are poisonous and their bite can on rare occasions be fatal. Adders are relatively short (rarely exceeding two feet in length) and stout.

They usually keep away from open water and as far as I am aware they do not climb. The colour can be very variable, from dark brown, through red to green and pale grey but the zig-zag stripe along the back is diagnostic and its generally stouter build identify this snake.

Adders and grass snakes take a wide variety of prey, though the adder is mainly a nocturnal hunter (which seems odd in the cold blooded animal), whilst the grass snake is diurnal (hunts by day). Frogs, toads, lizards, mice, voles and even slugs have been recorded but the grass snake must take more young birds and eggs. Why else would it be such an able climber in the shrubbery?

No matter that you may loathe them, snakes are fascinating and often elusive members of our fauna. Unprovoked, the adder is harmless and the grass snake is absolutely harmless. Stories of being chased or attacked by snakes in Britain are totally unsubstantiated.

In my experience both adder and grass snake prefer the quiet life, the less they see of we interfering humans the better it is for them and they certainly should not be persecuted.

August 2007
Bracken

PTERIDIUM AQUILINUM is almost certainly the toughest and by far the commonest and most widespread fern in the British Isles. And bracken, as it is more commonly known, can become something of a problem if it blankets the whole hillside and smothers virtually all other vegetation. It does seem to be spreading inexorably and it just loves the deeper, moist soils of west Wales where its fronds can sometimes grow to a height of 2 metres.

Having created something of a miniature forest the only really effective control over large areas of difficult terrain, might be spraying. On flatter or at least on easier ground, regular cutting over a period of years will effectively weaken it and livestock may trample and even graze upon a few of the fresh and tender shoots. This despite a degree of quite serious toxicity if too much is eaten. I have also heard recently that pigs and especially wild boar might be a partial solution as they are fond of rooting out and eating the succulent rhizomes. Presumably the pigs are immune or the rhizomes are a less toxic part of the plant? However, pigs or wild boar are not really a practical solution in the average situation in west Wales, so I suppose we should be grateful that bracken rarely, if ever, produces spores and all its progress is vegetative via those dense mats of rhizomes.

To the farmer, bracken can have few if any benefits and it has several, significant drawbacks. At its densest on the open hillside it smothers most other vegetation, though it may nurse and protect a few early flowering species, plants that can get most of their growth out of the way before the bracken really gets going. Long vegetation of any sort and bracken in particular is liable to harbour ticks. Horrible little creatures that can carry Lymes disease, they are a familiar problem to the farmer, the walker and any dog owner. At its most annoying, bracken also effectively hides the sheep from both the farmer and dogs and can make any gathering-in, a most frustrating and time consuming business.

Does it have any benefits? On easy ground, it can be cut and baled and used for winter bedding for livestock and at its densest it does provide cover and nest sites for quite a range of bird species. Of note in the winter are woodcock, which often roost throughout the day in areas of dense cover, bracken slopes included. In the summer a much wider range of species find it very attractive and of particular note would be yellowhammer, whinchat and tree pipit, all species that are in serious decline and particular causes for concern to the ornithologist. In late summer, after the breeding season, expanses of bracken can then be important feeding areas for a wider range of bird species. Redstart and some of the warblers seem to find it particularly attractive and I can only assume there is a good source of invertebrates in there somewhere.

Quite tender early in the year it does not take long for the bracken frond to harden and take on a decided degree of toughness through the summer months. Then, as it dies back in the autumn, we are treated to those beautiful yellowing fronds turning to a deep, reddish brown over and into the early winter. Apart from very early in the year, the fronds are tough and they can be quite problematic to handle. I will never forget tugging at a dead frond and cutting my finger virtually to the bone. Much safer and much more sensible to use a sickle or scythe and gather it in with a rake or garden fork, wear gloves too if you are going to be tempted to handle it at all. Armour plated gloves if you have them, and if you encounter any resistance at all, don't pull against it!

Keen gardeners will always find a use for dead bracken and I have in the past collected bags of bracken litter for use as a weed-resistant mulch around shrubs and some of the more frost-tender plants. Otherwise, we regularly once used it as bedding for the ducks and geese, before we lost them to old age, the polecat, fox and who knows what other predators we have around here.

Bracken may be despised by most land managers but it is virtually impossible to ignore and it is easy to see why bracken is often so successful. It is tough, it is vigorous and at its most vigorous it might even push fronds up through several inches of tarmac.

If it has few practical uses now, it is at least an important habitat for quite a range of wildlife. Though we could probably do without the ticks!

August 2015
Bracken #2

Bracken control is an on-going and increasing problem all over the UK and it was interesting to watch one treatment method on Foel Fawr* recently; bracken crushing/rolling using real horsepower.

A lack of grazing here (for several years) has allowed the bracken free rein and initiated almost a mini rewilding of the hillside. Bramble has also taken off and a wide variety of flowering plants, grasses, sedges and rush have appeared in some open areas where in the past they were grazed down, if not entirely out, by sheep.

The bird population is also changing with more linnets, fewer meadow pipits, and more whitethroats, the latter particularly enjoying some impenetrable brambly areas.

Tree seedlings are appearing all over the place and not surprisingly there seems to be a natural determination to eventually revert to woodland of some description.

The dark green fritillary butterflies no doubt appreciated the violets, their larval food plant. Violets have increased over the past several years and in some areas where bracken has previously been cut and managed they are particularly abundant.

Another attractive and delicate flower is the harebell. This was hardly ever seen flowering in the past, but since grazing all but ceased on the Foel, the pale blue flowerheads have become a common sight alongside the coastal path and roadside verges.

*Foel Fawr 'fridd' habitat restoration by conservation grazing using cattle and horses has followed on from the period of transition outlined in the article above.

August 2007
Peregrine

PEREGRINES are without doubt, birds of prey par excellence. Extremely powerful, built for speed and with a wingspan of a metre or thereabouts they are top birds. And, as with many birds of prey, the female is quite noticeably larger than the male.

That famous stoop on to prey, when peregrines may reach anything up to and over 100mph, and their seasonal depredation of racing pigeons are, however, all that you tend to hear about.

The stoop sounds spectacular and no doubt it is, but I have to admit that I have never witnessed a stoop and I might suggest it is by no means the preferred method of making a kill, for this admittedly, most charismatic bird. It undoubtedly does occur quite frequently, but if you think about it you can see that it does have significant, attendant risks for the peregrine. Striking another moving target, a bird that at any time might take avoiding action, at such a speed is not a tactic to be taken at all lightly and the possibilities for personal damage must be considerable.

I have watched many peregrine forays after food, most recently a bird over Aberystwyth attempting to take breakfast from the flocks of starlings leaving the pier early in the morning. Persistence and patience are great virtues of any predator and although I did not see a conclusion to this hunt, I have little doubt that this bird eventually picked off something. Perhaps one of the stragglers as the weaker birds were leaving in less confusing numbers!

And I still vividly remember watching a greenshank as it was feeding along the edge of the Dyfi Estuary. Very distinctive with subtle grey and white plumage, greenshanks also have quite a long and slightly upturned bill and of course, greenish/grey legs. Seen more commonly in the autumn as they stop off on their return from breeding grounds in the north, the greenshank is noticeably larger than the more familiar redshank, a bird which can be found breeding at a few sites in west Wales, notably around the Dyfi Estuary.

This particular greenshank obviously had its wits about it, as a marauding peregrine just failed to catch it by surprise. The peregrine persistently swooped low and back and forth but the greenshank sensibly waded out into slightly deeper water and just kept ducking under the surface at each pass of the peregrine! I watched as this evasive action went on for several minutes before the aggressor eventually gave up and went off in search of an easier meal.

More recently and virtually at the same site I watched as a female peregrine tried the same tactics on a black-tailed godwit. As it was probably the only 'black-wit' on the estuary at the time and they are one of the most attractive and elegant of wader species, I was muttering under my breath, "stay in the water, stay in the water". Unfortunately, either the water was not deep enough or the godwit lost its wits, at any rate its nerve soon broke. It took to the air and in less than 20 metres it was seized by the peregrine. It was made to look so easy and it was.

On other occasions I have witnessed other tactics, such as beating low and fast over fields where lapwing and other species were breeding. The chances are that something or other will see the peregrine's approach, raise the alarm and something or other will then take to the air. If it does and it is more or less in front of and in the line of travel of the onrushing peregrine, the chances are it will fall victim. On the Dyfi estuary peregrines have also been seen taking birds on the ground and contrary to some popular opinion, it is not always going to be a clean kill. Particularly if it is a large and tough prey species such as a mallard. I watched as a peregrine took over 20 minutes to subdue and finish off a mallard out on the saltmarsh. I did not see how the mallard was taken but the ensuing struggle was not exactly lunchtime viewing or the typical dashing and spectacular quick kill associated with such a predator. Nature is definitely red in tooth (or should that be beak) and claw and any method that yields results will be used, even if you are a top predator such as a peregrine.

December 2016
Otter

AMONGST the larger UK mammals (if you discount deer) the otter is probably one of the most elusive, and make no mistake about it, your average adult otter is a sizeable and heavy beast - dog otters weighing in at anything up to 15kg, the bitch or female always being smaller.

Despite their elusive nature, their presence will often feature on any interpretation board wherever otters might occur. They are such an iconic species, an animal that even the most ardent fisherman must in some ways admire.

I often think it must be quite a disappointment to many a visitor when otters fail to put in an appearance or perform but if you are out on the riverside, especially towards dusk, you at least have a chance of a sighting. Low slung, with a bounding, running gait (typical of all mustelids), sleek waterproof pelt and an amazingly muscular, thick tail, once seen they are easily identified.

In west Wales there is now thought to be a reasonably healthy population with the relatively few fatalities being restricted to motor vehicle collisions and very occasionally accidental deaths from inshore marine fisheries, (nets and pots). During any survey work near water I will always look for signs of otter as they are a top predator and, if present, good indicators of the health of the immediate environment. Otter runs into ditches and pools are easy to ID.

The tunnels through rank grass and rush will be about 20cm in diameter and inevitably lead to where they want to be, down into the water. And almost certainly there will be spraints and/or droppings somewhere on any bank that divides two sections of water linked by an otter run.

Having located some droppings, I will usually have a look to see what they have been eating. Fish bones and scales are typical but in my recent experience on some west Wales river systems, not nearly so common as one might imagine and an indicator that all may not be well with the fish population. Small mammal and frog bones usually figure prominently and, especially during spring and summer, there may be feathers as well. Birds, mainly wildfowl and young waders can occur quite frequently on the prey list at times. You only have to see the panic amongst a group of wildfowl on the water, when an otter enters the scene to realise the threat they must pose.

Near the coast and in the estuaries they are partial to crabs, shrimps and even shellfish, sometimes in great quantities and to the exclusion of almost all other food sources. On ditch systems and floodplain marshes in summer they have also been known to take large numbers of dragonflies, which they must find at night when the dragonflies are roosting/resting on the vegetation and relatively easy prey.

While surveying for water voles on Cors Fochno, myself and another fieldworker watched three otters working a wide ditch together and coming up so close we could hear them crunching on sticklebacks, or more likely dragonfly nymphs? So you could be lucky, don't give up on ever seeing an otter but do keep an eye out for those signs.

October 2005
Fox

OVER THE YEARS I have had quite a few encounters with foxes.

One of the most attractive animals in what is the rather impoverished mammalian fauna of the British Isles, equally one of the most admired and despised by different sections of the community. Admired for its resilience to persecution and for its undoubted adaptability, despised for its depredations by the game and shooting fraternity and by many sheep farmers, for obvious reasons. Though I do know of several farmers who are happy to have 'their own' foxes settled on their land, as long as they are not causing too much damage. They only become a potential problem to sheep farmers at lambing time anyway, otherwise they do sterling work for the farmer by keeping the rat, vole and rabbit populations under some control.

Several years ago I watched a fox run through a flock of sheep in broad daylight and the sheep never turned a hair nor blinked an eye, as far as I could see. If it had been a dog and a well behaved dog at that, I suspect the reaction would have been somewhat different.

I have also watched a fox watching a shepherd and his dogs. While descending a mountain I noticed a fox lying on a grassy shelf some distance below. It in turn was peering over the edge at the shepherd and his dogs, working the sheep a further 100 metres or so below.

Closer encounters with truly wild foxes are relatively rare and generally fleeting. But in recent years I have had occasion to be out at night actually seeking them out. Fox surveys can be done by walking a transect route and with the aid of a powerful torch it is possible to pick out the reflection from their eyes, and the eyes of anything else that happens to be out and about for that matter. For example, I was quite seriously thrown one evening to observe a pair of distant eyes slowly lifting and lowering what I knew to be quite some height. Not exactly spooked but decidedly puzzled, I was glad to finally work out that it was a very dark horse that I had not realised was in the field. Peacefully it continued grazing as I walked on, somewhat relieved.

Foxes I came across at fairly frequent intervals, particularly when cubs were out and about exploring. There is a technique sometimes used for calling-in foxes so that they come within range of rifle or shotgun. By sucking on the back of your hand you can make a squeal or squeaky noise, something akin to that made by a rabbit in distress, or so they say. Having tried this on several occasions I can say it does work, sometimes! Some of the more wary foxes will disappear like a shot but others are certainly attracted by the prospect of an easy meal and it can be quite disconcerting, having the glowing eyes of a fox homing in on you and approaching you in the dark.

Cubs are more inquisitive, naïve and much easier to approach without causing alarm. On one occasion I watched three quite large cubs that had obviously just emerged from a nearby earth. One remained very wary, one interested and one was downright cheeky, or foolhardy perhaps. I could have lifted my foot and literally pushed it away, it came so close.

Encounters in daylight are few but I guess, as with the shepherd watching fox, it is more often a case of being watched than watching, for we humans.

One encounter does however come to mind. It was in the foothills of Pumlumon, not far from Llyn Nant y Cagl. I was out early and taking a breather, leaning back against a fence, part way up a steep, grassy slope with forestry trees providing a bit of background camouflage. If you keep still and the wind is in the right direction to carry your scent away, even a fox might accept you as part of the scenery. This particular animal appeared from nowhere and began slowly working its way up the slope towards me, pouncing and feeding on what I assumed to be invertebrates in the grass, probably craneflies/daddy long legs, of which there were many.

I watched it for at least ten minutes as it continued its slow approach, absorbed in its breakfast snacks. Perhaps it had been a poor nights hunting? Only when it was within 15 metres or so did it stop, look up and take any note of me. After a brief consideration it departed in no great haste across the slope without a backward glance. On another occasion I had been sheltering for quite a while in a natural hollow high on an escarpment, sheltering from a biting east wind. On getting up to stretch and ease some stiff muscles I was surprised to see a splendid fox, little more than eight metres away. It too was stretching and actually yawning and I can only assume it had been sleeping in a small but dense patch of rushes that lay between us and off to one side. It looked at me with disdain, yawned again and trotted off seemingly unconcerned, though this one did stop and look back at me a few times before it disappeared through a broken down fence and into a jumble of fallen boulders. He or she, (even at such close quarters I was not sure whether it was a vixen or a dog fox), was obviously off looking for supper, or should that be breakfast? I still had a while to wait for dusk and hopefully some nightjars to put in an appearance.

Encounters such as these should be treasured- instances when we almost get in touch with really wild life in its own element, no matter how modified by man it might be.

Foxes are omnivorous. When there are no lambs, carrion, chickens, eggs, young birds, small mammals or rabbits to be had, they will eat insects, worms, fruit, berries and even leftover takeaways. Adaptable in the extreme, it is little wonder that they are such a successful species.

January 2016
Pine Marten

I went recently to a community engagement event in Pontrhydfendigaid (Bont) regarding the pine marten recovery project. Well attended with well over thirty in the audience we were treated to a very informative update from David Bavin of the Vincent Wildlife Trust (VWT).

Twenty martens (10 males and 10 females) were translocated in 2015 from NE Scotland and more recently nineteen (10 males and 9 females) have been released, having been translocated from NW Scotland. The VWT intend to further bolster this mid-west Wales population in the autumn of 2017, the intention being to establish a viable breeding population of at least forty individuals in the longer term. Some of the 2015 releases did produce young (kits) though the litters were small at only one or two kits per female. However pine martens are longer lived than your average small mustelid and they typically do have small litters. A male pine marten can have a head and body length of up to 52cm and a bushy tail of half that length again.

Males also have large home ranges that often take in parts of several female home ranges. Most of the released animals have GPS/radio collars and intensive tracking is beginning to reveal what they get up to and where exactly they might prefer to be. More detailed analysis is still to be done and will no doubt reveal more interesting information.

Information such as it is, of seventy den sites so far found, over 40% were in grey squirrel dreys! There is evidence from Ireland that pine martens do not tolerate grey squirrel presence and some recent Welsh video footage of a female marten and two kits with a dead grey squirrel would seem to point to that as a distinct possibility. It would be a great plus point if the martens could at least dent a burgeoning grey squirrel population, a population that damages young trees and also damages a lot of other wildlife.

Volunteer effort has been crucial in tracking, monitoring and scat (droppings) searches and it is probably true to say that without this volunteer effort the amount of information gathered would have been very much reduced and the VWT would like to thank all the volunteers, landowners and land managers and others that have made the project the success that it is so far.

Pine martens, like most predators, will take what is available and easy to find, catch and consume. Scat analysis has established that the 2015 releases were taking in something of the order of 27% invertebrates, 32 % small mammals (including grey squirrel), 20% birds and 20% carrion/fruits etc. The majority of the birds taken were young corvids (crows) and any effect on resident songbirds was therefore thought to be minimal at worst. In all likelihood there is going to be some slight positive benefit if the corvid population has another natural control in operation.

Some of the 2016 releases have dispersed similarly to the 2015 animals but the majority have remained relatively local to release sites near Pontarfynach (Devils Bridge). One true wanderer has ended up near Abergele in north Wales and there is some suspicion that there may be a remnant marten population surviving up there and within Clocaenog Forest anyway. Most appear to have followed river corridors where native broadleaved woodland occurs and there is a wider variety of potential food sources. Martens have also been tracked over to Nant-y-Moch, been found again in Clarach and followed further north into Cwm Llyfnant, Cwm Cletwr and Cwm Einion.

Monitoring will be on-going through the winter period though martens go into a slow-mo mode and may only be active for four to five hours out of the twenty-four- I know the feeling! There will no doubt be further interesting footage via night-vision cameras at dens and feeding sites- roe deer and red squirrel have already been recorded as a by-product of the monitoring. Hopefully there will be a good winter survival of martens and more kits produced in the spring. Sufficient numbers perhaps to make it even more difficult for all those volunteers to keep track of exactly what might be going on?

January 1993
Badger

THE BADGER, Meles meles, is by far the largest British carnivore, at up to 40lbs it easily outweighs the fox and the otter and its much smaller relative, the weasel.

In Wales it is many years since I last watched badgers at a sett and the last live Welsh badger I saw was in a bit of a hurry! Near Llyn Plas y Mynydd, a very dirty-looking badger (it had obviously been digging in peat) raced down from Pen Creigiau'r Llan, crossing the road to disappear into the forest plantation opposite. What exactly it was up to, steaming across the open hillside in the late morning, I have no idea but I will be forever grateful to this particular beast for giving me such a marvellous view of one of the shyest members of the British fauna.

Unfortunately there are others who hanker after even closer encounters with this largely harmless member of the mustelid family. I say largely harmless because occasionally, I have no doubt, they may take a chicken or even a lamb and I suspect a badger may have been responsible for demolishing my bee-hives more than once. However, to suggest that badgers habitually take domestic livestock is, I believe, a gross exaggeration and I would suggest any remains found outside a sett indicate a fox as 'lodger'. Foxes are untidy and probably barely tolerated by the average badger, which is noted for its cleanliness.

The 'others' looking for closer encounters are the 'diggers' and 'baiters'. Archaic thrill-seekers who think nothing of putting a brave terrier into a sett whilst the diggers get to work.

Alan Durrant, the local badger contact, informs me that diggers have been seen and disturbed recently at a sett on the outskirts of Aberystwyth.

Unfortunately I can only assume the practice is widespread in Ceredigion. I would urge anyone who knows of a sett: do keep an eye on it. If you see anyone with spades and/or dogs at, or acting suspiciously near a sett, do inform the police. Certainly *do not* confront any diggers actually in the act, but get help and that means the police, who are well versed in how to handle these situations.

The badger now has a reasonable degree of protection and basically no-one can interfere with a sett without a specific licence to do so. Dogs, implements and vehicles used in badger digging may be destroyed or confiscated and fines of up to £2,000 (per badger) may be imposed. So the law, at last, seems to be on the badger's side. You can do your bit by keeping your eyes and ears open for any suspicious activities that may threaten a sett and its occupants.

On a frosty Christmas Day we visited a long disused sett only to find all the signs of intense activity. Clearly loads of fresh bedding (bracken) had recently been taken into the sett complex and a badger or two, I have no doubt, are back in residence.

Pairing occurs in July or August, but due to a phenomenon known as delayed implantation, active development of the embryo usually takes place from the beginning of the next year, that is, about now. Cubs may be born between February and April, so we will be keeping an eye on this particular sett from now on, hoping for a view of the cubs in Spring.

November 1998
Woodcock

A FEW WEEKS ago I was writing and hoping for a colder, dry spell. All in aid of dormouse hibernation, as unseasonal mild spells are liable to cause premature awakenings which are thought not to be helpful to dormice. I have also moved several bags of grit and salt to beside the dodgy bits of our hill, bits that become a sheet of ice in frosty weather.

That last should have really done it, no chance now of a colder spell! Or perhaps there is time yet, we still have at least a couple of months for the weather to turn and show us what a winter should really be like.

As it is we have snowdrops in flower and even the daffodils are well advanced and having a look around, but sensibly no sign of them opening. Temperatures have often been well above normal though some very strong winds have occasionally had a northerly bite. And often a leaden sky has released copious quantities of rain, such that you begin to wonder, will it ever dry out?

At least this warm and wet weather is appreciated by the woodcock. One of our most enigmatic birds, it is certainly a difficult species to get a handle on. Last summer I travelled extensively in Wales involved in nightjar survey work and was expecting to come across a few woodcock in at least some of the forested areas we visited. But only at one site, south of Brecon near the Talybont reservoir, did we find woodcock. This was in a mosaic of planted conifers with some clearfelled areas and a scattering of mature broadleaved trees. Exactly the sort of habitat looked at elsewhere and by no means uncommon in north Ceredigion.

In the late '70s they were still a regular breeding species at Ynys Hir, RSPB reserve. And in the summer it was a delight to be out at dusk (less tempting at dawn) to see and hear them during their rather strange flights, low over the woods. Known as roding, this involves the male beating a regular circuit around a favoured area and is accompanied by some rather frog-like croaking and the occasional higher pitched clicking or squeak, depending upon how you might like to describe it. They have been recorded as breeding here since then, but only infrequently during the '90s.

I have no idea why they have declined, and in some cases, disappeared as a breeding species and as far as I am aware, neither has anyone else. But at least we have them in some numbers for the winter. Most come over from the continent to escape their harsher winters. Snow and deeply frozen ground spells serious trouble for woodcock (and many other species) and so each autumn I look forward to some colder weather as I know coming in ahead of it will be the first of the wintering woodcock.

Now you might flush them from almost any woodland cover but you are most unlikely to see them before they are in flight and weaving their way up through the trees. Their beautiful black and rich brown, cryptic colouring and extremely secretive nature make them perhaps the most difficult bird to spot, at least when on the ground. I usually only have the briefest of glimpses in the car headlights as we wend our way up Foel Fawr coming home at night. They regularly use one particular wet flush and shallow ditch beside the road. Better views may be had by going out at dusk and sitting somewhere with a lot of sky as backdrop. Then, if you pick the right spot, you might be lucky enough to see birds silhouetted against the sky as they flight out from cover and on to the fields to feed.

Built along similar lines to a snipe, the woodcock is altogether a heavier bird with wider and more rounded wings and a much slower flight. Unlike a snipe, when flushed from cover the woodcock invariably remains silent although if flushed from woodland it may do a bit of snipe-like weaving to avoid the odd branch. With a long bill suitable for quite deep probing, it should be no surprise to find earthworms form a large part of the diet. These the woodcock can find in abundance on the wet fields.

It has always been a favourite quarry of the shooting fraternity, two woodcock with two barrels being the ultimate achievement. But how anyone can justify shooting such a magnificent bird is quite beyond me. The hunting instinct prevails but surely it must be weakening by now and this bird should definitely be taken off the game list.

Many years ago I was told of a winter fall of woodcock on the slopes of Pumlumon. Over the wider area there must have been a quite massive influx of exhausted birds dropping down into the heather and longer grasses, seeking some respite, rest and recuperation after an arduous flight from somewhere quite distant, maybe even non-stop from the continent.

Some of these birds were walked-up several times before eventually falling to a gun. Apparently they could barely fly 30 yards before having to come down to ground again.

Not exactly sporting, but a very interesting story and not likely to be repeated. In those days (sometime in the 50s or early 60s ?) there would certainly have been better heather and a few more grouse on Pumlumon. Nowadays you would have to be a very optimistic gun to bother taking your 12 gauge onto any mountain in the area. The heather is sparse and localised, the grouse have all but disappeared and you could never rely on coinciding with another fall of woodcock.

As a breeding species they remain quite rare in Ceredigion, although, being mainly nocturnal they are no doubt under recorded to a degree. Some shoots still take a bag of woodcock from lowland woods and no one knows if they are local birds or not. Much better give them a rest and leave them in peace. Watch them flighting out to the fields at dusk and then perhaps once again we might be able to enjoy the spectacle of their strange roding come the summer evenings.

1995/2005
Dotterel/ Pumlumon

I had thought that perhaps I might have left it too late. The past records I could lay hands on referred to the first two weeks of May and here I was on the 20th setting out for Pumlumon in search of dotterel, Hutan y Mynydd.

Pumlumon is my local and certainly one of the most reliable migration sites in Wales and each spring I try to set aside a day to go and meet up with some of them. There must be a steady throughput of dotterel and by spring I suppose I mean somewhere between the 6th and 22nd of May. Late for the birds down at lower levels but for denizens of high elevations with destinations much further north, quite early enough I suppose.

Smaller than the garden plover but larger than the ringed plover, the dotterel is recognisably of the plover family. On Pumlumon in May, a sizeable, somewhat dumpy looking bird, (imagine a mistle thrush without the long tail) is likely to be a dotterel. Be aware they are very active when on the ground and feeding, running in a typical plover fashion, hither and thither as they chase up invertebrates. When on the wing, flying usually quite low and fast, their long and pointed wings are diagnostic as is their rather soft, drawn out call. A trill or phurr-r-r, quite unlike any other bird call that I am familiar with.

On migration these fast flying birds use traditional routes and stopping off points. These might be particular fields on the eastern seaboard or as here in Wales, typically involves mountain hopping. Apart from on Pumlumon, dotterel are also seen on Cadair Idris with some regularity. This too has a long, stony saddle which is virtually bare of vegetation and just the type of habitat they like. Northward, spring migration is usually in early-mid May, the return in late summer-autumn is less predictable or, at least as yet, less well known. My only autumnal encounters with dotterel have been on the east coast of England, and once when I came across a single bird on Foel Fras, that rather strange, rocky, northernmost outlier of the Carneddau in north Wales.

Despite its rather rounded outline, Pumlumon *is* a mountain and deserves a degree of respect. Being so close to the Cardigan Bay coastline, the weather is generally quite mild but typically fickle and it can change very quickly. Driving and drenching wet snow is not what you expect in mid May, but that is exactly what I experienced, admittedly some years ago and before there had been any talk of global warming. Unpleasant in the extreme, this was the only day I had available and although the chances of seeing any dotterel were virtually nil, I went.

In some quite atrocious weather I was amazed to see the hardy Welsh mountain sheep lambing high on the mountain but after reaching the summit cairns I very quickly descended. Wet, bedraggled but otherwise satisfied that I had at least made the attempt at seeing some dotterel.

To get to Pumlumon we can take a long and winding road from beside the Dyfi estuary, through forestry plantations and then alongside and around the huge Nant y Moch reservoir, source of the water for the Dinas and Rheidol hydro electric schemes.

Pumlumon attracts relatively few botanists as the acidic soils support a rather uniform and dull flora that has long been overgrazed by too many sheep. However, a small herd of highland cattle have recently been turned out on to the lower slopes and hopefully the sheep numbers will be reduced and a greater degree of plant diversity will be the result. We will have to wait a few years yet to see the results of this experiment!

On the higher slopes and on the plateau you do find virtual carpets of clubmosses, namely the fir club moss, Hyperzia selago and more commonly, the alpine clubmoss, Diphasiastrum alpinum. And on a few of the most inaccessible ledges to sheep you might also find wood sorrel, wood anemone and even a few harebells. Relicts of a more diverse plantlife that might once again flourish, should the sheep ever be taken off or their numbers be drastically reduced.

My most fruitful hunting ground for dotterel has always been the rock-strewn, bare ground just to the east and south of the summit cairns and trig point. Here the dotterel can feed or shelter in any one of many hollows or amongst one of the equally numerous piles of stone. Being an incredibly tame and inquisitive bird it is usually easy to observe them for quite a while, once they have been located. Always bear in mind, these are birds on migration and Pumlumon is in effect a rest and recuperation spot. So view from afar and let them get about their business. Like as not, if you sit quietly and watch, they will approach you as they scurry about picking up invertebrates from the sun warmed rocks.

On colder, wet and windier days I have almost trodden on birds, huddled together and sheltering in one of the hollows, decidedly reluctant to fly. I then always retreat and leave them in peace.

Having got up to the summit, found dotterel or not, what do you do next? Never being one for wasting height gained, I will usually try to take in a little bit more, often setting off past the source of the Wye and following the fenceline to Pen Pumlumon Arwystli. From here it is barely another two kilometres to another minor summit and cairn from which you can look down upon the peat hags and bog surrounding the source of the Severn.

Interesting, but wet, so I will then bear westwards and begin the trek back, my first objective being the distinctively tall and slender cairn on the north side of the entrance to Cwm Gwarin. This fantastic vantage point gives an uninterrupted view down the wide valley of the Afon Hengwm. Having taken in the view you can pick a way down through natural cliff terracing to the valley floor where the remote and ruined farmsteads of Lluestnewydd and Hengwm Anedd continue to slowly moulder and crumble into the earth.

The Hengwm is an unusually wide and relatively shallow river for this area. Wildlife remains sparse but there is always the chance of seeing a dipper or grey wagtail, or perhaps even a pair of common sandpiper. Alas, as with much of our wildlife, not so common nowadays.

The whole circuit from Maesnant via Pumlumon Fach, Pumlumon Fawr and the return via Cwm Gwarin and Nant y Llyn amounts to about twelve kilometres. There is certainly not a lot of variety in the birdlife but even if you miss out on dotterel it would be unusual (for the observant) not to see buzzard, raven and a red kite or peregrine falcon. Most of the small, brown birds will be meadow pipits and you can still hear a few skylarks up here on fine spring mornings. Also remember to look out for the wheatears on the stony summits and other bouldery places. Buff, pink and grey with a bold white patch over the upper tail, apart from dotterel that's about as colourful as it gets on these often wet and windy high places of Ceredigion.

Local Area

June 1993
The Dyfi

THE DYFI ESTUARY has to be one of the 'crown jewels' in the Welsh landscape, less dramatic than the Mawddach perhaps, the Dyfi makes up for it on sheer size.

Dyfi Junction station is almost exactly 10 kilometres from the river mouth and the tidal reach extends well inland of even here. From the junction the northern section of the Cambrian Coast railway, to Aberdyfi, Tywyn, Barmouth and Pwllheli takes you right beside the estuary.

The views are breathtaking and the wildlife seen from the train can be interesting too. And, more often than not you will see sailing craft moored and/or canoeists exploring the mid reaches, certainly in the vicinity of Frongoch boatyard.

Occasionally I am persuaded to make the effort to get our canoes in the water and often Frongoch will be our destination. Quietly drifting downstream on the ebb tide has to be one of the most relaxing ways possible to birdwatch*. Red-breasted mergansers allow closer approach and it is interesting to see the males now in 'eclipse'. That is, moulting their splendid winter/spring plumage, looking scruffy and barely distinguishable from the grey/brown females.

Fifteen years ago Canada geese were a rare sight on the Dyfi, now there are nearly 300 adults and they are breeding prolifically, apparently causing problems with some local farmers by grazing recently sown grass and crops.

They are also of concern to the conservation organisations as they are very large birds and they tend to be quite aggressive towards other, more welcome waterfowl.

The cutting and embankment some half a kilometre north east of Frongoch has been home to a small colony of herring gulls for many years. We counted about a dozen nests and briefly visited the nest of one very foolish or brave pair, right on the tide line at the foot of the railway wall. Two massive, dark, olive-green eggs with blackish markings, I had forgotten how large they are.

Towards Frongoch we passed a tideline strewn with 28 dead sheep, mainly ewes but some lambs too. A sad sight but evidence of just how dangerous estuaries and saltmarshes can be, and not only for sheep! A fisherman setting up his gear was a good indication that the tide had turned and we could expect some help upriver back to Glandyfi.

We waited on a secluded beach and as the tide reached us noticed a hole in a curtain of ivy overhanging the cliff. Closer investigation produced a few white feathers with brown tips and I have no doubt we had found the entrance to a Shelduck's nest. They use rabbit burrows, nest under walls, boulders or rockfalls, even share a badger sett, often a long way away from the coast. The young on hatching then have to make a perilous journey down to the estuary or the sea.

Shoals of mullet come up with the tide, feeding on the shrimps that swarm in their millions in the shallow water at this time of year.

Soon the young mergansers will join them in partaking of this nourishing shrimp soup and I look forward to seeing the confusion which can occur when two merganser families meet. They certainly can't count nor do they know their own offspring.

*Bill Condry and RS Thomas were well known for birdwatching from a drifting boat on the Dyfi Estuary.

July 1993
Craig Yr Aderyn

MANY IS THE TIME that I looked with envious eyes at walkers using the footpath that follows the Afon Dysynni from Abergynolwyn to Pont Ystummaner. Only recently has it been convenient, and I have had the opportunity, to tread this well-used path myself.

On the outskirts of Abergynolwyn a footbridge over Nant Gwernol sets you on the right path, past Gamallt Farm and over two stiles along the south side of the river, to a magnificent viewpoint. A smoothed rocky outcrop marks this spot, almost immediately opposite Nantmyniawyd which joins the Dysynni, far below and on the north side.

These outcrops are of particular interest for three metal rings set in the rock.

Puzzling, but after some fanciful considerations it was decided that they must have been used for tethering livestock, probably cows. Adjacent to each ring-stake (made of one inch diameter bar) the rock has been carved out to a depth of 3-4 inches, presumably to take a small amount of feed, perhaps to keep the cows happy while they were milked?

Nant Gwernol has by this point been absorbed into the more substantial Dysynni whose source is Llyn Mwyngil, better-known perhaps as Tal-y-llyn lake. Dippers, mergansers and grey wagtails frequent all these rivers and streams and on a recent visit I have also found signs of otters. On such quality waters this is only to be expected and I hope the fishermen do not begrudge sharing their sport with such magnificent creatures.

From Pont Ystumanner you should be able to make out the ruins of Castell y Bere, a 13th century castle, thought to have been built by Llywelyn ap Iorwerth. The rocky outcrop on which the ruins stand is a fantastic vantage point from which to take in the main Dysynni valley. It does not take a great deal of imagination to visualize the flat, bottom fields either flooded by high tides or at least very marshy in the 13th century. Apparently the sea level has fallen some 60 feet since the days of Llywelyn ap Iorwerth!

South west and down the 'old estuary' lies Craig yr Aderyn (Bird Rock), an enormous dome of rock, home to a thriving colony of cormorants, kestrels, jackdaws and chough. At six miles from the present coast, it is a unique cormorant colony. The spectacle of these enormous black birds wheeling about their nests high on the cliff face is something not to be missed.

February 2005
Murmurations

HIGH ON THE LIST of wildlife spectacles on offer in Ceredigion has to be the winter starling roost under the pier in Aberystwyth. Through late summer, autumn and throughout the winter vast numbers will gather.

Sometime in the late afternoon, (it can be as early as 3.30 pm on dull, wet days) large and small flocks may be seen flighting in from all landward quarters, though the vast majority seem to come in over the town from the east. Lesser numbers will come in over the cliff and sea from the north but I have only ever seen quite small numbers approaching along the coast from the south.

Occasionally some of the flocks can be huge, consisting of 1,000 birds or more. Anything of this size is likely to have formed at a pre-roost gathering from which the final evening flight in to the pier is made en-masse. More modest flocks may number only a few tens of birds, maybe a few hundred. These I have watched wave hopping as they swoop in low from the north. With such large numbers of birds on the move (the roost can total anything up to 10,000 to 20,000 birds) it is no surprise that a few predators are attracted. You may be lucky and see a peregrine as we did a few years ago. We watched it make two unsuccessful attempts at incoming starlings, while we enjoyed the comforts of the lounge bar of one of the several hotels towards the north end of the promenade. However if you want to take in the whole event you really need to be out in the weather, wrap up warmly and it could be well worth it.

How far do these birds come each evening? Are they always the same birds? Do they leave in the same smaller groups in the morning? Is information passed from group to group or individual to individual? Do they return to favoured feeding areas? Or is it all disorganised and much more random? Lots of questions we might ask but we have very few answers.

One answer we do have and it might surprise a lot of locals. The vast majority of these birds originate in north eastern Europe. Ringing recoveries over a number of years have established that our starlings travel to and fro between west Wales and Scandinavia and even further east to many of the Baltic states. Continental Europe can be notoriously cold, so the much warmer and often wet coastal areas of Wales become very attractive destinations for starlings and a whole range of winter migrants. Starlings can roost safely under the pier and disperse daily to forage over the lowland fields and upland pastures. Combined they must consume an absolute mass of invertebrates over the course of a day never mind a whole winter.

And watching a flock work an area can be every bit as fascinating as watching swirls of birds going in to roost. With a continuous chattering a flock may appear to almost roll over the ground. Probing the soft soil with their quite long beaks they seem frenetically busy but progress can be slow. Those at the back of the flock soon get impatient (or fed up with leftovers) and so they fly to the front. So it goes on, a continuous roll-over of the flock until they run out of space or more likely there is an alarm of some sort and a mass movement as they all take flight and with a whirl of wings they are off to the next feeding site.

I have recently seen some sizeable flocks (500 plus) high on the hills above Pontrhydfendigaid, around the Teifi Pools area. On a cold and frosty day they were taking full advantage of the sun having thawed out the south facing slopes. Were these Aberystwyth birds? I suspect they may have been. Twenty five kilometres from the pier as the crow and starling might fly. Probably not too far to go looking for food, especially if you can make it over here from the Baltic states for the winter. Others might stick to the lowlands and smaller flocks can often be seen associating with waders on the saltmarsh and wet fields beside the Dyfi estuary. In fact it is sometimes quite difficult to differentiate between waders and starlings when they combine in flight, as they often do.

Adaptive and mobile as they are, the starling has become a cause for concern. Numbers have crashed, particularly breeding numbers in Britain and elsewhere in Europe. A range of causes has been speculated. Amongst them, lack of winter stubble- they will take a lot of grain and other seeds if available in winter. Lack of nest sites- we do have a habit of filling in holes in buildings and clearing up natural hole nest sites in the form of old or dead and woodpeckered trees.

Amazing birds, they can be very noisy and aggressive at a bird table. Their long beak, rather upright stance and swaggering walk can make them unpopular. But they are stunningly speckled and glossy plumaged when seen at close quarters. Do not take them for granted. Like most of our wildlife, they are under continual pressure.

October 2005
Mines & Quarries

WHILST I MAY BE FASCINATED by wildlife and wild places I also take more than a passing interest in the past industrial activities of we humans. Possibly because the disruptions caused by all this activity almost inevitably creates a whole range of micro-habitats and environments that a range of wild species will somehow seek to exploit.

You must marvel at the landscape of north Ceredigion where it borders on Montgomeryshire and Merionydd, scarred over millenia and often into the quite recent past by human activity of all kinds.

Paths, tracks, railways and tramways, leats, mines and quarries scattered all over the map and over the ground. Now most are defunct and derelict and indeed fading, if ever so slowly, back into that self same landscape now largely given over to farming or forestry and increasingly to tourism.

Those major visual scars left by mining and quarrying are only part of the story. Such activities also inevitably effect the flora and fauna in the immediate surrounds and in some cases can have quite serious and prolonged affect on invertebrates, fish and watercourses far downstream.

The Afon Ystwyth and Afon Rheidol still occasionally feel the effects of all the mining activity long ceased at Cwmystwyth and in the Rheidol valley. However, on the plus side some rather interesting plant communities often occur around old mine sites, particularly on some of the less hospitable, leftover substrates such as the spoil from mineral ore (copper, lead and zinc) processing.

Thrift or sea pink and sea campion are two species very much associated with coastal habitats and both are quite abundant and add a brilliant flash of colour to the old cliffs around Aberystwyth Castle grounds in summer. They, along with moonwort and forked spleenwort (both small ferns) can also be found at one or two of the many mine sites in Ceredigion. Rarely in abundance and somewhat out of context, these and a few other species can make a plant identification trip to a mine site, just that little bit more interesting.

I have also heard stories of spoil being taken away and used for paths and in concrete mixes for barn walls. It looks ideal, but don't do it! Both practices apparently had quite serious consequences for the chickens that picked up the grit and the cattle that were in the habit of licking the wall! In fact I do believe you may need a licence to disturb mine spoil at all, because of the potential release of heavy metal residues.

If anything, the adits of mines can be even more fascinating, though most are now blocked for safety reasons. Preferably blocked with a substantial grille or gate with at least an opening for the bats and other creatures to gain entrance. Bats seek out sites with very stable temperatures and old adits make good substitutes for natural caves where at any great depth the temperature can remain remarkably stable. One question does occur to me as I write this, how does a bat know when conditions are right to emerge or that it is the right time of year, when it has been in such a controlled and stable environment for days, weeks or even months?

Having over the years been into a few adits, I am always amazed at the conditions those miners had to endure. Dark, dangerous and dusty and if not dusty then dark, dangerous and decidedly wet! Some system of pumping out or draining water was always essential it seems.

Last week we scrambled up the steep southern slope of the Llyfnant valley, having been given good directions and an assurance that the luminous moss, schistostega pennata, was luminescent just a few weeks previous, we confidently found the cave in which it occurs.

It is a 'cave' only due to a huge overhanging slab of rock that must weigh tens of tons. The enormous boulder has peeled away from the crag and created a deep, dark hole into which it is quite easy to walk. Right at the back a rather eerie, greenish-yellow glow was unmistakably the luminous moss. Quite startling, we were looking for shafts of sunlight at first but there was nothing apart from the light at the entrance to cause this effect. It was one of the most unusual sights I have ever seen and it quite made up for the previous times I had been here and failed to see the phenomenon! Many of the caves in mid-Wales are of this type, formed by overlying boulders rather than true caves.

Slate quarries were little different in that they were equally dangerous places of work though, I suppose, the quarry worker did benefit from seeing the light of day for longer. Assuming that is, they were not deep underground in some cavernous working such as might be found near Corris and Aberlleffeni or that slate mecca - Blaenau Ffestiniog. Open quarries can be good hunting grounds for ferns, though the rather nutrient-poor conditions of west Wales slate quarries often restricts the range of species that occur. Dimly lit, sheltered, frost free and often wet rock faces are just what they like but don't be tempted to go seeking them out in quarries. They can all be found and seen in much more comfort and safety on roadside rockfaces or within the many wooded valleys that flank the Dyfi Estuary or which, further south lead more directly to the sea.

Old quarries and indeed mine shafts are also the sometimes haunt of choughs, that red billed and red legged member of the Corvidae or crow family that is more commonly seen disporting itself along the coastal cliffs of Ceredigion. On a recent visit to the Monks Cave coastal area, between Llanrhystud and Aberystwyth, we had a pair of chough somewhere near or often overhead for much of the afternoon. They were making full use of a sunny if windy day and we also saw several species of butterfly doing likewise, including small copper, common blue, wall brown and small tortoiseshell. A narrow strip of ungrazed or lightly grazed grassland was all that was required to give the butterflies enough shelter from the wind and the foodplants, flowers and nectar sufficient for survival.

Choughs like to feed on invertebrates that they find by probing, with their almost sickle-like bill, in the very short, sheep grazed turf or in shallow and often eroding soils at the cliff top and along old field boundaries. There is, as usual, at least the potential for a conflict of interest here and indeed elsewhere where I have seen management for choughs (admittedly a rare species) seemingly take precedence over all else. Is it ever sensible to manage an area for the benefit of just one species? A balance has to be struck somewhere and I personally hope that the butterflies and all manner of other flora and fauna are taken into account when deciding on management of such a unique and scenically beautiful area as Ceredigion's coast.

October 1993 & October 2006
Dyfi Estuary

The Dyfi estuary is one of the best places to witness bird migration or birdwatch along the whole west coast of Wales. Not that it's easy: it is always a bit of a gamble where you might do your bird-watching with access/viewpoints at a premium given that the estuary is something like 10 kilometres in length (from the sea to Glandyfi) and at its widest it reaches three kilometres.

As the tide rises (there were some exceptional tides in mid-September) waders are forced off the sand and mudflats and may resort to moving higher up-river and regularly end up on the raised ground of the saltings of Ynys Hir RSPB reserve. If the tide is pushed up by westerly winds or there is a lot of fresh water in the river, then they may even be forced over the railway embankment into the floodplain fields. This did not happen on the last high tide series, but Ynys Hir is always a good bet (especially when the weather is a bit iffy) as there are several hides overlooking the estuary in which to shelter.

At the mouth of the estuary in late summer /early autumn there is always the possibility of terns and offshore there may be gannets. Typically the terns are likely to be sandwich terns but occasionally there will be a common/arctic tern among them. The two species can be difficult to determine, hence the catch-all 'comic' category. If you are really lucky you may even get a little tern. The nearest breeding colonies are now on the north Wales coast though they did breed on the shingle at the mouth of the Dysynni, just north of Tywyn, into the 1980's.*

Amongst the waders, dunlin and ringed plover prevail but autumn is also good for rarities such as curlew, sandpiper and little stint and I was pleased to hear a distant whimbrel off Ynys Hir during one of those recent high tides. Whimbrel, for some reason, are much more reliable on spring migration and can be seen on the foreshore, estuary and fields near Ynys Las, sometimes in good numbers in April and May. Lesser birding sites going northwards include Aber Dysynni (Broad Water) near Tywyn, always a favourite spot with the possibility of eider duck an added attraction just off the point. I recently managed a walk down Afon Cletwr, a significant tributary of the Dyfi on the south side. Here, as the tide was rising, there were marooned sheep, several little egrets and two greenshank. The latter are medium sized waders, very loud and slightly larger than the redshank. Their plumage is pale-grey/white and their presence a sure sign of winter's approach.

Even more interesting were the grey mullet creating ripples and occasionally breaking the surface with tail and dorsal fins as they cruised the shallow water. At about a foot/15 inches long they were nothing like the size of some seen near the harbour mouth in Aberystwyth recently, but I was quite impressed and pleased to see them nevertheless.

A brief clearing of the sky just recently had me out looking over the estuary from Y Foel, Ffwrnais. The summit is only a little over 700 feet but it is quite spectacular, rocky and broken. It stands out as truly mountainous despite being dwarfed by much higher, rounded, grassy mountains nearby. After more rain and with a weak sun filtering through a grey sky the estuary looked a very wet place, even with the tide out. In the mid-distance on one of the firmer, muddy banks I could just make out a moored boat, but my eyes failed to pick out the cockle-pickers I knew would be there. Some days previously I had actually ventured onto this vast expanse of sand, mud and water for a closer look at their work. And what work, in all weathers, ruled by the tide, raking up cockles into net bags which are designed to let the smaller cockles fall through, back onto the beds.

Most of the pickers were down here from the Dee, where the cockle beds are virtually worked out. Recently I had heard a similar story from a fisherman in Morecombe, Lancashire. Over-exploitation has caused the once prolific Morecombe Bay shellfish industry to collapse.

Whilst out on the Dyfi I tagged along with the sea fisheries inspectors as they checked the catch. On this occasion all were over minimum size, but I imagine that sometimes theirs is not the most popular of jobs. Nevertheless, it is necessary when there are obvious dangers of over-exploitation. This time there were 15 pickers, but there had been 50 earlier in the year!

Using a simple tenth of a square metre frame and a small garden sieve it was easy to take samples from the beds. One sample extrapolated to 540 cockles per square metre. This seemed like an amazingly high number to me, but earlier in the year the inspectors had found well over 1,000 cockles per square metre on a nearby bed.

Cockles have been an important food source for many years, although it is only in the past 18 months or so that serious, commercial fishing has been resumed on the Dyfi.

Some fifteen years ago I discovered a dump of cockle shells, partly buried deep in the conifer plantations at Lodge Park, near Tre'ddol, a relatively short walk from the estuary and the beds now being worked.

Whether the landed gentry were eating them or whether it was the estate workers' fare I have no idea. It does show however that cockles have been taken from the Dyfi previously, in some quantity.

It is to be hoped that the present much more intensive exploitation is having no long-term detrimental effects upon the estuary ecosystem.

*One of the first jobs I did in Wales, in 1977 and '78 was collecting the little tern wardens' hut from the army camp in Tywyn and helping erect it in rather an exposed position on the shingle ridge at the point. Several poor breeding seasons due to high tides and the depredations of kestrel and probably foxes, allied to increased human disturbance saw this enterprise fail, some time in the early to mid '80's.

October 2016
Dyfi Ospreys

Alongside the A487, between Glandyfi and Machynlleth, the Dyfi Osprey Project, its website and facilities have certainly been appreciated by a wide range of the general public.

I remember the first nest platform being erected in the top of a tall spruce tree about a kilometre downstream of the present site and being phoned by a local farmer, who had seen a large bird on the nest.

This turned out to be a bit of a false alarm as it proved to be a Canada goose - amazing where these birds get to and quite a feat of aeronautics to land safely! My knowledge of the present Osprey Project site goes back much further, to the late '70s /early '80s when, with the Forestry Commission (FC), I looked at a relatively small, dense spruce plantation with a view to its wildlife/conservation potential. Clearfelling and eventual conversion to such as the Osprey Project were never on the agenda at that time.

It was difficult to penetrate and the conifers were well grown, having been planted on ploughed ridges and further freed from a high water table by a system of ditches and dykes. These had a sparse growth of phragmites (common reed) along them but the only plant I remember of note was the royal fern, not exactly common in the wild, but occurring locally and in some quantity nearby at Cors Fochno.

After being sold by FC to a private buyer and the felling of the spruce, the area was allowed to regenerate near-naturally for a while. Later, several pools were excavated and the first boardwalk was put in by the Montgomery Wildlife Trust (MWT). By this time the phragmites had spread and bog myrtle (myrica gale) had also appeared in quantity alongside embryo birch and willow scrub. For several years it became a favoured haunt of barn owl, grasshopper warblers and nightjar amongst many other species. The birch and willow requires constant management to prevent the whole area becoming a wet, broad leaved woodland. This, on occasions, has required the grazing and trampling effects of the popular water buffalo but it also needs the assistance of a band of volunteers and MWT staff.

The present boardwalk gives access to the lofty 360-degree observatory which in turn gives excellent views of the osprey nest, distant over the nearby Cambrian Coast rail line. Technology feeds high quality pictures to the reception centre and on-line and has allowed detailed observation of activity at and near the nest. A five-year summary of fish brought in shows that grey mullet provides around 46% of the catch, sea trout a further 24% and flounder, something like 20%. What this translates to in weight terms and calories is more difficult to determine but attempts are being made to establish these facts as well. Bass and brown trout combined account for a further 8% and quite a wide range of other fish species the remaining 2%. Roach and perch have figured in their diet and I know perch occur in Llyn Penrhaeadr, which can be approached from the Llyfnant/ Glaspwll or Einion valleys.

On sunny days the board walk is a great place to see common lizards and here they literally are common. The darker edging strips are preferred basking sites and with a regular throughput of visitors the lizards are tolerant of passers-by and often quite approachable.

They vary greatly in coloration and, while some will be almost garish green, others are dun and dull browns to virtually black, but they are all the same species.

The ospreys have raised young in each of the past six years, no mean achievement when you consider the vagaries of the weather and regular trains passing by within 100 metres or so. Hopefully they will be back in late March/early April 2017. Their return from wintering in Central Africa is always eagerly awaited by a host of volunteers, project staff and visitors alike.

May 2005
Pwll y Gele

IT'S SOMETHING of a longstanding joke on our travels. Comment, "That looks like an interesting valley/ woodland/ river/ mountain, have you ever been there?"

"Well yes," (more often than not I have). "Mind you it was a long time ago."

I must admit that in the course of one job or another, perhaps a wildlife survey, outdoor pursuits or just natural curiosity, I have been about a bit in mid and north Wales. However, I was recently pleasantly surprised to come across something outstanding (and new to me) in an area I thought I knew well.

One of the most attractive small bodies of water you could ever imagine. An oversight on my part, almost slap-bang in the centre of my old stomping grounds – Coed y Brenin (King's forest) near Dolgellau.

In fact I was returning from a visit to the arboretum below Glasdir, beside Afon Las. Hereabouts the douglas fir must be some of the best in Wales. Impressive, towering straight trees of high value, I am sure more of these quality trees could be grown on the better ground in other forest districts. And could we look to progress to Continuous-Cover forestry on some of the very best sites?

Two foresters I have spoken with in recent months have expressed more than a passing interest in this type of forest management. Given the right thinning regime in the early years of a plantation's life I see no reason why it would not be feasible to create a more 'natural forest' on selected sites.

On my return from Glasdir on this occasion the complex of minor roads around Llanfachreth had me confused for a while. I had no map! So it was that I came across Pwll y Gele, two miles (as the crow flies) to the east of Llyn Cynwch, familiar to anyone who knows Precipice Walk. In the early 80's I passed through this area frequently (involved with survey and conservation work for the Forestry Commission), but I had never taken this particular by-road to pass Pwll y Gele.

It was early April and the showers were decidedly wintry, snow and sleet! From the shelter of the car I could see two female goldeneye, and just off the near bank a little grebe called and soon appeared out of the reeds. Pwll y Gele is generally shallow with emergent vegetation almost in mid-water.

More recently I called back again, back-tracking my route, as again I had forgotten my map! A beautiful spring day with wood anenomes, primroses and the first bluebells in flower, the 28th of April and I also heard my first cuckoo. Now a pair of coots, and a pair of great crested grebes were in residence. Fish were rising and the water was mirror smooth and so clear that the rosettes of water lobelia were easily recognisable on the stony bottom. An idyllic scene with lots going on, but so peaceful and tranquil, it was almost magical.

I will certainly be calling in again to see how the grebes get on and to have a look at the lobelia and water lilies. Also to pass a few quiet moments in contemplation perhaps!

Outings

November 1991
View From The Ridge

LATE IN OCTOBER I was fortunate enough to spend two days camping in north Wales just a few kilometres south of Yr Wyddfa, Snowdon.

Hardly a breath of wind, nor rain, plenty of sunshine and spectacular views to the summits – absolutely incredible! We approached Snowdon via Cwm Llan which has obviously seen a lot of activity in its time. Mineral mines and slate quarries are found along the length of the valley. The slate quarrying was sufficiently important to make it worthwhile building a substantial tramway and incline to get the products out.

Now it is the walkers rather than any mine or quarry workers that frequent Cwm Llan and the old tramway makes an ideal walking surface.

It is part of one of the less popular routes for the energetic aiming for Snowdon's summit. For the more easy going a nose around the quarry workings, a look at the waterfalls and the spectacular scenery is often enough.

On our way to Snowdon's summit this particular day we saw several flocks of fieldfare coming to settle and rest for a while on the sun-warmed slopes. What a difference from another October day I well remember on the Carneddau to the north.

Carnedd Llewelyn is only a few metres short of Snowdon in height and I recall walking across this windswept mountain through rain and thick cloud.

On this particular day even the birds were keeping their feet on the ground as much as possible. Chaffinches, obviously as determined as ourselves, boulder-hopped through the rain, against the wind, determined to get over the ridge and down into some safer haven. Birds only a few metres from our group, totally engrossed in crossing that sodden mountain! However, back to the sunshine and Snowdon. At the summit, eight ravens performed and played in the wind currents and we even had two butterflies (small tortoiseshells) as we lunched in sunny luxury.

The views from Snowdon are often joked about, cloud, swirling mist, visibility near-nil and all that. This particular day the view was tremendous though not quite the best I've seen.

On the way up we had the good fortune to see a 'Brocken Spectre'. Within a rainbow halo our shadows were cast onto the clouds hundreds of feet below. Quite eerie and certainly a spectacular effect.

At times the spectres seemed three-dimensional as a wisp of cloud broke from the main mass and it appeared that the shadaows were reaching up towards us. Apparently the phenomenon takes its name from the Brocken mountains in Germany where these effects are said to be quite commonly seen.

It's easy to see why walkers in their thousands head regularly for the hills and Snowdon in particular. I just wish they could have the good fortune of getting up there on a clear day.

My hit rate stands at somthing less than 10%, but for all those disappointing misty days the occasional clear day can compensate.

October 1992
All At Sea

SINCE THE BEGINNING of the summer holidays we have had very few fine days when the wind has moderated. Unsettled weather, squally showers, more persistant rain and high winds have combined to keep the boats in harbour more often than not.

We, however, were extremely lucky to choose a fine, bright evening recently. An evening to take a boat out from Aberystwyth, ostensibly seal and bird watching. First we headed south. Beyond Blaenplwyf transmitter, dramatic, eroded boulder-clay cliffs give way to higher, equally spectacular mud-stone cliffs favoured by cormorants, shags and fulmars in the summer.

The caves, stacks, and sheltered coves are attractive to seals and we saw something like twenty grey seals observing us with some curiosity if not disdain.

Leaving the seals in peace and the cliffs to the roosting cormorants we headed out to sea in search of more birds. As the setting sun fell towards a far horizon we had distant views of a piratical skua harassing a kittiwake, otherwise it was quiet and at this point the latent hunting instincts of the passengers took over, could we have a go at fishing?

The rods were brought out and in an amazingly short time the first fish was boated. A spotted dogfish which was unhooked and returned, likewise fish number two, a small dab.

Then it was all systems go, as mackerel and herring took the baited lines on both sides of the boat. A whiting, a tiny grey gurnard and a splendid tub (or yellow) gurnard added variety as did a lesser weaver, one to be handled with gloves and care!

The gurnards were returned but I did not see what happened to the weaver (being pre-occupied untangling lines). I assume it too was returned to the sea. Eight species in something like an hour, a surprise to me and a delight to see species such as the 'tub' at close quarters. An amazing fish with pectoral fins adapted to feeling its way along the sandy bottom, 'sensing out' the hidden crabs, small fish, shrimps and other crustaceans on which it usually feeds.

The 'tub' or yellow gurnard can vary greatly in colouration but always has a reddish tinge. Our tub was decidedly pink and I immediately assumed it was a red gurnard but I was reliably informed that the smaller, red gurnard is really, *spectacularly* red!

Where the tub gurnard gets its 'yellow' alternative name from I did not think to ask but we all certainly enjoyed the fishing, the sea air, the seals, the birds and the most spectacular sunset.

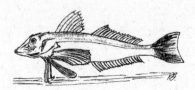

June 1993
Wood Ants

IN WALES the plight of the red wood ant formica rufa is apparently a cause for some concern. Relatively few nests are recorded and these are concentrated in Gwent, north Cardiganshire and areas adjacent to the River Mawddach in Meirionnydd.

Over the next two years the Countryside Council for Wales (CCW) hopes to survey and collate information on the distribution and abundance of these fascinating insects.

I say fascinating because only recently while walking in Coed y Brenin forest, which surrounds much of the upper Mawddach, we saw several of their substantial nest mounds.

Absolute 'hives' of activity on a warm, sunny day. The constant coming and going with nest material and food items is a sight to fascinate anyone.

We had ventured up the minor road leaving the A470 just north of Ganllwyd. This takes you over the River Eden at Pont-ar-Eden and continues through magnificent forest, alongside and often high above the Mawddach, towards the Gwynfynydd Gold Mine.

The Forestry Commission has recently made a substantial car park at the end of the public road, and for visitors and locals alike it makes a splendid walking base.

The Mawddach here is often enclosed in a rocky gorge, and looks very dramatic surrounded as it is by huge douglas firs and western red cedar. You can almost imagine you are in the North American Rocky Mountains! Although an environment much altered by man, it has its attractions, and the Forestry Commission has gone to considerable lengths to make it accessible, providing many way-marked walks.

A footbridge crosses the Mawddach at Grid Reference 734251, less than one kilometre upstream from the confluence with the Eden, and it was here that we had the most fascinating and closest encounter with the red wood ant. A veritable army was passing to and fro along the north side of the bridge, those heading east laden with spoils! This was not nest material, which could presumably be gathered from much closer to the nest, these ants were laden with food!

Wood ants are excellent hunter-gatherers, and by crouching on our hands and knees, much to the surprise of passing walkers, we could get a closer look and some idea of what food they were finding.

A few were struggling under absolutely massive loads, considering the ants' own size of about one centimetre long. Beetles and spiders caused great problems, though it appeared that many of the larger items had been divided up at source. Most however were carrying small, pale-yellow aphid-like insects that were no problem at all.

We followed their trail over the bridge and located a moderate-sized nest, a heaving mass of ants and conifer needle litter, on a roadside bank. Apparently an average nest of up to one metre in diameter may consume as many as six million food items each year. As 99 percent of this consists of woodland invertebrates and their larvae it is hardly surprising to hear that Scandinavian foresters positively encourage the wood ant.

April 2015
Coastal Birds

ON SATURDAY, 14th March, I saw a swallow, heard that it was the lowest winter Arctic sea-ice coverage ever recorded and was reminded that the west Antarctic ice sheet was under threat.

Inevitably, we are becoming ever more concerned about climate change - perhaps we should just say global warming and be done with it, as there seems to be little doubt that it is happening.

The swallow was easy enough to remember as it was seen on a trip to The Victoria Inn in Borth to watch that Six Nations epic against Ireland - a trip that inevitably and unnecessarily added to our CO_2, emissions and our carbon footprint. On 20th March (eclipse day), we were a little more environmentally friendly and took a morning train on the northern branch of the Cambrian Coast from Machynlleth. Soon, we were looking over a very full Dyfi Estuary, which was more like a mill pond with hardly a ripple on the water.

A very high tide that morning not surprisingly coincided with the partial eclipse and combined with some mist it all made for a very atmospheric light.

We planned to leave the train at Morfa Mawddach for an easy walk across the bridge into Barmouth, but first the precarious looking cliff section before Fairboume and Morfa is usually of interest.

Lots of herring gulls were back and beginning to sort out nest sites, some very close to the railway. It has in the past also been a site for fulmars, but there were none to be seen. However, the bonus bird on this trip was a peregrine - nonchalantly perched on one of the many retaining walls that support the track on this precipitous section. It was the briefest of glimpses as the train passed by, literally within a couple of metres of the bird.

Without doubt, it is the closest I have ever been to a wild peregrine, albeit from within a passing train. The driver must have had a fantastic view.

The eclipse was over by the time we were on the bridge and walking towards Barmouth, the tide rushing out with a vengeance far below. Typically, there was little bird life on the water or on the emerging sands, just a few cormorants, oystercatchers and a pair of great black-backed gulls.

The Mawddach is a very sandy and clean estuary (with very little mud and associated invertebrates) and as such it rarely attracts or holds very many waders as the food is just not available. After a coffee and some discussion it was decided to gain some height and head for one of the many viewpoints above the town- new territory for me.

Dinas Oleu (Fortress of Light) was the first ever National Trust property, gifted to the Trust in 1895 by Fanny Talbot. At something less than five acres, it is hardly one of the largest NT estates but its significance in starting a trend was well ahead of its time.

This rocky hillside overlooking Barmouth has numerous paths weaving their way between dense patches of gorse, developing scrub and alongside some immense drystone walls.

These massive walls immediately reminded me of Kyffin Williams' Welsh landscape paintings. Dark, hard, blocky and very angular with all the material quarried from the surrounding bedrock.

It was sunny and warm enough to detect a faint scent of gorse and several wheezy yellowhammers were singing and setting up territories. The whole hillside looks like excellent habitat for this declining bird and we would like to think that the National Trust will bear yellowhammers in mind when managing these few precious acres of a very rugged landscape.

February 2016
Porthmadog

I can think of numerous reasons to pay a visit to Porthmadog, the rail journey from Machynlleth being just one. It has to be amongst the top-ten most scenic in the UK and, as it takes the best part of two hours, there is time to relax and take it all in. Then there are the Ffestiniog and the Welsh Highland Railways, two major attractions for any steam enthusiast. Unfortunately on my last visit (early in January) there were no scheduled trains but as usual there was still some activity. Track maintenance and loco movements between the excellent (and seemingly always open) facilities at the Ffestiniog terminus and the locomotive works and sheds at Boston Lodge are always on the cards.

Another attraction is a walk along The Cob. Built by William Maddocks and completed in 1811 it allows for some close-up views of a variety of waterfowl and waders. Indeed the birds are now so inured to walkers that it takes quite an event to see them fly off in alarm. Any disturbance is more likely to be a passing peregrine or sparrowhawk looking for a meal, rather than any humans admiring the views up towards Glaslyn, Cnicht and Yr Wyddfa/Snowdon, walking the dog or birdwatching. On this particular day the tide had barely turned and water was being released via several sluices from the freshwater marsh behind the Cob. Not a lot of mud or shallow water was available so the wader count was low and bar-tailed godwits (barwits) were conspicuous by their absence. On another day this has to be one of the best places in Wales to observe this elegant bird. Unusually they have a slightly upturned bill and although in winter their plumage might look somewhat nondescript, in summer the plumage changes to a rich chestnut, almost red.

Cob Records (another reason) has been going for nigh on fifty years now and supplies vinyl, CDs and DVDs to a worldwide customer base. Amazing to browse their collection of LPs but my best record find was discovered in the Oxfam shop which is tucked away behind the park and not far from the attractive harbour. I had been on the lookout for this particular track for decades, ever since my vinyl single went astray.

Llyn Bach (what I have heard referred to as the inner harbour) is another feature and viewed via a circular walk easily accessed by a footpath that starts just behind Cob

Records. Little grebe overwinter here and there is always the chance of goldeneye, goosander and red-breasted merganser. The latter two are sawbills and fish eaters that have been coming in for some flack from certain quarters of the fishing community. Apart from on overstocked fisheries and fish farms I cannot see that their effects on fish stocks could be anything but minimal. If we want to point an accusatory finger regarding declining fish stocks my guess would be that we need to look in the mirror and reflect on some of our own damaging fishing practices.

On the way up from Machynlleth it was great to see fulmars soaring and exploring the cliffs above Fairbourne, a very early but sure sign that spring really is on the way. Here on the return journey we also had very close views of a peregrine, happily perched and preening as the train slowly passed by.

Where else can you get within 2 metres of a wild peregrine without disturbing it in the slightest? Then there are the long sweeping beaches, Harlech castle, the views towards Cadair Idris from Barmouth bridge, sunset over the Llŷn Peninsula and Ynys Enlli/ Bardsey Island. Yes, a trip to Porthmadog should be on everyone's agenda.

April 2016
Coast Path

RECENTLY I made some time for my annual Borth to Aberystwyth coastal walk. Initially I had hoped to do it partly along the beach but the time and tides were against that, so the cliff top Coastal Path had to suffice. This, on later reflection, was probably no bad thing as several miles of shingle beach and boulders would not have done my dodgy knee any favours.

About the middle of March and in the midst of that very welcome dry spell, there was a brisk northeasterly blowing and the sky was clear blue.

The sea was still slightly disturbed and a typical khaki colour, despite the surface being almost unruffled.

In sheltered spots (and there are a few, even on the clifftop) it was decidedly warm, but despite several stops for a breather at likely spots and to take in the views, I saw no sign of any butterflies.

For several days I had been half expecting to see a small tortoiseshell or maybe a peacock (at least in the garden), but they have been ominously absent, even up to the end of the month, by which time the fine weather had broken anyway. In fact the only butterfly that I had seen by the end of March was a solitary comma. This butterfly has gradually spread north and westwards and only been around in west Wales since perhaps the mid-70s. I can remember seeing one of the first in the summer of 1977, flying across the Dyfi Estuary.

This latest one (obviously a hibernater awakened by the warm and sunny weather) was also seen near the Dyfi. It was a bit tatty looking, which is saying something for a comma as it has a very scalloped wing anyway, but you have to give it full marks for surviving a quite exceptional winter. The exceptionally warm and exceptionally wet conditions have been less than conducive to hibernation and survival for a butterfly.

Back on the clifftop, the gorse was almost in full flower with stonechats and dunnocks making full use of its spiky bushiness for song posts. Thickets of gorse and wind-cropped blackthorn are ideal for both species as they provide suitable nest sites and protection from predators and refuge from any disturbance by coastal path walkers.

They can be literally impenetrable to us humans. One bonus of such a mild winter has been the better than average survival of small songbirds such as these.

Out at sea there was not a lot to be seen bar a few gulls and the occasional cormorant. Two common scoter (both males) were notable as they were quite close in to the shore. Flocks of several hundred can be seen in the winter months off Borth, but they are generally much further out.

Absolutely jet black with a hint of yellow on the beak they are regarded here as sea ducks, though they nest by freshwater lochs and lakes in Scotland, Ireland and more commonly in Scandinavia and northern Russia.

A brief glimpse of a male peregrine and a pair of chough cavorting in the wind near Wallog were other highlights, but again I was to be disappointed at not seeing any fulmars. These close relatives of the albatrosses really are true seabirds, only coming to land to breed. An iconic species, but north Ceredigion seems to have lost them, for quite some years now.

From the top of Consti I was able to point out likely spots for purple sandpipers (on the prom wall) and black redstart (on the Old College) to an interested walker/birdwatcher.

I had a bus to catch, so decided to leave them for another day.

October 2012
Lindisfarne

VAST SEA SCAPES and the distant Farne Islands with Bamburgh Castle looming out of the sea spray just a few miles down the wildest of coastlines are all visible from the battlements of Lindisfarne Castle.

It was still something of a spur of the moment thing to ring the National Trust Working Holidays phoneline. Working holidays with the National Trust can vary from all manner of energetic estate management projects to the rather less physical, room stewarding in what are often quite large properties. It was the latter we were looking for as we have more than enough physical labour in our respective jobs and we were looking for a change.

My phone call just a day or so after the brochure was out was just in time to book the last available fortnightly slot, in October.

October is *the* month for migrant birds passing through on their way from northern Europe to warmer climes in the south. In mid to late October most of the wintering wildfowl and wader species would already have settled in on the vast inter-tidal sand and mud flats sheltered by the island, and the thrushes, finches and perhaps some other, rarer species might be around and about or passing through, given the right weather conditions.

It is well over 300 miles from our place on the west coast of Wales to the vast skies and impressive seas, backed by wide dunes and the expansive beaches of Northumberland. They left a deep impression that contrasted markedly with our milder west coast experiences of mountains, streams, wooded valleys and the calmer waters of Cardigan Bay.

As the day of departure approached the weather had been ideal for quite some time, high pressure and light north easterly winds, ideal for incoming, autumn migrants to a north east coastal site. The possibility of coinciding with some Scandinavian and north European migrant birds appeared to be quite good and as we arrived, a group of obvious twitchers at Beal near the start of the Lindisfarne causeway merely confirmed that. We hadn't been on the island more than a few hours before we were made well aware of the juvenile roller (a rather heavy-looking, central European, bluey-grey, jay like bird) that had been causing quite a stir amongst birdwatchers for several days before our arrival. Apparently it was only the second county record since the 1950s. We caught up with it several days later, possibly proving that I am not a twitcher?

The birders couldn't have been more helpful, especially the two that pointed out the roller which was still using a scrubby line of trees and some set-aside field margins several days after our arrival. They were not overly impressed with my equal interest in a covey of grey partridge in the field over the road when there was a roller to see, but I was equally thrilled to see some partridges- they are extreme rarities in our part of Wales.

Twitchers might-be something of a problem when they descend on the island in large numbers. Most of the shrubbery and cover for small birds tends to be in the larger, private gardens and it did seem quite odd and not to say inconsiderate to see a group of twitchers at the gates of some of the most popular gardens for holding rare birds.

Much of the island is treeless and it is only within and around the village that there is any significant shrubby cover. Sycamores are virtually the only large trees and most of these are also found in private gardens, around the car parks and in the village near the ruins of the Priory. Having lost most but not all of their leaves, the upper branches of these hardy trees were often being scanned by birders seeking out that rare bird (perhaps a redbreasted flycatcher or barred warbler) which in turn was seeking out its next meal, presumably an insect of some sort. Hawthorns heavily laden with bright red berries, particularly along the Straight Lonnen (lane), also had their attraction. During our stay they were always good for lots of blackbirds, redwing and occasionally a few fieldfare. Especially first thing in the morning as recently arrived migrants from over the sea sought shelter and a much needed rest and refuelling before departing the island and heading south and west over St Cuthberts Isle and the wet expanse of Fenham Flats to the mainland.

Twitchers en masse can be quite intimidating, but on Lindisfarne they did seem to be a likeable bunch. Very often dressed in camouflage gear and laden with all manner of optical equipment and tripods and informed constantly by the ubiquitous mobile phone and the internet, they really are a breed on their own. It still remains very much (but not exclusively) a male dominated pastime with just a few, sometimes bored looking partners tagging along, patiently waiting as another rarity is looked for.

With the causeway closed, nothing is likely to be using the roads and several times we were able to cycle along St Cuthberts Way down to The Snook at the western extremity of the island. Cycling along St Cuthberts Way you can look out over a narrow strip of developing saltmarsh to Holy Island Sands and in the distance, Fenham Flats. Particularly famous for large numbers of wintering brent geese and waders such as bar-tailed godwit and grey plover, this vast expanse of wet mud and sand holds equally vast numbers of other wildfowl and waders, more than enough to keep even the most discerning birdwatcher happy.

Grey seals are often hauled out on the sandbanks at low tide. These originate from the nearby Farne Islands which are usually visible some 10km distant and on the SE horizon when viewed from the village. As the tide ebbed and flowed we would often watch seals using the current and numerous channels, commuting back and forth to the open sea past and far below the castle battlements. What was also noticeable was how wary the birds were- once a seal disappeared under the water any bird within about 50 metres or so would take to the air and settle in a safer spot some distance away. At low tide the seals low moaning (singing - you must be joking) might be heard from several kilometres away. Hauled out on the sandbank next to the main channel they can be viewed quite easily with binoculars or telescope from the small beach near St Cuthberts Isle. We counted about 60 or perhaps as many as 70 but really it is difficult to tell where one seal might end and the next might begin within such a tight bunch.

The tidal channel between Lindisfarne and the tiny St Cuthberts Isle, off the southwest point near the Priory, was always worth watching. St Cuthberts is a favoured roost for waders at high tide and a small group of brent geese also regularly came to graze on the eel grass beds nearby. As the tide raced swiftly in or out we often saw redbreasted mergansers and goosander in the channel, occasionally a red-throated diver but best of all I was able to reacquaint myself with the slavonian grebe. In winter plumage they do look very similar to black-necked grebe but here you could get really good views and determine the pure white down the front of the neck, diagnostic of slavonian.

We did not chase or seek out the rare and elusive bird species but we did make a point of looking for short-eared owls and on more than one occasion we watched as at least two hunted in the evening twilight over the fields and sand dunes. Ghostly in the half-light they are always a joy to find and once found they do tend to be fairly reliably located.

Finding waders was no problem at all, identifying some of them, maybe! Sitting on a bench at the top of the harbour beach you might see half a dozen species in front of you and at almost any state of the tide, always assuming any dog walkers have their charges under at least a modicum of control. We never saw sanderling here but saw nigh on all the others. Sanderling seem to like a wider, more exposed and sandy shore. Small flocks of this very obliging bird were found on the North Shore near Snipe Point and within Sandon Bay.

The closing of the causeway does bring an incredible peacefulness to the whole island. It was almost as if, cut off from the mainland all those that remained took time to relax, before the next influx of the human race. Watching the tide slowly sweep in over the sands and mudflats, disturbing the feeding birds and dislodging the seals could not be anything but peaceful and relaxing.

For those of a twitchy nature we logged 85 different bird species without trying too hard and missed out on what would have been several 'lifers' for me. Not to worry, the thousands of starlings to and from the reedbed around The Lough, at dusk and most spectacularly at dawn with the castle black against a fiery sky were possibly my highlights.

'The Birds of Holy Island', a booklet of some 88pp by Mike Kerr is essential reading for anyone interested in the natural history or indeed some of the wider history of the island.

Baseline

January 2015
Shifting Baselines

IT IS A TERM that has been in common usage for quite some time and basically it points out that any comparisons may be confounded if we do not (or cannot) refer back to reliable data from the past, i.e. we do not have a reliable and fixed baseline. For instance, I can remember when species, such as lapwing, skylark and even the grey partridge were literally all over the place. So much so that we took little notice of the fact and virtually no one thought to study or count them.

The same might be said of house sparrow and starling, so commonplace that they were virtually ignored until the late 20th century when it was realised they were in steep decline.

Anyone now coming into environmental studies, ecology, studying almost any aspect of natural history, merely bird-watching or even fishing will have difficulty understanding what was around in the not too distant past.

They may be able to read about past abundance of this or that but will they really believe it if there is only anecdotal evidence and (more importantly) they cannot experience it?

Without that actual experience, it is often difficult to grasp what it was like. And so, today becomes 'the norm', hence a new (shifted) baseline may be established.

I have been told of Welsh streams and rivers full of wild brown trout - I have never seen it but can well believe it.

Most watercourses now seem quite sparsely populated but even allowing for a fisherperson's exaggeration there has to be some credence to those claims of past abundance.

In the UK as a whole and here in Wales the declines in some bird species are now well documented but for most species we only have really good data going back something like half a century, if that.

Clearly things have radically changed since the Second World War with the advent of mechanisation, they were changing markedly in agriculture up to that point as well.

More recently, in the past few decades, we have forest plantations maturing and being felled/replanted. Hedges have disappeared and many have now reappeared under environmental schemes, broadleaved woodlands remain neglected, mixed farming has all but disappeared, fewer and cleaner (less weedy) crops are grown and of course silage has replaced hay as the staple winter fodder.

Think brown hares, flower rich meadows, bumble bees and other insects.

Taking lapwing and skylark as a case in point, in the early to mid 20th century they were at near to maximum population levels.

We always must bear in mind that prior to agricultural expansion (over many, many centuries and over a range of habitats) they were both probably quite scarce species as they require open habitats and quite short vegetation.

When one looks at the Welsh landscape now there seems to be no shortage of that, so why have they declined so much over the past forty to fifty years or so?

Lots of reasons, but much can be traced back to a vastly increased human population, increased pressure on the farmed landscape and an ever increasing agricultural efficiency, leaving little time or space for some of our most iconic bird species to raise any young.

Your average lowland field could go from being tightly grazed then perhaps rolled or scarified-aerated, fertilized, grass growing rapidly and being harvested for a silage crop within less time than it takes a pair of lapwing to raise any young to flying. There is always the possibility of further silage crops following on immediately which may rule out the whole spring and summer breeding season. So is it little wonder that few lapwings survive in the wider farmed landscape?

The same could be said of skylarks, though their time on the ground may be a few weeks less they still do not have time to raise young on your average lowland field and they remain for the most part, restricted to the semi-improved, grazed land on the hills.

If we accept our present (shifted) baseline we have both species virtually extinct in lowland fields and it is difficult to see the situation changing much despite various agri-environment schemes targeting these declines.

December 1985
A Very Interesting Outing

THE LAST SUNDAY in November saw the Young Ornithologist Club members out and about birding. Although a cold morning we were fortunate in choosing a virtually windless day which allowed birdwatching without too much discomfort. First notable sightings were a pair of wary bewick swans standing out elegantly and very conveniently in a field close to the roadside.

These winter visitors from breeding grounds in the Arctic are rare and usually brief visitors to the Dyfi Estuary.

Next on the agenda, although you never know the agenda in advance at this game, was a female merlin. This small falcon now so rare in its breeding haunts of upland Wales often occurs near the coast during the harsh winter months. After dashing across the golf course and reed bed near the Ynys Las turn, it too posed for our better viewing on a grassy tump before proceeding to flush a snipe from the marsh. Then unfolded a dramatic climbing, spiral chase with the Merlin gaining quite rapidly. Clearly a change of tactics was called for and the snipe got the message and made off in a straight line still hotly pursued with only about six feet separating the birds as they disappeared from sight.

Off the beach at Ynys Las were quantities of great crested grebes and an elusive diver. After a good number of attempts a few members were able to identify it as red throated, getting a brief look at the slightly upturned appearance of the bill. Amongst the dunes were several stonechats, so familiar to anyone walking the cliff, and coastal paths in summer. Brief stops on the return journey took in substantial flocks of golden plover and lapwings again conveniently close to the roadside.

Finally a short stroll along the lower reaches of the Afon Clettwr found a dipper and that bane of the wildfowler, the redshank.

Just some of the highlights of a very interesting outing, emphasising the great variety of birdlife locally, not to mention the mammals. Grey seals, porpoises and what appeared to be a school of pilot whales all added to the day.

Everyone found the merlin exciting and the evening chase riveting, personally I hope the snipe got away but have grave doubts as to whether it did.

July 2015
Where Has All The Wildlife Gone?

RECENTLY, I spent the best part of five hours walking in rural, central Wales. Chilly to start, it soon turned into a clear, June day and for the most part it was pleasantly warm.

What really struck me was that in the whole five hours, I only saw two butterflies.

Although we have had some poor summers (some very poor summers), when I see only two butterflies in a whole morning's walking in mid-June with the sun shining, I am bound to wonder, what is going on?

One butterfly was a painted lady and the other a white, probably a green-veined white. The painted lady was almost certainly a recent immigrant, possibly a precursor of an influx of this species sometime soon.

I had been noticing that a lot of the nettles at the field margins had been weed-killed and all the hedges were very tightly and tidily trimmed. The fields without any stock in them were ready to be cut for silage and there was very little to be seen in the way of flowering plants (bar grasses), other than some red clover. In the west, it is often wet and the land is good at producing grass.

To an urbanite on holiday, it looks a green and not unpleasant landscape, possibly even very attractive. But to a naturalist, insect, bird or most mammals (other than humanoid, sheep, cattle or horse) the chances are it is approaching a near-desert, as far as their own, long-term sustainability is concerned.

Silage is so much more reliable than hay that it was inevitable it would take over as the winter feed of choice. To a degree, it means that we now have landscapes drained, (sometimes literally drained, remember the rain) of wildlife and that oft-used term, biodiversity. Very recently, I was in Aberystwyth when I was assailed by a well-known shop tannoy extolling the range of weedkillers and insecticides available and how using them might lead to a more colourful garden.

I am not against herbicide use (I do use them when required, sparingly), but I would suggest there is no excuse for the widespread and sometimes indiscriminate use that they are often put to.

Virtually all organisms on this planet have enough on their plate without having to also cope with the chemicals and poisons which we seem to want to spread about the place.

Perhaps we may be going too far in our efforts to get a few more kilograms of meat off the land and perfect plants in our gardens?

During that perambulation in the countryside, I also covered quite a length of riverside and was impressed by how little wildlife (associated with the watercourse) there was. Apparently the fish population (in quite a substantial river) is so low that the angling club members no longer take up their fishing rights - although I did see a couple of goosander fly past, I saw no fish rising and, perhaps most tellingly, no dipper or grey wagtail.

On checking beneath mid-river boulders I could find no invertebrates at all, no caddis, no mayfly, no stonefly no nothing!

No wonder the fish, anglers and bird communities were lacking in numbers. This was a substantial watercourse and clearly something is amiss. I was informed there had been suggestions it was due to afforestation in the upper reaches and the effects of acid rain but I feel there is a whole lot more going on here and the use of herbicides and pesticides in all their forms cannot be entirely off the radar.

The fact that most of the watercourse was grazed to the edge can also not be ignored, as this often leads to erosion and chemical pollution and increases in downstream silt accumulation.

We perhaps need to think longer-term and ease off a little in the use of damaging chemicals and damaging practices.

We owe it to ourselves, the wider environment and we owe it to future generations to better look after what we have here, now.

June 1989
Wind and Weather

'ASH BEFORE OAK - in for a soak, Oak before Ash - in for a splash.' As we have had few splashes lately and certainly no soaks, it would appear that we may have a country saying proved true this year. In fact the Ash was so far behind in coming into leaf that it must be called a no contest.

Here in North Ceredigion a mere 22 millimetres of rain fell during May with the temperatures averaging 20C for the latter half of the month. For comparison the last four years have seen 36, 66, 76 and 67mm of rainfall in May, 1984-88 respectively.

This may well have suited the sun worshippers on the beach but for the farmer and gardener such a start to what might be a long summer, must be viewed with some trepidation. Late frosts aside, the mild winter allowed a multitude of plant pests to survive. In particular aphids, which over-winter as eggs, have had a good start and if past experience is to be relied upon we ought now to look forward to an increase in the ladybird population. Both larvae and adult ladybirds are major predators of aphids. It was a good few years ago, perhaps 1984, that we had a briefer but otherwise similar hot spell and I well remember the tide line at Ynys Las being littered with stranded ladybirds, blown onto the beach and into the sea by hot offshore winds.

In Britain it is most unusual to have such a long spell of easterly influenced weather and all manner of things may eventually be affected. Already these winds have brought early records of painted lady butterflies and even a humming bird hawkmoth in the Dyfi area. The estuary too has played host to avocet, marsh harrier and hoopoe, all East Coast and Continental birds in normal years.

More importantly these easterly winds will have presented West Wales with a lot of airborne pollution from the industrial midlands, the Black Country and even further afield. Much of this pollution, will have settled out in the extensive conifer forests which clothe many a hill hereabouts.

When the drought breaks this dry deposited material will be washed off the trees and during its percolation through already acid soils this dilute acid solution will release trace elements such as aluminium, particularly toxic to fish. Such a combination of events is thought to be the cause of one of the most easily seen effects of so-called 'Acid Rain'. Namely the scarcity of fish, invertebrates and dippers on heavily forested river systems.

The hydrologists studying the interaction of pollution, weather, forests and river systems at Staylittle to the East of Pumlumon will be awaiting the drought's break with as much anticipation as the farmer but for very different reasons. Of course the root cause of 'Acid Rain' is too much pollution. It remains to be seen if we really have the will to get to grips with reducing the amount of pollution, atmospheric and other, that our society produces.

May 1993
Maps

INTEGRATED ADMINISTRATION and Control System (I.A.C.S.) applications (for EU farm payments) have to be in by the 15 May. Having had a glimpse of the I.A.C.S., 50-page instruction booklet and some sample field data sheets, I am not surprised there are problems.

In the distant past I well remember sweating over and being confused by an altogether different type of integration (and differentiation) at technical college. Somehow or other I managed to force the basic process into my head, go through the motions and scrape a pass. I suspect the farming community will have to do something similar, grit their teeth and work methodically through the paperwork, I wish them luck!

One of the main problems has been the lack of up-to-date maps drawn to a sufficiently large scale with the 'new' field numbers marked. Changing acres to hectares is not a great problem, even I can cope with that; multiply it by 0.42!

The detail on the old maps is very precise and looking at Ysgubor-y-Coed, 1 to 2,500 (25 inches to the mile) is a pleasure as well as an eye opener.

There have been tremendous changes in the parish over the past few years and certainly since 1905. Even in 1905 many woodlands were identified as plantations, having (according to the key) a significant proportion given over to conifers.

After the First World War and particularly since the 1930s the spread of plantation, 'monoculture' conifers has been more significant. Many fields and some of the 'mixed woods' on the 1905 map have been 'conifered'. But whilst there have been some not insignificant losses there have been (more recently) some gains.

The Forest Enterprise arm of the Forestry Commission seems determined to get to grips with countering some of the conservationists' criticisms.

In the not too distant future, Cwm Einion in the parish of Ysgubor-y-Coed will change yet again. It is planned that conifers between the minor road and the River Einion will be felled. Some small groups of very large trees and small areas of larch may be retained but for the most part clear-felled areas will be allowed to naturally regenerate with natural broadleaved tree species. A welcome development and enlightened action on the part of Forest Enterprise.

Hopefully it will go a long way towards helping Cwm Einion live up to its other name Artists' valley. More importantly it is not only in such public places that sensible, environmentally sensitive actions are taking place.

Forest Enterprise has a mammoth task and the possibilities nationally are practically endless. Of course finance will be the limiting factor but I look forward to seeing the new maps continue to show environmentally sound policies are being followed.

December 1993
Snipe Makes a Comeback

LOWLAND MARSH was once a commonplace habitat, but over the past 15 to 20 years it has been disappearing fast! Fortunately the Countryside Council for Wales (CCW) has recently been able to purchase 240 important acres of surviving marsh and wet fields just west of the Afon Leri near Borth. Aber Leri fields were once part of a huge bog which extended way up the Dyfi estuary from Cors Fochno and even far out into what is now the sea. Clay overlain with a thick layer of peat and the remains of birch/pine forest can often be seen along the beach near here and tiny fragments of undrained bog can be found up to and beyond the point of highest tides on the Dyfi.

Access to the Leri and around these wet fields is by right-of-way across Borth Golf course. A track crosses the old (true) course of the Avon Leri some 150 metres north of the clubhouse. Another public footpath then follows the west bank of the canalised Leri to the railway bridge, south of the boatyard. Bounded by the railway and the embankment these low-lying fields have always held water despite past drainage attempts.

Now the CCW has the opportunity to manipulate the water-levels and control grazing, effectively increasing the wildlife interest.

The flora has already been studied and shows a noticeable gradient from fresh water/marsh species to brackish, almost maritime species. An indication of saltwater seepage either though the shingle bank and under the golf course or perhaps through the Leri embankment?

Old dykes fringed with common reed add further interest and the outlook certainly looks good for aquatic invertebrates and amphibians. The birdlife has also benefited from some simple controls of the water level.

Snipe (a bird I had thought extinct as a breeding species in North Ceredigion) have returned and although the 1993 season was poor, I am sure the Leri fields will continue to attract this secretive bird in summer.

Several other, more conspicuous waders also increased in numbers, (redshank, oystercatcher and lapwing) birds that have been hard-pressed to hold their own as breeding species in Ceredigion of late.

During spring and autumn, passage birds such as black-tailed godwit and whimbrel use the fields and now, in the depths of winter they again become a favourite haunt of snipe. Important as it is to control water levels it is also vital to control grazing. Purchase has allowed the CCW tight control of a management regime intended to retain and encourage a diverse and interesting ground flora whilst keeping the vegetation at a suitable height for the snipe. It is early days yet but the potential of these wet, rushy fields is enormous.

At the moment the public are obviously welcome to use the rights-of-way but please do be careful if you cross the railway bridge. Also please do keep dogs under close control, preferably on a lead, livestock are free to graze the Leri embankment, they and any wildfowl on the fields will not enjoy dogs running amok!

June 1995
Better Days for the Bay?

AS SUMMER PROGRESSES I often find myself down at the coast. Here it is cooler, I can have a paddle or even a swim and there is always lots of activity, holidaymakers and locals enjoying the beach and the waters of the bay. Plenty of wildlife to enjoy as well - gulls and oystercatchers on the beach, with shearwaters and gannets patrolling and foraging some way out from shore.

On the shingle a few ringed plover may have persisted to raise a brood, despite the attentions of we humans and our dogs. The flowers of the dunes, the shingle and the cliff top are at their best and at the tide line there is always something of interest to be found.

Recently I was watching an oystercatcher at mid-low tide on, what I had always presumed to be, pure sand with little or nothing living within.

Every 50 metres or so along the wet sand this bird found and extracted (but inexplicably did not eat) a bivalve known as the banded wedge shell Donax vittatus.

It is one of the commonest found washed up at the tide line, twice as long (up to 3.5cm) as wide, with a clearly toothed edge. According to the books, it favours firm sand in large, open, exposed bays, at lower shore and below.

Bivalves have a shell consisting of two halves (valves) held together, when alive, by elastic ligaments. They range in size and form from the familiar mussel and cockle to the elongated razor shell and piddock. Since they sieve or filter small particles of food from the surrounding water, they can be useful indicators for water quality. They take in so much water when feeding that any impurities or pollutants may build up in their tissues to significant if not dangerous amounts. Good news for bivalves, fish, dolphins and, we humans is that the new sewage treatments works at Aberporth is open and that 'the state of the art' technology at Aberystwyth will be up and running by the end of June.

This will be of great benefit to the whole bay and effectively points the way forward for sewage treatment at other coastal towns. With Clarach also connecting to the

Aberystwyth facilities it means a huge stretch of coastline should see immediate benefits. Surfers and bathers will feel a whole lot better about taking to the water, I am sure.

Thanks to Dwr Cymru/Welsh Water for their progressive and enlightened attitude and thanks to Friends of Cardigan Bay (FOCB) for their campaigning which kept the pressure on for a better solution. As a voluntary organisation, FOCB can probably claim to have done more than any other to effect an improvement in the environment locally.

Friends of Cardigan Bay are also concerned about oil and gas exploration and deeply involved in educating the public and user-bodies about threats to the bay and coastline and they welcome new members.

Perhaps one day in the future (when we have found a solution to the plastic problem), we might visit the beach and pick up nothing but naturally occurring flotsam and jetsam, banded wedge shells and their like. What a day for celebration that will be!

July 2007
Bird Reports - Ups & Downs

MOST BIRDERS, birdwatchers, twitchers, ornithologists (call them what you will) have been made well aware that over the next few years there is another period of Atlas surveying planned. That is, an Atlas of the Breeding Birds in Britain, and for good measure there is also a winter Atlas starting in November this year too.

The British Trust for Ornithology (BTO) will be encouraging volunteers to get out and put in countless hours of observation and record taking.

Are populations of a particular species stable or soaring like a lark? Or are they plummeting like a gannet into the waters of Cardigan Bay?

Here in Ceredigion and other parts of west Wales it may be problematic getting adequate coverage for the Atlas, particularly in some of the remoter parts of the Cambrian Mountains and other sparsely populated areas. On a smaller scale, looking at the latest issue (2004 and 2005 combined) of the Ceredigion Bird Report there were 138 individuals who sent in records, a considerable number considering the overall population.

All records are of importance so keep them coming in. Usually the report is published annually but several factors conspired and it was decided a combined 2004 & 2005 report was the best option. So, for £6.15 (incl p+p) you can get two complete years and 90 pages packed with easily understandable, ornithological information relevant to Ceredigion. Some of it may be invaluable if you are considering contributing to the BTO atlas work, as grid references in the report help point you in the way of most of the best bird watching sites and areas.

Almost all the Ceredigion records give quite detailed references to the numbers, the where and when a particular species was recorded. Quickly skimming through some of the older reports it is apparent that some species are being more frequently recorded whilst others do seem to be on the decline.

Definitely on the plus side we now have little egrets breeding at Ynys Hir on the Dyfi Estuary in the far north of the county. Quite an exotic and once a very rare visitor, they first bred in 2004. Now there are thought to be at least four pairs and birds are appearing more frequently at Cors Caron too.

Some of the increase in the scarcer seabirds recorded might be put down to the increased interest of some particularly dedicated birdwatchers.

Sea watching is quite a specialism and not something I excel in but I do always note the thousands of shearwaters and lesser numbers of gannets that any time now will be appearing offshore of Aberystwyth and Borth. The shallow waters of the bay are favoured feeding areas for the massive breeding populations of these birds on the islands off the Pembrokeshire coast.

On the other hand it appears from the report that numbers of wintering red-throated diver and great-crested grebe have plummeted of late and so we await the arrival of the shearwaters with some added interest. Will their use of the bay decline too? Are the fish stocks that they utilise still there?

The BTO only recently organized a simple tawny owl survey and mainly because we have them breeding regularly in the garden, high up in a nest box fixed to a japanese red cedar, I took part in that. But what about the barn owl, how is that faring? Where are the long-eared owls and for that matter, the wintering short-eared owls? Little owls have always been either under recorded or remain very scarce in the county.

Why do some species thrive and why are others struggling? We know some of the answers but quite often we just do not know enough. We can guess, but only from more detailed monitoring and recording can we begin to understand more of the factors that might be involved.

If you want a copy of the 2004+2005 Ceredigion report, they are still available from Hywel Roderick*. 32 Prospect Street, Aberystwyth, (£6.15 incl p+p). This bumper issue has information on over 220 species and articles on specific species and bird ringing in the county. Now, if ever there was one, there is a species on the brink of local extinction, bird ringers!

All the income is invested in future editions and it is the only comprehensive account of the state and change in the bird populations within the county. Without it, no one, no matter how dedicated, would have as nearly true or as full a picture of the birds in Ceredigion. They make ideal birthday presents for anyone interested in birds or visiting the area and in need of just that little bit of encouragement or information to get out there, explore and perhaps more importantly, record!

* Hywel Roderick (1954-2009) who, alongside Peter Davis (1928-2019) was one of the editors of the Ceredigion Bird Report and co-authored the book Birds of Ceredigion.

January 2014
Bird Atlas

THE British Trust for Ornithology (BTO) has just published the latest 'Bird Atlas'.

That is the Bird Atlas (2007 - 2011) relating to the breeding and wintering birds of Great Britain and Ireland (GB-I). It is the fourth atlas covering that area following on from Breeding Atlases in 1968-72 and 1988-91 and a Winter Atlas of 1981-84.

This is by far the most ambitious project and the resulting tome has over ten times the data within it of any previous Atlas, extends to over 700 pages and weighs in at something like the average mute swan, I would think.

It must have been an absolutely mammoth task putting it together, and amazingly over 40,000 volunteers contributed their time, from data input and time spent literally 'out in the field'.

Although for 'field' you might read anything from coast and saltmarsh to extensive heather moorland and barren mountain top, and include everything in between, including urban environments as well.

Regional representatives (also volunteers) were the links between headquarters and field-workers and orchestrated much of the work, and over the four survey years a few contractors were also employed, to cover those areas (usually particularly remote) that volunteers could not cover.

Heaven knows how many hours of work that totals up to, but it does emphasise what is achievable with commitment and volunteers.

Various maps detail the breeding and wintering distribution of all the bird species (wild and feral) found in GB during the period 2007-11, others show the breeding and winter distribution change compared to previous Atlas work.

As I was involved in other bird research (curlew) over that period, I only managed a couple of survey areas for the atlas, and to tell the truth, I had a job completing them.

After a week's work in the uplands of mid-Wales following curlew (a seriously declining species) the last thing I was looking forward to at the weekend, was another excursion into the hills looking for anything and everything in the bird line.

Anyway, I managed to get in my minimum visits within time limits (I did have several years to do it) and although it may not have amounted to much, at least it helped fill in a few blank squares on the map.

Atlas and similar survey work is well within the average bird watcher's reach, and it does give that extra bit of purpose to any time spent out in the field. And I would recommend it to anyone as there are ongoing BTO surveys to suit almost all abilities and tastes and whatever time might be available.

At the moment the Winter Thrush Survey is in its second and final year. The Wetlands Bird Survey has been going for years, Garden Birdwatch has been up and running since 1995, and that can be done from your kitchen or living room window.

The Welsh Chat Survey is ongoing, as are many more; nothing to do with social media or the WI, chats in this context are whinchat, stonechat and their near relative, the wheatear. Both whinchat and wheatear are long-distance migrants wintering in Africa, whereas the stonechat could be classed as resident and overwinters in Britain in some numbers. All three like very different versions of open habitats.

Wheatears go for the sparsest ground cover, short vegetation and stony or rocky areas. Stonechats prefer more of a mixture of open ground with gorse and maybe the odd brambly tangle, such as on the clifftop slopes along much of the coastal path, where you might see them now. Whinchats (a species in serious decline), prefer large areas of rank grassland. Rhos (wet) pasture and occasionally bracken will suffice, and if it is lowland, so much the better.

This type of habitat has been disappearing from lowlands, and whinchats have had to move into less suitable and less productive habitat at higher elevations, and it is difficult to see them making much of a comeback without a change in land management practice.

The whinchat spends our winter in tropical and sub-tropical Africa and there may well be some problems on migration and in the winter quarters, but habitat loss here in Wales is almost certainly another big driver in a decline that is so markedly shown in the Atlas.

Although I have not been involved in the chat survey specifically, I have noticed (over many years) a distinct decline, and lately, almost a total lack of whinchats on my travels about north, mid and west Wales.

On the plus side, the Atlas reveals an astonishing spread of buzzard from strongholds here in the west to now occupy virtually all of mainland UK and large areas of the Irish

Republic. Also on the up are red kite and little egret, with the former now widespread through reintroductions that for the most part have gone well.

Little egret, on the other hand, have done it all themselves, perhaps with a little help from climate shift.

In Wales a little egret was still something of a rarity not much more than a decade ago, now they are almost a common sight around suitable coastlines where they seem to prefer estuaries with saltmarsh creeks and gullies in which to feed, and many pairs breed within and alongside established heronries of the more familiar, and much larger, grey heron. Little egrets are one of the most elegant of the heron clan. With such buoyant flight and that brilliant white plumage, it is easy to see how in the past its plumes might be much sought after for society women's headgear.

Protection of great crested grebe, little egrets and other species from such exploitation was a prime mover in the establishment of the RSPB in 1889, and we all know what a massive organisation that has developed into, concerned with wildlife and wild places throughout the UK and some far-flung places throughout the world via its international department.

The BTO is much, much smaller and primarily concerned with research into birds within the UK. It has been established since 1932 but it does not have a portfolio of reserves or protected places, managing just a small amount of woodland and wetland around the headquarters in Thetford, Norfolk. The BTO only relatively recently opened a regional office based at the University of Bangor, N Wales.

What else can the Atlas tell us? Well loads, I have barely scratched the surface since it arrived on the doorstep. There are worrying declines in many bird species (cuckoo, yellow wagtail, turtle dove, curlew, tree pipit, woodcock, ring ouzel, red and black grouse, redshank, swift etc) across a wide range of habitats, and we have little, or sometimes no certainty, as to what is driving some of these declines.

There can be no doubt that the pressure on wildlife, wild places and natural resources worldwide is increasing, and there seems to be little political will to really get to grips with this problem.

Citizen science such as produced this latest Bird Atlas is but one way to get at least a small part of the message across and I am sure it will be well used to inform numerous debates.

June 2011
Unpredictable Weather

DESPITE ALL THAT SNOW and ice, it was a dry winter and it merged into an unusually dry spring. As springs go, 2008 was wet, 2009 and 2010 were dry but 2011 was exceptionally so.

A roasting over Easter and all those Bank Holidays was good for the tourist trade but a biting wind made some of the bird monitoring difficult, to say the least. A real drought has hit the south and east whilst here in west Wales we have at least had some rain towards the end of May and the rivers and streams are getting back to something like normal levels.

This unpredictable weather has consequences for the wildlife. BBC Springwatch based at Ynys-hir until mid June must have been hoping for some sun and settled weather to assist the film crews.

I have been told of broods dying in nestboxes for lack of food and have noticed myself how noisy many chicks have been in natural nest sites. On the one hand this might encourage the parent birds to greater efforts in supplying food but on the other hand it is a poor if not desperate gamble on the youngster's part as all that vocalisation can be a signpost for all manner of predators. Cats can be particularly troublesome at this time and they will soon follow up such obvious signals, foxes have big ears for a good reason and many a ground nesting bird will have fallen foul to their predations, this and every spring.

Survey work also takes me to various wetlands and although it is nice to get around without a boot full of water it is worryingly apparent that many wetland birds have suffered due to the previous dry weather.

Wader species such as lapwing, snipe, redshank and curlew have been declining for years and this breeding season is unlikely to help reverse that trend. Birds arrived at regular breeding sites but all the indications are that many fewer than normal stayed around to attempt breeding. This begs the questions, where do they then go and what do they do for the remainder of the season? Some with a bit of luck may have pushed on to breed elsewhere. Others I guess (no one really knows), will have given up and conserved resources in the hope of breeding in more favourable circumstances next year, they are after all quite long lived species generally.

Of course all that sunny, dry weather was good for the butterflies and it is difficult to remember a better early season, though there were exceptions and small tortoiseshells and peacocks have been very scarce. Green hairstreaks were particularly numerous on some days in the uplands and it would appear they have had a good season.

Some of the moths have done well and we recently saw hundreds of lackey moth caterpillars in 'protective' webs on blackthorn and other shrubs along the coastal path between Borth and Wallog. Actually almost all the caterpillars were on the outside of the webs so I suspect they are otherwise unpalatable or they would have been food for the numerous whitethroats and stonechats that love that low, dense protective habitat of prickly gorse and blackthorn thicket that thrives on top of the cliffs.

We walked back along the beach but do not try this unless you are familiar with the tides and time you might take, and on no account try climbing the cliffs. That cold winter and freeze thawing has caused numerous cliff falls and exposures of new cliff face and there really is no safe exit up the cliffs along this stretch of coastline. I particularly wanted to see if there were any fulmars breeding. Some years ago and there would usually have been a handful of pairs between Borth and Wallog. As I suspected there are none there now. No herring gulls either and no cormorants though one or two occasionally flew past offshore. Is this an indication of a declining food source in this part of Cardigan Bay?

A few gannets, thousands of shearwaters and a few hundred gulls seen feeding avidly on a sprat shoal close in to Borth at the start of the walk might suggest otherwise. A great sight to see but all that frenzied activity was soon over, which was hardly surprising considering the number of birds involved.

It certainly has been a strange past few months, we now need it to settle down and hope some rain gets to the south and further east.

January 2016
Soils, Climate and Weather

IF AT ALL POSSIBLE, I try to steer well clear of weather forecasting.

In Wales it has always been a bit hit and miss and if the experts can get it wrong so often, why should I imagine I can do any better? Often the safest bet on any exposed western seaboard is to wait for morning and take it from there.

In October we had high pressure, blue skies, some sun and even the faintest touch of frost on a very rare occasion. Thinking ahead, I might have predicted a cold spell before Christmas, but November was a total contrast and December has been much the same, generally overcast, un-seasonally warm and wet, wet, wet.

We have to expect some stormy, wet weather, but the last couple of months might be described as particularly depressing if not (more than a bit) worrying. The ground has been super-saturated for weeks on end and water has been pouring out of places where it had never appeared before.

With the Paris Summit on climate change long gone, and commitments made, the big question has to be - is what we are experiencing now just the vagaries of our UK weather, or is it climate change making itself felt already?

Even the waterfowl and wader species will not have appreciated this dismal, drizzly wet weather and during some of the prolonged spells I have also noticed the garden birds struggling to cope. Sometimes, they have appeared almost as stressed as when there is a covering of snow or a few days of frost.

Mammalian hibernators such as bats and hedgehogs may also have been tempted to emerge due to the higher than normal temperatures, not good in the so called 'depths of winter' when despite the record high temperatures there will not be much food about.

It appears that December 2015 was the warmest and wettest ever in parts of the UK. Agriculturally, it is also very problematic and farms with some higher, drier ground must consider themselves fortunate. Others with low-lying, level fields and/or poorly draining soils have had a real problem of pulse after pulse of rain with virtually no let up. It must be a delicate balance when assessing whether to drain land and then risk drought conditions in the summer.

Then, there are the nutrients- artificial fertilizers are expensive and liable to be leached from the soil during periods of prolonged and heavy rainfall.

2015 was the Year of the Soil, often a very thin and fragile membrane of productive material that takes decades and centuries to form. It only exists (in any usable quantity, quality or depth) on a relatively small part of the Earth's surface and I get the distinct impression that we have become more and more divorced from its significance to us all. Perhaps we should assume every year is the Year of the Soil, it really is that important, though it is not much use without an adequate supply of water.

If you live in west Wales, the chances are that you will have had more than the average experience of soils, climate and weather.

It is just a fact of life that someone living and working in a large urban area, in an office or in industry will probably have little or no connection or conception of just how important this stuff (soil, earth, dirt) is, unless they have a decent garden or allotment to go home to of course.

A miraculous combination of factors, features and conditions has allowed an incredible diversity of life to develop here in unique circumstances and we humans have taken advantage of that in all manner of ways, all in what amounts to the blinking of an eye on a geological timescale.

There have been some huge changes in the past; glacial periods, eruptions, earthquakes, tsunamis, floods and even meteor strikes apparently. You just have to wonder if we might not be at the beginning of another major one due to climate change with this one driven by our CO_2/fossil fuel and other greenhouse gas emissions.

March 2016
Invasive Species

Often it can be quite subjective, what we deem to like and appreciate and what we might otherwise take quite a dislike to. Just now I have it in for grey squirrels and American mink, amongst a range of other things in the environment: plastics are certainly high on that list (and growing) along with a whole lot of other human rubbish, but most of the other dislikes are plants.

Invasive Non-Native Species (INNS), however introduced by human activity, should not be here. The reason they can be so invasive is that their natural controls are usually lacking.

Allied to some genuine escapes, the release of mink from fur farms by animal rights activists was also a big mistake. The introduction of grey squirrels from the 1870s into the early 20th century has been disastrous for the native red squirrel and for broadleaved tree regeneration.

I can hear people rhapsodising about the cute and clever grey squirrel, but at the end of the day it is causing immense problems. Having recently taken on part responsibility for some broadleaved woodland it has again been brought home to me just how much damage this pesky rodent can cause.

Like rats, they like to nibble things, and the bark of young trees can come in for a lot of attention. In the short term, trees can be killed, but even if they survive, in the longer term they can become extremely dangerous as squirrel-damaged branches are severely weakened and liable to break off.

I have also been involved in a lot of water vole work. This brings in the American mink, a distant mustelid cousin of our stoat, weasel, otter and even the badger.

As a youngster I can remember water voles as widespread and in many instances quite common. You could easily find places where you might watch it gnawing vegetation held in its paws. With the acute hearing of youth it was not unusual to hear them, even if you could not see them. A mini-beaver really, no dams though.

At Cors Caron the water vole population has recently crashed and it is almost certainly due to an increase in the mink population. There are schemes already in place to control grey squirrels around Tregaron and Llanddewi Brefi with the aim of aiding the recovery of a relict population of red squirrels in the Brechfa Forest and also proposals to monitor and possibly control American mink around the Cors Caron area with a view to aiding the recovery of the water vole.

This is good news for the native wildlife of the area as mink and grey squirrels assuredly do a lot of damage, damage that for the most part might go unseen. Mink are known predators of reptiles, amphibians, fish, birds and other small mammals. But in the UK they are particularly well known for being able to knock out water vole populations at the drop of a hat almost.

Grey squirrels carry, but do not suffer greatly from, squirrel pox, a disease that is usually lethal to our native red squirrel and they also do a lot of damage to nesting birds (taking eggs and young). They also annoyingly strip the hazel of nuts each year, well before any are anywhere near ripe.

Good news, from the Vincent Wildlife Trust, may be in the form of the release of 20 pine martens in the Rheidol Valley last September.

Already, radio-collared/tracked marten have been found near Llandre and in Cwm Cletwr, near Tre'r-ddol. Maybe the bonus will be their effect on grey squirrels. Anecdotal evidence from Ireland indicates that where martens move in, then grey squirrels move out. Apparently red squirrels are relatively unaffected, but I remain to be convinced of that and it remains to be seen how effective this reintroduction might be. Personally I can't wait for a pine marten to appear in the garden here, and start sorting out the grey squirrels. We shall see.

Political
Gains & Losses

June 2016
Human Interference

HOMO SAPIENS as a species is truly unique on this planet. No other is as all-pervasive, influential or interfering as the human.

On the whole, we are rarely satisfied for long and given the least opportunity we will go to extraordinary lengths to relieve boredom, to get what we think we need, think we deserve or merely hanker after.

Admittedly this hyper-activity has brought enormous benefits to much if not most of the human race, but as in all races there are going to be losers as well as winners.

We have major problems associated with the seemingly inevitable pursuit of economic growth allied to increasing population pressures. So much so, that I can't help thinking that we could be heading for an implosion of some sort, perhaps not too far into the future.

Boom/bust is a common feature for all manner of organisms, from algae to jellyfish and lemmings and locusts to rabbits, and 'the bust' often boils down to population increase and resource depletion, or an epidemic of some sort. Somewhere in there will be humans, we are as much a part of the worldwide ecosystem as any other species and ultimately we are governed by much of the same rules.

However, we might be tempted to bend them, or be able to 'buck the trend'!

If (it is claimed) we are struggling to cope with Syrian, Afghan and other refugees, what will happen if climate-change really kicks in?

Surveying in upland Wales recently, I was coming across a super-abundance of field voles (a boom that soon went bust). Field voles are familiar but distant rodent-relatives to the lemming, but much smaller.

Staple fare for all the owls, kestrel, fox, weasel and buzzard amongst others, a field vole is the mammalian equivalent of the meadow pipit when it comes to food webs, it might individually be small, but in numbers it makes up a substantial part of the diet of many predatory species.

Recently, we took on responsibility for some bits of land that included a field where several years' worth of dead vegetation had formed a protective mat (thatch) that large numbers of field voles were enjoying as cover.

Herons were seen frequently in the field but it was a while before we realized what was going on, the herons were taking voles as they dashed across open areas heading for the next nearest available cover. Herons have a very catholic diet but I had never imagined that they might take voles so regularly.

To take nutrients out of the fieldsystem and diversify, we were advised to have the field cut and since then it has been cut again, so most of the vole habitat has now gone. This did cause a bit of a dilemma as cutting has to be one of the most destructive of operations imaginable, especially if you are an insect or even a vole making use of that habitat.

The vole population is now much reduced and along with most of the insects, more confined to the rank margins of the field.

The herons and owls now need to look elsewhere for a snack as that particular habitat has been radically altered, not to put too fine a point on it - for the most part destroyed, by interfering humans.

I hope enough has been retained around the margins to encourage re-colonisation over coming years, and before the cutting, we did make an effort to move peacock and small tortoiseshell butterfly caterpillars out of the firing line and deep into some areas of nettles at the field edge.

So we did (marginally) do something to ameliorate the effects of management.

Nature is opportunistic and there will be a resurgence of sorts, dependant to a degree on what we humans might decide to do next, what management or grazing regime it is decided to follow. No doubt a degree of patience is going to be required before we approach anything like a conclusion on this project.

One thing you can be sure of, along the way, there will be winners and losers whether we decide to interfere or not.

October 1987
Nuclear Power

Letter to the Editor

I feel bound to pick up on a few points in your Editorial of 16th October. First of all, why should anyone be reassured by the radiation experts' report? In May 1986, parts of Wales ONLY received a dose of radiation from the Chernobyl cloud comparable to 25 YEARS of nuclear bomb-test fall-out. I'm afraid the experts fail to re-assure me with such comparisons.

No-one, not even the experts, knows what the long term consequences of ever increasing radiation pollution will be, they can only guess.

Elsewhere in the News we hear of a renewed call, from another expert, for testing of soil and livestock radiation levels in the Pumlumon area - long overdue as your Editorial rightly states. The assumption was and always has been that no news is good news as far as the nuclear industry and this issue is concerned.

With the go-ahead for Sizewell B and some other older reactors such as Trawsfynydd limping along and Sellafield still polluting the Irish Sea with nowhere near a sensible or safe solution to waste disposal, I repeat no-one can be reassured that the future of anyone or anything on this planet is secure with nuclear power.

November 1988
Woodcock and Conservation

THE WOODCOCK must be one of the least understood of our native birds, mysteriously appearing in summer and only at dusk or before daybreak to patrol its territorial boundary. This 'roding', seen by few, is accompanied by peculiar grunting noises heard by fewer still.

As a breeding bird in west Wales the woodcock seems to be declining but as winter approaches their numbers are swelled by migrants fleeing the bleaker winter months of continental Europe and Scandinavia.

I saw my first immigrant woodcock of '88 recently at Spurn Point, that incredibly narrow neck of land threatened by the North Sea on one side and the Yorkshire Humber, arguably the most polluted river estuary in Britain, on the other.

Here I was told that parishioners earlier this century went to church with their shotguns as winter approached and if the woodcock were in they were impatient for a speedy service.

Such remorseless pursuit of weakened birds thankful for landfall must have taken a heavy toll on the population. Now with perhaps more controlled hunting, a depletion of suitable woodland and wetland habitats poses the biggest threat.

On returning to north Ceredigion the first serious frosts as usual preceded the first fall of woodcock.

A moonlit night produced my second sighting of the birds, flushed from the byroads of Cwm Einion - a favourite haunt in winter.

Two days later and what do I pick up in the streets of Aberystwyth but a woodcock. Only recently deceased, seemingly undamaged having probably died from exhaustion after long hours of flight from who knows where.

This find gave the opportunity for close examination of the fine plumage, browns, chestnut and black providing perfect camouflage for birds in winter and summer. The bill is fine and long (70mm) for probing in the mud and wet fields for worms.

If about at dusk keep an eye out for the surviving woodcock as they emerge from the woodland to feed at night on the flooded fields or riverside marshes.

Their steady flight is like an enormous broad-winged snipe, direct and usually silent. Not at all like when flushed from their daytime retreats of wet, leaf-littered woodland - flight rapid and fast climbing to put trees and branches between themselves and any potential threat.

I have watched birds leaving Cwm Einion quite high, clearly heading for the environs of the Dyfi Estuary to probe with the other waders either in the wet fields or estuarine mud.

It was interesting to see the recent letter in the Cambrian News pointing out the problems of farm and human effluent and its possible effects on the Dyfi, perhaps thought of as one of the 'cleanest' estuaries in Britain.

The aforementioned Humber estuary has graver problems with large populations, busy ports and heavy industries releasing all manner of pollutants ultimately into the North Sea.

Surely the Dyfi is clean? Well, last summer I happened to be involved in a rudimentary study of animals living in the slack-water saltmarsh alongside the afon Leri/Dyfi confluence. The smell of this area left something to be desired and it definitely was not a healthy saltmarsh smell, it was tainted with sewage either human or farm, probably both if the aforementioned letter is half correct.

The Dyfi is famous for its sea trout and sometimes salmon runs, but the local people should not be complacent about the health of the Welsh environment.

It needs protection, constant vigilance if it is to be preserved for future generations. And the same goes for the rest of Britain's threatened environment - even the Humber still has salmon attempting to reach the cleaner upper reaches although a once thriving shrimp industry has died here within the last 20 years.

Nature certainly is not going to go down without a fight and it is about time we put down our arms and put our shoulders behind the environment and its healthy maintenance.

It would be nice to think that more of the wintering woodcock would stay here finding our woodlands, marshes and estuaries just the place for them to summer. Perhaps then more of us would be familiar with the term 'roding'.

August 1988
Ploughing and Reseeding

IT HAS BEEN CALCULATED that it takes between 100 and 2,500 years to produce an inch of soil. Ploughing and reseeding has been the norm since man began cultivating in earnest but in recent years the impetus and equipment available to reseed has grown apace. Several years ago I witnessed the sloughing off of good topsoil from a recently reseeded steep slope which had been ploughed, at no small risk to the operator I might add. On the other hand however, the effectiveness of some of these operations is quite obvious from a glance over the improved fields and hillsides leading up into the Pumlumon range.

The bright greens might be anathema to the conservationist but it certainly looks impressive to the grazier when compared to the dull unpalatable grasses and herbs left on the overworked pastures the other side of the fence.

However, ploughing and reseeding with ryegrass/clover mixtures can have its drawbacks. A typical local example I observed had a slope of some 20° (not exceptional hereabouts) and the soil loss the best part of a foot (12"). To lose such a depth of soil on what is already likely to be a 'thin soil' could be catastrophic.

Compaction must make up much of the volume loss and presumably our old friend the earthworm will remedy some of that. Sadly a fair amount of soil must also have made its way into the streams and rivers to be lost forever from the land. The plough also throws up a lot of stone, laborious to clear, and bare ground at this time of year is easy prey to the invasive thistle, dock and nettle, the grazier's big headaches.

The conservationist and naturalist have mourned the loss of hay meadows along with hedges and woodland these past few decades and not withstanding the ESA (Environmentally Sensitive Area) status afforded most of N Ceredigion, hay meadows and species-rich pastures are still likely to be lost.

Ryegrass/ clover mixtures may be nutritious but older leys containing a variety of grasses, herbs and clover ought to be treasured. With a tight sward keeping out invasives such as thistles, it is worth looking at alternatives to ploughing to increase nutrition and yields.

The lime subsidy, now long gone, perhaps ought to be resurrected in some form and would certainly be preferable to reseeding whilst at second hand it could improve the quality of some of the west Wales waters by buffering the acidification caused by airborne pollutants.

Some of the small inconspicuous herbs found in old leys have also been found to be important sources of trace elements, those bits and bobs such as copper and other minerals without which we might all feel a bit off colour. Perhaps it's no coincidence that now many a shepherd arms himself with the hypodermic to supply some of the missing nutrients, especially at crisis times such as lambing.

Whatever the answers, it's worth thinking twice about massive disturbance of top soil. Is the sward ok now? Would an application of lime be more beneficial and less costly? Am I prepared and able to cope with the thistles, dock and nettles which might invade and will there perhaps be a loss of essential trace elements available to the stock? How much top soil may we lose in a typical downpour? Is it worth it? Does it really make economic sense? If the pasture is of ESA grade, can I get a grant to maintain it as it is now?

Lots of questions all farmers must ask themselves, difficult calculations and decisions to be made as they will affect farming for generations to come.

September 1991
Sharks in 'The Post'

EVERY WEEK throughout the season the Football Post Newspaper arrives here in North-Ceredigion, usually on a Tuesday, courtesy of my younger brother. The Nottingham Football Post that is, a must for Forest or Notts County fans wherever they may be.

The edition on 24 August was particularly interesting and not just because Forest had beaten Notts County 4-0 - I have a soft spot for County too. The Post covers many sports from the hockey to boxing and even cricket but what caught my eye this particular week was the fishing pages.

Detailed accounts and advice on angling covers two inside pages every week. For anyone at all interested in wildlife these pages have a special attraction. Coarse fishing predominates as the East Midlands has many quality waters, reservoirs and rivers well populated with a wide variety of fish species, 'slightly' different to Ceredigion!

However it was the sea fishing section that I dwelled on, with its account of the Nottingham Sea Specimen Group and its recent visit to Aberdyfi. Apparently out of five booked boat trips they had lost three to the weather. Hardly surprising as the weather, until just lately, has been unreliable to say the least. According to the columnist on their most recent successful trip to Aberdyfi they boated 14 tope, the heaviest of which weighed in at 38lbs. All were returned to the sea after weighing.

Tope are members of the shark family often coming inshore during the summer months after spending the winter in deep water.

Later in the week two members managed to get out again from Aberdyfi. They caught 39 sea bass up to 7lb 8oz and 30 of these were returned to the sea!

They also returned a porbeagle shark, estimated to weigh some 90lbs- obviously the scales could not cope with it!

Apparently a porbeagle may have as many as seven 'rows' of teeth. As a front tooth loosens, so another moves forward to take its place. We humans seem to have lost out here in the evolutionary race having to make do with just the two sets of teeth!

What struck me about these accounts was the number of fish returned to the sea virtually unharmed. Greater concern for the environment and all that exists within it is still, commendably, on the increase.

Now we need the water authorities to continue cleaning up more of the inland and coastal waters. With recent Cambrian News headlines in mind, nothing short of a comprehensive sewage treatment works should be acceptable to Aberystwyth or any other coastal resort for that matter. After all, without a sea to safely bathe in there appears a great black mark or hole in Aberystwyth's potential.

Long-sea outfalls are as unacceptable as short-sea outfalls in the light of present knowledge and I certainly hope public pressure will prevail to ensure a final, satisfactory solution. Maybe then the Cambrian Coast and all its 'cleaner' resorts will continue to attract the anglers and holiday makers from the East Midlands and even further afield.

April 1992
Coastal Concerns

IT WAS HEARTENING to see the Cambrian News editorial commenting forcefully on the continuing appalling state of Britain's coastline. Within two years we may well have done away with the sewage outfall into the harbour at Aberystwyth but as the editoral states: 'there are many more outfalls requiring urgent attention along the Cambrian Coast and elsewhere'.

The Norwich Union Coastwatch, quoted in the editorial, serves to highlight the magnitude of the problem and quite frankly the state of the Cardigan Bay foreshore must be a cause for concern.

Plastic, in the form of discarded netting, rope, bags and bottles is the most obvious and unsightly flotsam deposited on the beaches. Wood, even sawn timber, never seems to be so displeasing to the eye somehow. Glass in the way of bottles, jars and often lightbulbs and tubes is a downright hazard to all. With the enthusiastic help of some visiting London schoolchildren I recently picked up bags-full of glass within minutes along a short stretch of beach at Ynyslas.

The coastwatch, which took place over two weeks early last autumn, apparently identified a welcome downward trend in the number of oiled birds, 32 found as opposed to 49 in 1990. I do not want to be a gloom and doom merchant but I find it almost impossible to believe that nationwide only 32 oiled birds were discovered during the survey period in 1991.

On 25 March, I walked the stretch of beach from Borth lifeboat station to the car park at Ynys Las turn. Most of the time along this 3½km (just over two miles) stretch I was not searching for anything in particular but as usual I became curious and took the opportunity to follow, for a time, one of the higher tidelines on the shingle. I soon found the skeletal remains of a long-dead black-headed gull but more ominously four auks, absolutely covered in thick, clinging oil. Never before have I come across such grossly oiled birds. These three guillemots and a razorbill could have been made of tar or pitch, absolutely no feathers being visible at all.

It is easy to imagine how 'oiling incidents' could be overlooked. The sooner we re-introduce a monthly, coordinated beached bird count or coastwatch survey at selected beaches around Britain's coastline the better.

Only then will we obtain enough raw data to be able to say with any confidence what is happening out there on the seas. The results should be published regularly- nationally and locally- what about it Friends of Cardigan Bay?

If I could find four oiled birds without really trying then a thorough search, I am sure, would have found more. Let us also not forget those which never reach shore and those which find a last resting place on one of the many inaccessible beaches beneath the cliffs.

What I found was the proverbial 'tip of the iceberg'!

I do not pretend to know where the oil is coming from, maybe a passing ship cleaning its tanks, who knows? Wherever it comes from it is inexcusable. The plastic and glass is equally inexcusable and nothing short of a comprehensive clean-up and education campaign is ever going to see the seas and beaches clear of this mess.

September 1993
Roads and Railways

I much prefer to travel by train, but if I have to go by car, the journey to see brothers and sister and their families takes me beyond Telford, onto the A38 to Burton and Derby.

About six or seven miles south of Derby the new Toyota factory appeared some years ago. Much heralded as a creator of jobs, this was sited conveniently to take much of the skilled workforce laid off by Rolls Royce and British Rail Engineering Ltd of Derby.

It is an enormous complex, more like a small town than a car factory. It was built because the Japanese wished to make further inroads into the European car market, and was welcomed locally for the jobs it created in an area hard-hit by the recession. But it really amazes and annoys me that although you can get green-field sites and taxbreaks to build a foreign car manufacturing facility, and to build new roads and motorways through 'protected' sites, British Rail still remains underfunded and undervalued by comparison.

Everyone in The Cambrian News circulation area must be aware of the continuing threat to the Cambrian coast railway, and the likelihood of closure will surely increase should the line be privatised. Closure would be an absolute disaster for Aberystwyth, Borth, Machynlleth and the many towns and villages serviced by the northern section of the line to Pwllheli.

The society in which we live is making it very difficult to retain any cohesive public transport system, especially in rural districts. This poses particular problems for the young and the elderly, who very often do not have private means of transport.

The furore created over the new relief road for Aberystwyth will hardly rival the battles of Twyford Down or the astonishment at proposals for 14-lane sections of motorway in England. However, it does show that some people do care about the social and environmental effects of transport decisions.

Many people do not want to see more roads driven seemingly indiscriminately across vast tracts of countryside, destroying forever some of our most valued landscapes.

I was also intending to comment here on the proposals for an out-of-town hypermarket, but I think perhaps I had better not.

Maybe this has been an unusual choice of topics for a Country Diary, but if you think the car, public transport and even supermarkets are nothing to do with wider countryside issues then you really are living in Cloud Cuckoo Land! And talking of cuckoos, if you see one in September it will without doubt be a young one. The adults depart quite early, leaving this year's fostered offspring to make their own way down to their South African winter quarters. Quite a remarkable feat, that!

Otherwise September is a very good month for birdwatching, and although the swifts too have already left, the swallows and martins are conspicuously gathering, while the first winter visitors have already arrived.

It's a time of year to savour mists, dews, a threat of the first frost, and the colours. Autumn is well and truly upon us, and - at least in my book - that is not unwelcome.

April 1995
Human Hands

In Britain there are few places unaltered by the human hand. A bit of coastline here, perhaps even a bit of marsh there and some tiny fragments of native woodland, but only in the most inaccessible ravines. Over the centuries we have altered the landscape irrevocably and, in parallel, determined what remains of our native flora and fauna.

On the world-wide scale the destruction and modification of the natural environment continues apace and, despite protestations from some quarters, the degradation shows no sign of slowing down.

I can understand (just about) if not agree with the short-sighted reasoning behind some debt-ridden, Third World country's need for cash and the consequent exploitation of its natural resources, (although it invariably appears to be exploitation initiated by some First World power in need of raw materials). But how on earth can rich, developed countries such as Canada, Australia and the USA justify clearcut logging in their remaining, ancient, native forest?

In South America, in Malaysia and in Australia we are talking about the probable extinction of many species unique to the country and to the world. We know it ought not to be allowed but how we begin to slow it down, never mind stop it is another matter.

Much nearer to home and on an altogether different scale it was recently brought to my attention how some of our own practices need improving. Contractors had made a mess of entering a small plantation, felled and extracted timber (some of which should not have been taken) and left the site partially devastated.

Incidentally all this activity had taken place over and around an active badger sett, which is hardly acceptable and may well have been illegal. Particularly as the sett could easily have been avoided and/or excluded from the felling license.

Since the early/mid eighties more and more forestry work has been undertaken by contractors. Humans being what they are, there are times when perhaps not quite enough care is taken and this certainly seems to be a case in point. It is quite possible that when the area was marked for thinning the badger sett was overlooked.

As it is, two of the entrances appear to be still in use, so perhaps the long-term outlook for these badgers is not so bleak. What it does highlight however, is the need for close cooperation, discussion, care and more stringent safeguards as regards what is acceptable practice.

Just a few years ago most of the damage wrought here would not have been allowed.

Foresters had their own patch, their own felling gang (almost) and were proud to keep up the standards. Now (with contractors) in many cases it is get away with what you can. Hence the abandoned petrol/oil cans, untreated, untrimmed stumps and (as here) damage to remaining trees. Whilst you cannot make omelettes without breaking eggs and you certainly cannot conduct forest operations without considerable disturbance there are ways of reducing the impact.

We have a major problem of deforestation worldwide. Here we effectively have no wild-woods left but we do have the expertise and the opportunity to improve our remaining semi-natural woods and plantations. We must not spurn any opportunity to ensure that Best Practice is put into operation worldwide and in our own backyard!

November 2011
Energy

WITHIN the next few weeks Mynydd y Cemmaes windfarm should be up and running, generating renewable energy into the future.

Although there have been problems and issues to talk through I am looking forward to this first commercial windfarm in Wales coming on-stream.

Certainly it is visible from afar and from within the Snowdonia National Park, but so too is Trawsfynydd, which won an award for its design and siting within the landscape, within the park. I know which I prefer. I do not wish to get deeply into energy policy, or this government's lack of policy, but it seems to me that privatisation and letting market forces loose on this one is a particularly risky business.

It is a complex issue that needs clear, 'unbiased' thinking if a sensible energy policy is ever to emerge. How this can be done now the generating industry has been privatised is another matter but here in Wales there are important elements which must be taken into account.

Without all the protests there is no doubt that orimulsion (bitumen-based fuel) would be burning in south Wales, increasing significantly the 'acid stress' factor on the environment.

Added to this we have the proposed increase in emissions from the nuclear reprocessing plant at Sellafield (Windscale) and the possible re-firing of Trawsfynydd.

Only a little further afield there is intense debate about pit closures, imported cheap coal and open-cast sites. It all adds up to a rather 'dirty' web of intrigue, and the wind-farm at Cemmaes looks cleaner, minute by minute.

Number one on the agenda must be an effective drive to reduce our power requirements, through energy conservation. How this can be achieved with a private, profit-orientated industry I do not know!

Number two, we should fit all coal and oil-fired power-stations with effective means of cleaning up the emissions, and until nuclear power can be produced without any threat to the health of the environment and an effective means of dealing safely with its waste is devised, there should certainly be no expansion of its use.

Number three, we must retain a viable coal industry. Despite its drawbacks it is the most abundant fossil fuel available to us as we approach the next millenium.

Number four, wind energy and other non-polluting forms of power generation must be developed and must be encouraged with further 'non fossil-fuel' incentives.

Years before the 'Chernobyl incident' and even before the 'acid rain' debate had got off the ground I had a graphic example of how the wind knows no boundaries.

Within Dyfi forest, high above Aberllefenni, is Foel Friog. Once an extensive sheep-walk, it had recently been planted with Sitka spruce and formed one of the larger plots on which I was monitoring the bird populations.

Early one morning I discovered a burst balloon to which was tied a label informing me there was a reward (£5) for the finder of the furthest from the release site, an industrial estate in Bristol. The sender won a tenner and I duly received my fiver from the organisers of the balloon race.

A harmless bit of airborne pollution, quite fun and profitable to all concerned. It also illustrates that we have no control over the airstreams and that we really must get a grip on what we release into the atmosphere.

Hopefully the Cemmaes project will have favourable winds and be producing clean energy, profitably, for many, many years to come.

June 1993
Joyriders

Even in the most remote parts of the uplands it is now quite common to see the signs of bikers. Not cyclists but the more intrusive and potentially more damaging, off- road scrambler.

It is now several years since I watched a group of six 'scramblers' negotiating the then footpath leading from Hyddgen towards Pumlumon and the ruins of Nant y Llyn. Two of the riders managed to get stuck in a sphagnum bog and left a nasty trail of extrication.

More recently (and only a few miles distant) I have seen the affects of 4x4 expeditionists on what was once a quite walkable footpath. Much more damaging than the scramblers, these heavy machines have left deep, peaty pools surrounded by a soggy morass and effectively closed the path to walkers!

Whatever the pleasures of this activity, if it destroys or severely damages the environment and impinges unreasonably upon other legitimate users of the countryside, then I really feel it must be brought under some control! I would not want to be a killjoy but these characters and their vehicles are destroying valuable and fragile environments. I enjoy speedway and the enduro motorbike championships but these are well organised events, well controlled and they do not indiscriminately affect the enjoyment of the great outdoors by others.

And into this damaging/nuisance category I am compelled to include the jet-skier! Perhaps the most intrusive newcomer to the beach scene and undoubtedly a despoiler of the marine environment. Their penetrating buzzing and thumping certainly does spoil a day at the coast. Notwithstanding the effects on seals, dolphins and other marine life, should freedom of the individual allow such an intrusive machine into everyone else's life?

I think not, and to all those involved in defining and enforcing local byelaws and legislation can I make this request? Think in the longterm, think of the environmental damage being caused and think of the hundreds, nay thousands who visit mid Wales each year in search of unspoilt countryside and coast and some tranquillity.

October 2014
Don't Bottle It

IT IS just staggering, the amount of waste and potential litter that the average human in the UK can produce in a day, never mind a week.

Discarded packaging accumulates almost exponentially and I suppose it might be understandable (but in no way forgivable) when some of it spills out into the great outdoors. All that plastic (and most of the rubbish is plastic) can come in a multitude of types, intricate shapes, size and colour, and some of it can even be attractive in a weird sort of way. In the streets, on the verges, in the fields, rivers and ultimately in the sea and beaches is where a lot of it ends up.

It is predicted that before too long a lot of our sandy beaches will consist of a good proportion of grains of plastic rather than grains of sand.

No matter how colourful, it soon turns ugly and it can cause massive problems for councils, wildlife, livestock and the community generally.

Although there is a move towards using more of the bio-degradable plastics, much of what we produce and use now will be around for decades and so we are looking at a problem that is only likely to get worse.

Recently, I was taking in some late September sun at the coast and thought I would check out the dune slack about a mile south of Ynyslas point. Here, there are pyramidal and bee orchids to be found in the summer, but in the past it has been the scene of some sorry messes.

This time, there was less broken glass, but a quantity of plastic bottles and empty snack packets. It did not take long to gather the first bit of circumstantial evidence to again indicate a local source: a child's bus ticket from Aberystwyth to Ynyslas turn on 26 September.

The information on a mid-Wales Travel bus ticket is quite impressive, it even has the time of issue (17.40) and the time of departure, (17.44). So they must have got on at the bus station in Aber. The shopping bags were further evidence of the origins along with large plastic bottles that had contained cola, lemonade and cider. Incredibly, someone ·had also thought to bring along several Ceredigion County Council recycling bags and using one of those, it did not take me long to clear up, apart from one glass bottle that seemed to have been deliberately smashed on a boulder. I have seen what broken glass can do to children playing in this area and it is not at all pleasant.

One youngster had even been filling in a Ceredigion Actif questionnaire and had ticked the boxes agreeing that 'we want to give opportunities to all children to develop their skills' and several other positive statements. Quite right, and I feel sure they would have ticked all the correct boxes had they got any further, but they had not. Perhaps the cider was kicking in by then?

It really is imperative that all youngsters such as these are made aware of the consequences of their actions and inactions.

Someone clearly had the right idea in bringing along the recycling bags but perhaps peer pressure dissuaded them from using them. They should have stuck to their guns and someone there should have cleared up.

Schools, parents, and in fact all of us need to emphasise that care for the environment is not just another 'take it or leave it' option. It is so important if they are going to have a half-decent world in which to live. Present circumstances throughout the world may not make it easy for a youngster to maintain a positive feeling about the future, but if the kids really do give up, then there is no hope.

Bright spots from this trip were four red-throated divers offshore (first of the winter visitors) with a few scoters and gannets further out. Even better and brighter, a young lad (possibly six years old) restored some of my faith in the fate of the human race by approaching me, a bearded stranger collecting rubbish, and deposited some plastic in the recycling bag.

Wonderful. There's hope yet!

December 1993
Privatised Forestry

Desperate for more cash to underpin our ailing economy, the Government 'drives on' by privatising the railways, despite almost universal opposition and a total lack of public confidence in the outcome.

Next in line may be the Forestry Commission - Y Comisiwn Coedwigaeth - a review body is at the moment looking into the possibilities of privatisation, and the debate has been hotting up.

Programmes on national radio and several articles in a variety of newspapers and magazines have pointed out some of the likely consequences of this particular privatisation. But despite this publicity I suspect many people are still unaware that the state-owned forest is freely accessible to the general public, who may walk or cycle along virtually any of the many miles of forest track in England, Scotland or Wales.

Once privatised, what price access? Some of the new owners might allow access, but I know from experience with new owners of ex-forestry estate locally, that the likelihood is that anything other than a public right of way will be closed.

And what about the recent, huge strides made by Forest Enterprise, the wood production section of the Forestry Commission?

I have been privileged to be party to some of the plans for the Rheidol Forest, and the amount of thought and work going into deciding felling coupes, their landscape and conservation consequences is phenomenal.

Although it has to be accepted that not everything will happen at once, the plans and the signs are there, and already a start has been made on the practicalities.

You only have to look at the Coed y Brenin, Ystwyth and Dyfi forests to see what we might expect, given time and some well-considered management. For example, work on river and streamsides has already been done within the Tarenig Forest. This can be seen from the A44 below Eisteddfa Gurig. Wide, clear avenues follow all the minor streams up through the forest from the afon Tarenig.

Closely planted conifers are deadly to a stream, because bank side vegetation is shaded out, the banks are then likely to erode, and aquatic vegetation and invertebrates die out.

Clearing the trees well back allows sunlight to reach the water and helps vegetation growth on the banks. If we are lucky, acid rain permitting, the invertebrates will return and perhaps even the wild, brown trout.

Who in a privatised forestry is going to be concerned with this, and with other wider environmental issues? Who is going to risk - and it is a risk - allowing the general public access?

Who is going to oversee the landscape implications of felling and replanting?

It is a frightening prospect, and I feel that the privatisation of forestry will be as unpopular as the privatisation of British Rail. Both have grave implications for the quality of life here in Wales.

The Forestry Commission looks after 2.8 million acres of forest, including thousands of recognised sites of conservation interest, and innumerable Sites of Special Scientific Interest and Forest Nature Reserves.

Over 1½ million visitors a year use these forests for recreation, and many enjoy the sense of freedom and isolation to be found there.

Undoubtedly, there is a lot more at stake in the future of the state forests than a few trees and political dogma.

July 1994
Sweet FA

THE FORESTRY AUTHORITY recently launched a new series of booklets aimed at landowners and woodland managers, emphasising the value and importance of the remaining 'semi-natural' woodlands in Wales. At the Builth Wells showground launch, the FA's Woodlands Officer for mid Wales, David Williams, and its Conservation Officer for Wales, Ruth Jenkins, addressed a large audience representing local authorities, planners, agents, Coed Cymru, Tir Cymen (CCW), conservation bodies and others with an interest in woodland and woodland management.

Semi-natural woodlands are composed of locally native trees and shrubs derived from coppicing and natural regeneration rather than planting. They are particularly important for the associated wildlife, and unique landscapes often depend upon their survival.

It was stressed throughout the presentation that these booklets are general guides - they do not offer specific guidelines for Woodland Grant Scheme purposes.

The Forestry Authority recognises that each and every woodland may need a different prescription if it is to produce usable timber and be retained into the 21st century and beyond.

The eight booklets deal with woodlands ranging from the 'Native Pinewoods of the Scottish Highlands' to the 'Lowland Beech Woods of Southern Britain'. While neither of these may have any application in Mid-Wales, certainly Upland Oak woods (Guide 5), Upland Birchwoods (Guide 6) and Wet Woodlands (Guide 8) are very relevant and give useful hints on management, wildlife conservation and potential wood production.

Based on the National Vegetational Classification (NVC), the guides take over from the 1985 booklet on broadleaf policy and identify five important basic principles.

Management must: Maintain and restore ecological diversity, maintain and, if possible, improve aesthetic value (ie a woodland's relevance in the landscape), maintain genetic integrity (ie no introductions of 'exotic' species), take appropriate opportunities to produce utilisable wood, and finally, enlarge the woodland where practicable and possible.

Whilst any of these aims may be impracticable in particular situations, they are all compatible with what is now recognised as good, sustainable management practice. They are beneficial to wildlife, beneficial to the woodland owner and beneficial to the landscape as a whole.

Leaving Builth afterwards and following the Wye upstream to Rhayader and Llangurig, I saw many examples of semi-natural woodland that has been unmanaged or under-managed for decades. Over much of Wales these woodlands are showing their age, with little or no natural regeneration.

Many are in desperate need of some attention and sympathetic management.

If you are considering the Woodland Grant Scheme (WGS) then these booklets give a good guide as to what might be expected by the Forestry Authority.

Semi-natural woodland restoration accounts for 80% of WGS projects in Wales, and the FA emphasises that positive management is always required.

There are useful hints regarding the need for management, the value of retained trees and dead wood, and methods of regeneration, site preparation, planting and coppicing. Further help and advice is always available at the local FA office.

These booklets mark another step towards creating woodlands in which young native trees will flourish for future generations to enjoy.

December 1986
Live Now, Pay Now

NANT Y MOCH is full again after baring its banks for many months. Few birds take to the waters of this upland reservoir, the driving force behind the Rheidol Power Station.

However, on a recent wet, windy, Pumlumon day, something stirred on the water. Shining like a beacon in the greyness a brilliant-white drake goosander accompanied another rather drab looking duck, a female goldeneye. Both had sought what little shelter there was, in the shallow, narrow finger of water that extends towards the ruins of Bwlchstyllen and the Aberystwyth water supply of Llyn Craig y Pistyll.

Having just flushed a couple of tired woodcock from the sodden slopes of Pumlumon, and speculated as to their probable origin, perhaps Scandinavia, I began to consider the state of Welsh Waters, both fresh and marine.

Rain-the life giver, or is it? A good question when one considers the effects of so-called 'acid-rain' and the aftermath of Chernobyl. And yet again catastrophic pollution has been in the news with the plight of the mighty Rhine grabbing the headlines, so what chance survival on this increasingly polluted planet?

In the sixties and seventies certain herbicides and pesticides were identified as responsible for the decline in a great many of our predatory birds. Grave mistakes have certainly been made in the past.

Perhaps now has come the time for another long hard look at what we intend to do to the environment we ultimately depend upon. Certainly in the light of recent findings it would be a foolish water authority that allowed extensive conifer afforestation of water supply catchments.

Apart from the probable acid-rain effects they would also have to take account of a high percentage of any rainfall evaporating from forest canopy, rainfall that would never reach the water supply reservoir.

As to the marine environment, the recent and continuing debate on nuclear products being found at sites around the Welsh coast must be a cause for concern.

The nationally advertised post by Gwynedd County Council, for a researcher with no axe to grind, either pro or anti-nuclear, will have been hard to fill. Most members of the public now have a healthy respect for, if not dread of nuclear power and all it entails, from Chernobyl to Trawsfynydd to Sellafield.

We can learn a lot from the status of the wildlife we might observe every day. The decline in dippers in many instances is thought to be related to the effects of acidification on the aquatic organisms they rely upon for food.

The decline in peregrines and sparrowhawks prior to controls on pesticides and the rise in their populations since controls took effect are well proven and accepted as fact. Pollution of whatever sort affects us all, eventually, and as Chernobyl and the Rhine disaster show, respects no boundaries.

Conservation also involves and concerns us all in a world of finite resources and it does nothing for my confidence to see recently over 40 television sets switched on for display in a single well known shop in Aberystwyth.

The thinking always seems to be live now, pay later. Unfortunately it will be our children and their children, if they survive, that will have to fork out the most.

The Farmers Union of Wales is only one of many to come to the conclusion that further steps along the nuclear way are too hazardous, declaring what amounts to 'No Confidence' in the nuclear industry.

With realistic conservation, effective 'save it' campaigns and more funding of alternative energy research, (e.g. Carmarthen Bay Wind Generators) we could at least call a halt to any nuclear expansion plans.

The Irish Sea now has the dubious honour of being the 'hottest' in the world, undisputed. The summer of 1984 will remain with me for the rest of my life -why? As a family we spent many hours basking in the late afternoon and evening sun, cooling off with a dip in the sea. Great, or so we all thought, but now I can't help feeling worried, to put it mildly, when I consider the nuclear controversy and recent findings potentially linking Leukaemia clusters and nuclear installations.

A nuclear scientist would no doubt tell me all about skin cancer, the effects of background radiation and of the sun. I would tell him or her, that mankind, and all other life of this earth, has evolved over thousands of years and to a great degree must have developed immunity to 'natural' environmental radiation.

However, we have not experienced long exposure, nor are we likely to have developed immunity to, the effects of the radioactive elements being discharged into the Irish Sea or those deposited by the Chernobyl cloud.

Pollution of waterways and the sea from mis-use of fertilizers, pesticides, factory/farm effluent, Sellafield or any other source should not be acceptable to anyone in the light of today's knowledge. The streams, rivers and coastline of Wales are one of the country's greatest assets, let them long remain so.

March 1991
Gulf War and Energy

IT SEEMS STRANGE to be writing of such 'inconsequental' things as the environment while we are confronted by the massive repercussions of the Gulf War. However the Gulf War was at best partly, some would say mainly, concerned with an environmental problem of massive proportions. Namely the world's dependence upon a relatively cheap, reliable supply of oil.

It is also worth remembering that whilst the more developed nations flinch at the associated oil price rises, to a poor, developing nation the price rises can be catastrophic.

Now if anything is to be gained from such a dreadful conflict it may be a realization that this love affair with oil and its by-products must be controlled. I cannot be the only one to notice the increasing traffic congestion in Aberystwyth and elsewhere, and all forecasters point to increasing car ownership well into the next century - we can look forward to even more oil-consumption, pollution and congestion. What is the answer? More roads, the car-lobby says, but all the evidence points to minimal long-term benefits for a massive loss of land to tarmac and concrete.

By-passes such as that relieving Cardigan are beneficial but what is needed is a radically changed transport policy with more emphasis on public transport and increased funding and use of the railways as a priority.

Market forces tend to be selfish and often short-sighted. After privatisation, who is going to promote a 'Save It' campaign in the electricity supply industry? A situation I find hard to come to terms with when energy-conservation must be a priority in all aspects of life.

Back to transport, it must make sense to get the railways back on their feet. I travel relatively infrequently by rail I must admit but I do make an effort whenever possible to use the railways. Over these several hundred miles per year how much freight do I see moved by rail? Virtually none. A few coal-trains for the power-stations and the regular oil-train on 'The Cambrian' to Aberystwyth. Otherwise everything, it seems, is moved by road.

Of course the road transport lobby is strong. It has been nurtured by successive governments and now the 'baby' is so big it will hardly fit in the pram and it is still demanding more food in the form of roads and oil-resources.

In Britain it is quite possible to be in a traffic jam and still be moving at 60-70 mph - try the M6 or M1! We must begin to move away from this conveyor belt mentality when the greater good of the whole environment demands that we take a long hard look at just what we have done and what we are doing in the name of progress!

February 2014
Reasons to be Cheerful

REASONS TO BE CHEERFUL, one of the emblematic songs of the late Ian Dury (Hammersmith Palais and Bolshoi Ballet). I remember himself and the original Blockheads performing at the Kings Hall in Aberystwyth, not so many years before it was demolished. As I have at least another nine or ten months before Christmas looms on the horizon again I thought it might be an idea to look at a few other reasons to be cheerful.

Well, the days are getting longer though sometimes you might begin to wonder if day has broken and the sun has really risen. Snowdrops are up and even in flower in sheltered spots. Birds are tuning up for that dawn chorus with mistle thrush, dunnock and robin being the main culprits and just this morning I heard my first chaffinch having a go, well before the end of January. The mistle thrush is not known as the storm cock for nothing, it has been belting out a rather discordant song for weeks, even during several squally blows that saw out January. Sure sign of spring on the horizon, or not? If this mild spell continues the frogs may even get it into their heads to set out for the spawning ponds. We (and the frogs) just have to hope that we don't get another sting in winter's tail like last year when we effectively lost a month of the growing season and some farmers in mid Wales lost a lot of livestock to snow and freezing winds.

Wild, wet and mild could describe what we have had so far, with less than a handful of ground frosts in between long periods of strong, swirling winds and heavy seas, but we all know that could change in a trice.

We have all heard about declines in bird species but there are some brighter spots in this rather dismal period and I thought maybe it would be timely to have a look at a few reasons to be at least a little upbeat, on the avifauna front.

An insatiable appetite for fresh, clean water has led to reservoirs being built over very many years and for a wide variety of reasons, from powering mining machinery to supplying drinking water and hydro-power generation. Large ones are rarely without complex, controversial elements (Tryweryn, Vyrnwy, Nant y Moch) but they do provide a unique habitat and have helped a few species spread their wings, notably goosander and great crested grebe. Both are fish eaters but the goosander is undoubtedly the greediest and sometimes thought to be a problem for the angling community.

A hole nester, the goosander prefers holes in trees but one of the first breeding records in Ceredigion was of a pair at Nant y Moch where there are few large trees and they resorted to nesting in a jumble of rocks well above the reservoir waters. Great crested grebes are rare on upland reservoirs as they prefer a weedy, reed fringed surround to breeding sites and as anchorage for their floating nests. Occasionally they may turn up and even attempt breeding but the only regular sites I know of are Llyn Glandwgan, Lake Vyrnwy and Tal-y-Llyn. They are also winter visitors just offshore of Borth and Ynys Las and elsewhere along the Cardigan Bay coast. The recent storms will certainly have been as problematic for them as they have been for the inhabitants of Aberystwyth and elsewhere.

A real exotic and an introduced species is the mandarin duck, another hole nester that appears to be on the increase and could be on its way to a river near you sometime in the next decade or so. I have been told of birds on the Dee near Llangollen and came across them myself last year on the Dee not far from Wrexham. They have also been seen and are suspected of breeding near Lake Vyrnwy and on the Mawddach near Dolgellau, so it would appear they are spreading westwards from the borders. Slightly bigger than a teal the males are quite off-the-wall as regards plumage, being all tufts and spectacular colours and, being more of a dabbler and apparently also partial to eating acorns and beech mast in the woods, it is a species of no real concern to the angler. So far they seem to be filling a niche in the UK and Welsh avifauna without any thoughts that they might become a problem, apart from the competition they present to other species for any suitably sized hole in a tree.

Little grebes too have benefited from our ability to manufacture smaller water bodies. While water vole surveying throughout north Ceredigion I came across numerous pools and ponds. Some were great for water voles, virtually all were also great for invertebrates such as dragonfly and damselfly nymphs and small fish, thus they were great for little grebe.

On to drier habitats, are there any left? Well woodlands and particularly forest plantations are drier so we can perhaps take refuge there. Forest plantations have always been controversial from proposal to planting and then even through to production and during the felling stages but as we are trying to be cheerful and positive here I will only mention a few of the bird species that have benefited. High on the list are siskin and crossbill and of course the goldcrest and coal tit. Redpoll would have been included a few decades ago but they prefer young, new growth and although there is quite a bit of replanting of felled areas taking place, they for some reason do not seem to take to these restocked areas quite so well.

Crossbill numbers will fluctuate- being such specialist feeders and dependant upon conifer-cone crops they tend to be nomadic and follow that seed source. Heavily built and perhaps a tad bigger than a greenfinch the males are reddish and the females a dull green. The crossed mandibles of the bill are a dead giveaway though.

The much smaller and more familiar siskin is another lover of mature conifer forest where it usually nests high in the canopy. Along with goldfinches, they seem irresistibly attracted to niger/nyjer seed and can be frequent visitors to garden feeding stations well away from plantations. Out of the breeding season they may also be found with redpolls as the two species often feed as a mixed flock, particularly on birch and alder seed.

Perhaps we can be at least moderately cheerful at the fact that a fair chunk of the winter is past and that spring is on the way, and some are apparently forecasting another decent summer. But best wait and see what the next couple of months has in store before we start celebrating!

June 2014
Returning to the Wild

I HAVE JUST revisited Iolo Williams and his State of Nature presentation, circa May 2013. It's well worth another look, on YouTube if you have the facility. Also and much more recently (May 2014) George Monbiot was at Aber Uni talking about the re-wilding of Britain. Not unconnected, as both lament the loss of diversity, species and habitats and refer to what might be adjudged mistakes in land management, ongoing-now and in the not too distant past.

Land use change inevitably affects us all and more directly affects those that work the land and all those organisms that live on that land or perhaps use it temporarily as a food source, as shelter or as a breeding site.

On my travels about mid, west and north Wales I get to see a lot of land and cannot help considering its value. Not in monetary terms, I have hardly a clue on that score, but from the point of view of the habitat, the plantlife, insects, mammals and birdlife and the overall diversity it supports.

We humans continue to have such a tremendous impact on the landscape and it is interesting to at least speculate on what any re-wilding might bring or mean. A spread of natural forest in some upland areas has to be a distinct possibility but I think we might rule out bear and wolf reintroductions. But what about lynx, beaver and pine marten?

It looks like beaver is definitely on the cards and just from a management tool perspective I have no problem with that. Lynx may be borderline but again in parts of Snowdonia, the Brecon Beacons or here in the Cambrian Mountains it has to be at least a long term possibility. Pine marten is perhaps the least controversial as there appears to be a small and widely dispersed population surviving in west Wales anyway, albeit possibly of some Scottish origin.

Rewilding means more than encouraging the regeneration of native woodland and specific reintroductions, it also means less sheep on the hills, at least some hills. Sheep may now be thinly spread on many hills but they do have a significant effect on the vegetation, grazing out the more nutritious grasses, tree seedlings, heaths and herbs. Mollinia or purple moor grass is Britain's only deciduous grass and it thrives in wet conditions and under sheep grazing, as all its more nutritious competitors are preferentially nibbled away. Another popular name for it is disco-grass and anyone who has tried walking through an expanse of mollinia will know immediately how this nickname comes about. High tussocks can be formed and it is sometimes debatable whether to step on top of a wobbly tussock or chance a boot full of peaty water by treading between tussocks. Farmers and fieldworkers alike will recognise and avoid crossing such terrain if at all possible as it can be exhausting and frustrating in the extreme. However it occurs over large areas of upland Wales and sometimes cannot be avoided- best then to follow the sheep trails through it, if there are any.

I have found curlew nesting in mollinia but they will steer clear of large expanses of the long established tussocky stuff as it is just so unsuitable for nesting. The young would have a real problem getting away on hatching and as they have to be up and about and feeding within a few hours of emerging from the egg they need to be near to better insect food sources. Often noisy but somehow secretive and enigmatic birds they appear to me to be the moorland equivalent of the wise, tawny owl of the woods. They certainly do keep an eye on things and know all that is going on in the vicinity of any nest.

The four recently hatched chicks in the picture (illustrated in the original article) were at a nest on the Vyrnwy Estate a few years back, Iolo Williams' old stomping ground, where curlew numbers have plummeted from near thirty pairs to less than a handful over the past twenty years. Why this should be we still do not fully understand but foxes are on camera as nest predators and crows are certainly a problem. Regularly overhead there are red kite and buzzard so youngsters like these still have a gauntlet of predators to face before they actually take to the air (fledge) after about 38 days. Interestingly, sheep were more of a problem and nest cameras showed them eating eggs and causing so much disruption at other nests that eggs were abandoned.

Curlew along with some of the smaller, sheep tolerant plants could lose out in any rewilding. If it happens, it will be interesting to see the conservationists arguing amongst themselves (and with the agriculturists), fighting their corner for whatever specialism they might be interested in. But perhaps we just have to be a little more pragmatic, do the best we can, accept there will be winners and losers and begin thinking on the landscape scale rather than at the species level?

December 2015
Shellfishing in Cardigan Bay

AN ABIDING MEMORY of mine is of commercial shellfish harvesters descending upon a rocky shore just south of Borth. This happened all of 25, maybe it was even 30 years ago. I watched as they stripped the rocks of an abundance of edible periwinkles. These are snail-like molluscs with dark brown and very strong shells, the very largest might just about reach an inch (2.5cm) in length.

At the time they could be gathered in by the bucket-load and soon numerous sacks were filled and awaiting collection, scattered all over the rocky shelves.

Since that day, the periwinkle population has never again reached anywhere near those proportions. The habitat has not altered but clearly something has changed, and so it is with some trepidation that I hear there are moves afoot to controversially open parts of the Cardigan Bay SAC (Special Area of Conservation) to scallop dredging.

No doubt encouraged by some celebrity chef on TV, there seems to be a market for scallops. The industrial way of getting them is to dredge. This entails dragging several wide and very heavy pieces of fiercely tined kit along and through the sea bed to gather in scallops to a metal mesh/net attachment immediately behind. It has to be one of the most destructive harvesting methods imaginable, in fact if you were thinking to destroy that marine environment, this is probably the best design and method that anyone might come up with.

It is akin to ploughing the sea bed and is known to leave a trail of dead and damaged organisms (including scallops) in its wake and how on earth the Welsh Assembly can be thinking of allowing this to happen in a Special Area of Conservation absolutely beggars belief.

April 2010
Marine Conservation Zones

COASTAL LANDSCAPES are forever changing and here on the Ceredigion coast we are not unaffected, but we are fortunate not to have the problems being experienced on many sections of the Yorkshire coast where the boulder clay shoreline is being eroded at the rate of several metres per year.

Here we might have the occasional slump of a section of cliff face or the erosion of some sand dune at the waters edge, damage that over time might naturally repair depending upon which way the wind might blow.

True, there are potentially much more serious problems on the horizon at Borth and elsewhere along other low lying sections of the coast but compared to the scale of things that are happening elsewhere around the UK coastline, most of these problems might be considered relatively minor at this point in time.

In such a dynamic environment of wind and wave the role of pioneer and stabilising plants is vitally important. The deep rooting marram grass is essential for holding together the dune systems at Ynys Las where there has unusually been an actual increase (accretion) in land area over the past few years. Okay, they may only be embryo dunes that could be washed away in a single storm tide but it has been fascinating to watch their quite rapid development.

And along the top of the shingle ridge the yellow homed poppy seems to be increasing while elsewhere, up and down the coast, sea holly appears to be getting a grip in some other, less than stable situations.

The Welsh Assembly Government is proposing to set up a suite of Marine Conservation Zones (MCZs) around the Welsh coastline by 2012*. They intend that these areas should be Highly Protected MCZs, which will bar commercial and perhaps even restrict recreational fishing.

Non-damaging activities such as surfing, boating and diving will be unaffected. Where that leaves jet skis remains to be decided I guess but I doubt many, if any, MCZs will initially be in the near Cardigan Bay area.

Amazingly, Wales at present has only one Marine Nature Reserve and even that is not fully protected. Skomer Island off the Pembrokeshire coast, best known for its seabird colonies and accessible from the Marloes peninsula, is a regular destination for the birdwatcher seeking out puffins and shearwaters amongst many other species.

Otherwise, and somewhat surprising to me, it seems that approximately 70 per cent of the coastline and 30 per cent of the near shore marine environment is already within Special Areas of Conservation (SACs).

Unfortunately an assessment in 2003 indicated that 60 per cent of the features being 'conserved' (ie habitats and species) were in 'unfavourable condition'. That means the site and designation is failing to provide adequate protection, hence at least part of the reasoning behind the need to establish MCZs.

A report into the environmental effects of fishing (Royal Commission on Environmental Pollution, 2004) advised that at least 30 per cent of UK waters should be designated as Highly Protected Marine Reserves but I very much doubt that Welsh Assembly Government will be tempted to go anywhere near that figure, at least not initially. The report is, however, an indication of the parlous state that some of our inshore waters are in.

It is to be hoped that a coherent network of MCZs will provide an opportunity for habitats and all manner of marine species to recover that the much larger and existing SACs are clearly not able to deliver.

The effects within MCZs can be considerable. A gain of over 400 per cent in biomass and 20 per cent in species diversity has been recorded within protected areas elsewhere in the world where similar measures have been taken and considering the mobility of most marine species, at least for part of their lifecycle, that is some increase.

The so called spill-out from a highly protected area can also be considerable with fishermen recording significantly increased catches adjacent to, but outside a fully protected zone. Bearing in mind MCZs are not all about fish, bigger fish and more of them (even in a quite restricted area) would seem to inevitably lead to more offspring and a healthier, more vibrant fishery all round.

The establishment of a MCZ does not have to mean a decline in any fishery, in actual fact it could, and should, mean a significant improvement in fish stocks in the wider area over the medium and long term.

Very recently, and after 18 years of debate, an agreement has been reached to seriously tackle the worldwide decline in species diversity/species extinctions.

The agreement of over 190 nations in Nagoya, Japan could be a breakthrough and the establishment of Wales' first Marine Conservation Zones could play a small but not insignificant part in bolstering that agreement.

The Welsh Assembly Government are seeking comments before they finally decide where any MCZs might be. All stakeholders are allowed to comment, and that means everyone living in Wales, visiting or interested in Wales' fantastic coastline.

*Currently (October 2023) there is still only 1 MCZ, around Skomer, the one and only Marine Nature Reserve (MNR) created in 1990, and reclassified as a MCZ in 2014. Cardigan Bay SAC is still dredged for scallops, and the entire West Wales Marine SAC has very few restrictions on damaging practices, but some rules for keeping a distance from breeding bird colonies and marine mammals.

August 2016
Planting Trees

THERE'S NOT A LOT to be optimistic about lately- party politics, referendum splits, atrocities worldwide, weather often diabolical and dull, most bird species have stopped singing and the butterflies (and many other insects) are conspicuous by their absence, all very worrying.

At least Welsh football, Andy Murray and now the Olympics have provided some distraction.

Apparently if you are found planting a tree, it is thought to be a sure sign that you are an optimist. After all, you have to be thinking long-term when you plant a tree.

Here in north Ceredigion and in west Wales generally we are fortunate in having a wide range of woodland types and a significant proportion of native broadleaves, usually the most important ecologically and for wildlife in general.

Forest plantations clothe much of the mid and upper elevations, but there is now a more relaxed attitude to broad leaved regeneration and even moves afoot to replace some conifer plantations with native broadleaves. How thoughts and woodland management aims and objectives can change in just a few years.

Hedgerows are another matter and despite a recent resurgence in planting under various, environmental 'guises', I get the impression we are still slowly losing hedges, mainly through neglect.

They are not easy to establish and maintain and always require some protection from livestock, probably double fencing. It also seems to be common practice to severely cut and trim even internal hedges annually and allow no flowering or fruit or hips to develop. Some periodic/rotational cutting over a number of years and more traditional hedge laying would allow a much more beneficial linear feature to develop.

Mature hedgerow trees are also of some concern as they too are slowly disappearing and little or no attempt is being made to see that they are replaced. Many will be very old trees, possibly 150 years old or more.

Statuesque in the landscape and likely hosts to important lichen communities and possibly other epiphytic plants, they also have a disproportionate importance for invertebrates and some of the larger, hole nesting bird species such as tawny, little and barn owl, stock dove and kestrel.

Boxes might be put up to offset the loss of natural nest sites but nothing can replace an old broadleaved tree when it comes to colonization by lichens. Many lichens are very particular about what species of tree they will grow on and where they might flourish. West Wales also just happens to have some of the cleanest and most moisture-laden air in the UK, which helps as well.

Nothing can replace that mature tree in the landscape and they will surely be sorely missed in the future if action is not taken soon to ensure that the next generation of big trees is on its way to maturity.

Over the years I have been fortunate enough to have been able to plant literally thousands of trees. Admittedly most of them were sitka spruce in commercial plantations, planted at the rate of anything up to nine hundred, or rarely, a thousand per day. In later years I have also felled literally thousands of trees, not at anywhere near a thousand per day, but yes they were sitka spruce and (fortunately for my peace of mind), they were not the same trees that I had planted some 20-odd years previously. These sitka had been planted on high elevation, deep upland peats where they were never going to flourish and as attitudes have changed it was decided to de-stock some of these substantial areas of upland heather moor. It seems doubtful if the golden plover, curlew and red and black grouse will be returning any time soon to such areas, but at least a substantial start has been made at rectifying a past planting mistake.

More recently we have planted various broadleaved trees and shrubs on a lowland site and even the beginnings of an orchard. In west Wales that really is being optimistic. As for apples and pears, I am not expecting a bountiful crop soon, if ever. However the mere act of planting a tree and watching it grow is something I would recommend to anyone, even a bit of a pessimist like myself can benefit.

May 2014
Planetary Kickback

THERE IS MORE TALK lately of ecosystem services - flood prevention, drought amelioration, water cleansing, C02 absorption and air cleansing are just a few examples.

What does it all mean? To me, it means we are at last beginning to truly value (albeit too often only in monetary terms) what the natural environment does for us and the other inhabitants of this planet.

I include the other inhabitants as we humans cannot go on as if we are all that matters, as if whatever we decide can be justified under the banner of the march of progress and that impossible dream of perpetual growth. Forever exploiting finite resources for our own immediate benefit without much thought for the long term, the serious effect it will have on a multitude of species and habitats is just not sustainable. I believe we all know it.

Anyone who has had chainsaw training (anything from reading a manual to extensive chainsaw use) will be familiar with the term 'kickback' and know how uncontrollable it is, and how dangerous. Before the advent of chain safety-brakes it was a cause of many serious injuries.

It seems to me we are getting some kickback from our planet on various fronts. Unless we start to handle things more responsibly, we are going to see some serious accidents soon. This planet is a very powerful organism and it needs to be handled with much more care and respect than your average chainsaw.

We have a population crisis, a housing crisis, an energy crisis, consumption and debt crises, a youth unemployment crisis, an ongoing banking crisis and, despite all our ingenuity, we can lose airliners, ferries can still capsize and conflicts continue to break out like a rash all over the place. Added to that is the present and impending climate change, and no-one knows exactly where that might be heading.

A plethora of problems, for individuals and for the world in general, and no easy solutions that are going to satisfy everyone, all of the time.

Occasionally, it helps if we can escape some of this madness, switch off completely and get out into the wider environment. A walk by the river or sea, in some woodland or a up a hill can help with general fitness and alleviate depression, or so recent reports suggest. There can be little doubt that most of the population feel the need to get closer to nature occasionally, though I sometimes feel we are diverging as a species and there is a growing majority that are more at home in a concrete jungle or immersed in their communication technology and social media.

Out and about, it is often the commonplace and less complicated that I find particularly attractive. Rarities they may not be, but the humble wood anemone, dog violet and celandine can take some beating. Along with the swallows, warblers, waders and other migrants, they are true harbingers of spring. And what a start to the season it has been. After a dismal and dull (but mild) winter, it was great to see the sun shining over both the Easter and the May Bank holidays.

One thing we can be sure of, no matter what a mess we might make of the next few decades (though we do not necessarily have to make a total mess of it), at least the natural world will keep on turning. It may well be that ecosystems will be radically changed, but in the long term, that is what ecosystems do: they evolve over many millennia, never remaining the same.

At the moment, we just seem hell-bent on exploiting, manipulating and moulding everything to our own benefit without a lot of thought for the future. If you can, get out and wonder at the complexity of the natural world that surrounds us- it's usually free and available 24/7.

Recently, I spent almost five hours on a bird survey in the uplands south of Builth Wells. I had almost forgotten about the mist and drizzle when I heard dozens of skylarks singing and several pairs of curlew were calling nearby. Unfortunately, I didn't actually see a single curlew during the whole survey (I blame the mist and the amount of ground I had to cover), but they were clearly well aware of me. What matters is that they were there.

At some stage, on a repeat visit, I have no doubt I will actually see them, hopefully with some youngsters. That is the next big trick, raising the next generation and leaving them something to work with. I just hope that we can manage not to make an absolute mess of that one.

Milltir Sgwâr

September 1998
Ysgubor y Coed

IN THIS, the northernmost parish of rural Ceredigion, we are fortunate to have such a wealth of wildlife surviving. But, along with every other parish in this somewhat overpopulated isle, we have undoubtedly seen a net loss in species over the past few decades.

Red squirrels were last seen in the parish in the late 60s and in compensation, or is it a punishment, we now have the grey, unassailably dominant and at times something of a pest and a nuisance. Several if not all of the fritillary butterflies, that were once quite frequent in many of the gardens, are now extremely scarce and although a few are recorded each year, it seems probable that some such as the silver-washed, dark green, pearl bordered and small pearl bordered are near to becoming locally extinct.

Few, if any, butterflies have increased over the last 25 years, though the comma may be one notable exception and we do seem to be experiencing more frequent occurrences of migrants such as the painted lady and clouded yellow, perhaps as a result of a changing climate and global warming?

The reintroduction of the brimstone at Ynys Hir seems to continue successfully and many gardens are treated to the appearance of this large and spectacular, sulphur-yellow butterfly, early in the year. However the overall impression is that although there may still be a wide range of butterfly species in the parish, the populations of the vast majority are at quite a low ebb. Agricultural changes and intensification combined with a lack of broadleaved woodland and hedgerow management, allied to a series of rather poor summers following on from cold springs may also not be helping. Moths occur in relative abundance with almost 400 macro moths being recorded in recent years, *(Russell Jones, RSPB Ynys Hir)*. Ashworths rustic and the Double-line moth are just two of several notable species that were attracted to light-traps on Foel Fawr, where they were subsequently released.

The parish contains sufficient semi-natural oak woodland to support significant and typical, western oakwood bird communities and the summer influx of pied flycatcher, redstart and wood warbler are major attractions for birdwatchers at the Ynys Hir nature reserve and elsewhere.

Conifer plantations of mainly sitka spruce, dominate large areas and particularly the higher ground. As most were first planted in the 1950s or thereabouts, much is now at the harvesting stage and several large holes are appearing in the canopy. Restocked areas are now quite common in the Einion catchment, as this large area of forest (once the core of Rheidol Forest district) begins to fragment and diversify.

Siskin. goldcrest, coal tit, crossbill, redpoll and goshawk have all increased along with coniferisation and although nightjars have ceased breeding on the bracken covered slopes of Foel Fawr , they too have benefited from the breaking up of the forest plantations. Large and small clearfelled areas seem well suited to this strange summer visitor and a few pairs are found using forest clearfells in most years.

On the other hand these extensive plantations are implicated in invertebrate and fish declines in some of the streams and rivers. Bird species such as the dipper have also declined as a result of the poorer invertebrate fauna on rivers such as the Afon Einion and Melindwr. The Afon Llyfnant, at the northern boundary of the parish, has a less heavily forested catchment, good invertebrate numbers, numerous trout and breeding dippers.

Although birds can dominate the scene, there is a wide range of other wildlife to be seen and enjoyed. This ranges from scarce, indeed nationally and internationally rare lichens, ferns and mosses to a very wide range of tree species. Mammals are also well represented and although we as yet have no deer, and red squirrel, pine marten and wildcat are absent, we do have most of the rest. Even the occasional grey seal and most rarely a porpoise has been known to come up on the estuary high tides as far as Glandyfi.

Otters have made a remarkable comeback from the pesticide residue induced declines of the mid to later 20th century. Although the animals are rarely seen, their spraint and other signs can be found from the estuary edge up all the major tributaries to the top of the catchments and frequently around many of the reservoirs and pools.

High in the hills beneath Pen Creigiaur Llan (511 metres above sea level) lie Llyn Conach and Llyn Penrhaeadr. Along with Llyn Dwfn and Llyn Plas y Mynydd these reservoirs once supplied various mining enterprises with water and hence power for machinery. Now they are fishing lakes, Llyn Plas y Mynydd being privately owned while the others are managed by the Talybont Angling Association.

Llyn Conach, and occasionally Llyn Dwfn, support a small colony of black-headed gulls and most recently both little grebe and tufted duck have been found breeding. The rush dominated margins around the reservoirs and the connecting streams also have small populations of water vole. Water voles are a cause for concern nationally and appear to have been lost from the lowland ditch systems on the Dyfi floodplain where they were once quite common.

Most of the more interesting ferns, mosses and lichens are found on the shaded south side of streams and rivers such as the Einion and Llyfnant. Both species of filmy fern, (Wilsons and Tunbridge) occur in restricted zones where the air is particularly moist and where they are protected from direct sunlight. Interestingly there is a colony of Parsley fern on the loose boulders of the dam of Llyn Dwfn. There are only about six other sites in the whole of Ceredigion where this attractive, but not nationally rare, fern occurs.

Native brown trout and eels have declined in quantity and in size over recent decades, though small fish in often small numbers may still be found in most of the streams and rivers. Seasonally you might also find bass, flounder, sewin (sea trout), salmon, mullet and other species in the tidal reaches of the Dyfi.

Amongst the scarcer mammals are the brown hare and the hedgehog. Undoubtedly getting quite rare, we do not know if their decline is as a result of increased road casualties, increased predation or perhaps some other cause. The mustelidae are very well represented with badger, otter, stoat, weasel and polecat quite frequently recorded but unfortunately we also have a population of their distant cousins, the American mink - a problem for breeding waterfowl, waders and many other species, and quite likely a major factor in the decline of water voles on the floodplain ditches.

Smaller mammals are equally well represented and distinctly more abundant, to the extent that some species are a recurring problem in many households in the parish.

Field voles and woodmice are the most likely culprits and make up the bulk along with common and pygmy shrews. Bank vole, water shrew and dormouse have a much more restricted distribution, the last two being particularly scarce. Dormice are known to occur on Foel Fawr, within Tyn y Garth forestry plantation, in some of the shrubby gardens of The Garth and around Cymerau Hall, Glandyfi, and also on Ynys Hir reserve.

No cereals have been grown in the parish for many years but we do have old records of harvest mice. These relate to nests found in marshy areas of rank grasses such as remain on parts of the reserve and around the fringes of Ynys Eidiol common.

Bats are small mammals and difficult to ignore on the numerous occasions when they occur in houses and outbuildings. The wide variety of habitats in the parish, including water bodies, general lack of agricultural pesticide spray usage and relatively good numbers of flying-insects (moths), probably accounts for a seemingly healthy bat population. Some rarities have been found, including barbastelle and lesser horseshoe. Larger roosts or congregations of the commoner pipistrelle species and long eared bats are more the norm. The lowland water bodies are particularly favoured by daubentons bat, a specialist feeder over water.

I am well aware that this account of some of the wildlife in the parish is very incomplete and I would refer interested readers to an excellent booklet written by William Condry *Wildlife in our Welsh Parish*. First published in 1993 to commemorate 70 years of Eglwys-Fach Women's Institute, this booklet is full of information and copies are still available.

And I really ought to at least mention the reptiles and amphibians. Slow worms are widespread and I suspect so is the common lizard although it is less frequently noticed. Adders are scarce and more or less restricted to Ynys Hir reserve where the grass snake is quite abundant. Toads and frogs are also very common, along with the palmate newt, and all three can often be found in most garden ponds with frogs and newts using even the smallest pond that might be provided. Most of a very long list of invertebrates have also been ignored but I might perhaps mention the several species of dung beetle. So common on grassy paths, busily burrowing and burying sheep droppings, where would we be without them?

Wherever you go in this parish there is wildlife of interest and often in some abundance. Although over the wider countryside this is by no means the norm, there are moves afoot and money is gradually being made available for more environmentally friendly farming and forestry practices. We really must ensure that the wildlife in this parish remains so interesting and abundant into the future. There will always be room for improvement but Ysgubor y Coed could almost serve as an example to which so many less fortunate parishes might aspire.

December 1988
Corvids

THE JACKDAW is one of the most familiar, sometimes amusing, often annoying members of the crow family.

One particular specimen went under the name of Dennis whilst in our hands. Not really a menace, though he/she did get into the habit of picking at shoe laces until undone. Named after his finder, Dennis if you read this - Dennis the jackdaw returned to the wild ok!

Having fallen down a chimney into the hearth he was salvaged and evacuated from cat-town for his own safety. In the country he thrived with us, developing his rudimentary flying skills whilst being fed on scraps, boiled egg, softened dog biscuits and bits of cheese, his favourite.

Eventually he took up with the local gang of jackdaws and for several weeks longer it was possible to entice him down from his pals but eventually the only response would be a loud 'chack'.

Many years ago my brothers had kept magpies as pets for a few months. Such activity is now definitely frowned upon and is in fact illegal but it must be admitted it's a wonderful way to get to know your bird. Raising a bird from injury or mishaps as in Dennis' case is allowed, although birds of prey come into a totally different category, and any possessed for however brief length of time, have to be notified to the proper licensing authority.

Anyway the crow family could prove very useful to the sponsored birdwatcher. Here in Ceredigion, in fact throughout West Wales we are fortunate in having all the British species represented.

Jackdaws are easy, small with grey cheeks and grey iris, often in flocks and always a few about town and village. Rook and carrion crow need to be differentiated, and at a distance can prove difficult.

Look out for the pale grey bill and face of the rook. This can give the impression of an abnormally long/large bill for the bird's size. Occasionally in winter the odd rook frequents the Aberystwyth harbour car park area and for close views of an often ignored species this may be the spot.

Closely viewed you also ought to note the beautiful purplish sheen on the plumage, much more elegant than the duller carrion crow.

The raven of Tower fame is common in Ceredigion, nesting on the sea cliffs, inland rock faces and in woodland. At this time of year they can often be seen flying high overhead or along cliff tops with powerful wingbeats, often audible. Note their overall large size, massive bill and head and wedge shaped tail.

Last and certainly least offensive of the black crows is the chough. Similar in size to the jackdaw but more delicately proportioned with bright red legs and a very distinctive, relatively long, red down-curving bill. Constitution hill or at least the cliff top between Aberystwyth and Clarach are favourite haunts for these masters of the air.

One question often asked of me is do birds play about. Well certainly the crow family has its inquisitive members and some of them undoubtedly do things for the fun of it. How else do you explain the black rag hanging upside down from the telephone wires? On approach the rag dropped, turned into a carrion crow and leisurely flapped off. Watch a flock of jackdaws. They are not just practising evasive action from imaginary predators, they wheel and tumble about for the fun of it. By the way, see if you can pick out the pairs- it's not difficult, most of the crow family pair for life.

Ravens always do victory rolls, perhaps to impress a mate, but more likely for the sheer devil of it.

Two of the crow family missed, but the magpie and jay are surely familiar to all who ever venture out of town and they are so different to their cousins they can be considered separately some other time.

November 1993
Life in the Valley

CWM EINION (Artists Valley) has always attracted visitors, artists of note and amateurs have never had a problem finding scenery to enthuse about.

Mixed deciduous woodland cloaks the riverside as the waters tumble from the more open course above Dolgoch Gorge. Less than a mile downstream from Dolgoch there is the even more spectacular Raven falls- Rhaeadrau cigfran, and of course, by the A487 the much photographed Furnace Mill and Falls.

Recently very significant changes have been taking place around the mid and upper reaches, above Dolgoch. A south facing field almost beside the river has been developed as an organic market garden and almost opposite, on the other side of the river we have a Tirwedd Cymru (Landscape Wales) scheme for Ystrad Einion mine. The valley has not seen so much activity for many a long year.

Ystrad Einion mine had a relatively brief and poor productive life in the 1890's, with very small amounts of lead ore, zinc blende and copper ores being mined. In 1977, when I first came to the area, Ystrad Einion was known to me as the haunt of a pair of kestrels.

They nested regularly in the ruins of the main building, using one of the empty sockets in the wall that once supported some substantial floor timber. Tirwedd Cymru has certainly put a stop to that, although it is no great loss as it is many years now since kestrels last used the building and Forest Enterprise have several, suitable nestboxes situated in the surrounding forest plantations. Dyfed County Council and the Welsh Development Association have combined on this enlightened scheme to landscape and stabilise the buildings, and surrounding site.

The remaining main building, looking not unlike a small castle-keep, stands out rather at the moment with its repointed walls. However, given a few months weathering I am sure it will begin to blend into the landscape again.

Two buddles have been retained and the tailings covered with earth (to be grassed presumably) to reduce any metal pollution from the waste reaching the nearby Afon Einion.

Situated within 100 metres of an already popular picnic site the whole area has the air of a 'honeypot' in the making. If the restored and accessible mine receives any amount of publicity I am sure the picnic site will be a 'hive' of activity during the summer months. It will be interesting to see how Cwm Einion copes with an increase in visitors.

Good for the market garden and good for the tea-room (Tyn y Cwm) but what of the road? At the very least the road will surely need more passing places if there is not to be regular grid-lock at busy times. Most visitors (and many locals) do not like reversing along narrow, unfenced roads with no kerb and a river alongside!

However these problems are not insuperable and I am sure many will appreciate the initiative of Tirwedd Cymru in recognising the site and ensuring its long-term preservation. We will have to wait and see how the people actually living in the valley view any increase in traffic!

December 1993
William (Bill) Condry

HERE I SIT writing another Country Diary column in the same cottage that saw William Condry begin writing his own Country Diaries for the Manchester Guardian in 1957*. It's a coincidence, and I would never claim to be approaching his inimitable quality of writing.

In Condry's book A Welsh Country Diary (Gomer Press, Llandysul) you can catch up on a selection of the best of his Guardian columns, taken from those 36 eventful years. Conveniently divided into monthly chapters, each chapter is illustrated with an atmospheric line drawing by Robert Gibson depicting some scene from the month. The whole book is easily handleable and takes a friendly if at times pointed look at man and his effect on the environment.

The very first diary concerns Rachel Carson's book 'Silent Spring'. This was a warning almost too late, but a warning that, perhaps even now, we should reflect on again, considering the plethora of chemicals we continue to invent and use. Not to mention the banned chemicals we still, immorally, feel free to export to the so-called 'under-developed' countries of the world. 'The Man who loved Curlews' and 'Shepherd of the Hills' are tremendous portraits of character, landscape and a time past - beautiful memories of real people and places which now need never be forgotten.

'The Lady with the Oxford Degree' comes in for some gentle criticism for her comments regarding Mynydd Mawr. There was "nothing of interest there" for a French scholar, perhaps, but to a naturalist, and particularly a botanist, such a wild mountain holds many treasures.

Steep rockfaces, safe from sheep, support globe flower, oak fern, roseroot and starry saxifrage, amongst others. 'A Fox on Gower's Cliffs' takes the reader slightly further afield, and occasionally other diaries take you over the border and even out of the British Isles. These excursions are rare, however, as for the vast majority of his topics William

Condry invariably returns to Wales, the Brecon Beacons, Snowdonia, Anglesey, Pumlumon or some other less well-known corner.

Another absolute gem of a story based on human character is 'A Treasure Refound', just one of 350 treasures to be found in A Welsh Country Diary.

You would need to buy the Guardian (Saturday's issue, usually!) for about seven years to obtain a similar number of contributions by W M Condry (Machynlleth). Here he has drawn together many personal favourites, and for a modest £7.50 you can curl up in a favourite armchair and while away the winter nights in the company of an expert.

This is an ideal Christmas present, and/or a relatively inexpensive treat for oneself!

*Bill & Penny Condry had lived at Felin y Cwm and, through talking to the landlord, later enabled Roy & Vic to rent it.

January 1994
The Beech Tree

NEARBY, BUT HIDDEN in the conifer plantation (on the opposite side of the valley), is a huge beech tree. Hardly a specimen tree but at breast height its circumference of five metres surely makes it one of the largest trees in the area.

At 10 feet above the ground it radiates into four enormous limbs, each one of which would make a substantial tree in its own right, and higher still its enormous grey branches continue to divide and spread ever wider.

In summer it casts a dense shade and little or nothing grows beneath its giant, spreading boughs. A thick carpet of shed leaves covers the ground and together with the shade this effectively prevents any regeneration of shrubs or colonization of ground flora.

In many ways this is a special tree, often an objective of a short walk and because of its hidden situation, almost considered 'our' tree. The common beech is native to the south east of England, parts of the midlands and possibly south Wales.

Here in the north and west it is an introduction although there is some evidence to suggest it may well have arrived here naturally by now had it not been for the general decline in broadleaved woodlands and perhaps some (more recent) overzealous woodland management practices that sees beech as a threat to oak and selectively weeds it out!

Christmas Eve and it had snowed, at least we had a fair sprinkling above the 600 foot contour, enough at any rate for the sledges to be brought out. It was lovely snow which had gently coated the dark conifers and given the brown hills the look of a sponge cake delicately dusted with icing sugar.

An absolutely magical atmosphere pervaded the upper valley, so still and so quiet, no wind or rain and at last we had some snow.

A couple of hours out on the hill, with excited shouts and heart stopping, cresta-run type descents, soon passed by. As the sun sank over Cardigan Bay the conifers looked ever darker but a bright moon put some sparkle back into the snow as the temperature plummeted below freezing again.

Time to retrace one's steps and seek out the milder climate of the lower valley. Without doubt the snow was good, at least for another day's sledging. Hope you all had a Happy Christmas and that everyone has many more magical moments to reflect upon as we head into 1994.

June 1994
Garden and Woods

IN THE AVERAGE garden there is often little space and almost always no welcome for weeds. A notable exception is the organic garden at the Centre for Alternative Technology, which is most a-typical in using weeds to divert and distract slugs and other garden pests from the crops and flowers.

Everyone ought to be able to tolerate some weeds, and here we have a carpet of speedwell to admire before the first mowing of the lawn. We also have a few nettles which I must admit can be a problem, though they do provide a nourishing soup on occasion.

We have no teasel to attract the goldfinch, but we do have dandelions and these on seeding have attracted a pair of very obliging siskins into our garden.

To watch these delightfully small finches stripping the ripe 'clocks' of dandelion was a treat and they were so tame there was no need of binoculars. The male is strikingly green, yellow and black, one of the most handsome of British birds.

Perhaps we ought to remind ourselves more often, just how colourful many of our birds really are? We need not go to the tropics in search of exotica, it is right here on the doorstep. To my mind nothing on the estuary or coast can quite compete with the shelduck. Brilliant white, glossy green/black head, chestnut breastband and a bright red bill.

In the woodland perhaps the jay, brilliantly named ysgrech y coed- scream of the woods- in Welsh, could be described as the most spectacular. Its harsh alarm call is so typical but do you, like me, note how secretive and quiet they become during the breeding season?

Soon we will be seeing (and hearing) family groups of jays when they and other corvids (magpies/crows) may present a major problem for shelduck.

Shelduck nest in rabbit burrows, old badger setts and in crevices, often well away from the estuary or coast. Upon hatching the ducklings then have a perilous journey to complete before reaching the relative safety and rich food supply of tidal waters. Many will not make it, some will fall prey to magpie or jay no doubt.

However, many will survive and I suppose we must accept this as nature's way of ensuring the 'survival of the fittest'!

August 2005
Butterflies and Moths

BUTTERFLIES AND MOTHS belong to a single order of insects, the Lepidoptera, which means 'scale wing'. The minute scales on the wings are flattened and give them their iridescent and distinctive look. Being so beautifully marked and for the most part absolutely harmless, it is little wonder that they are perhaps the most attractive and acceptable group of insects to us humans.

Moths around the bedside light might be a bit of a nuisance, and the caterpillars of the large white butterfly might make a mess of your brassicas, but what a dull summer it would be with no butterflies or moths about.

They are absolutely amazing creatures, so delicate but then so strong as they fly somewhat erratically about the place.

This year has been the poorest of a series of poor years for many species of butterfly. I have seen very few of any species, apart from meadow brown, gatekeeper, small heath, speckled wood and skippers, barely a handful of some species all summer, and some species not at all!

The buddleia (butterfly bush) in our garden seems well recovered from some drastic pruning, but even loads of flowers here have failed to attract anything like the number of butterflies we have become accustomed to expect. I have only seen solitary red admirals, a few green veined and large whites, peacock, small tortoiseshell and the occasional fresh, beautifully marked, copper-coloured and ragged-winged comma.

Many species have been in overall decline for a long time now. Habitat loss is always cited as a major factor and it cannot be denied, we have lost virtually all the flower-rich hay meadows and most of the best hedges and many of the associated banks.

Such places once provided food and shelter for butterflies and moths amongst a whole host of other insect species. Tir Gofal, and other environmentally-based schemes, may put some of the losses right by encouraging hedgerow management and wider, ungrazed field margins. But it will take a few years yet before we begin to see any great effect.

Sheltered banks and grassy verges help a whole range of species, and certainly not just the butterflies and moths. Few woodlands are now managed in anything like a sustainable manner. When did you last see any regular coppicing taking place? There is little or no market now for the produce, and therefore no incentive to manage in that way.

It is difficult to see a market for small round wood emerging, and so we are left with dribs and drabs of woodland glades in the occasional nature reserve. In the not too distant past most woods would have been hives of industry, and very productive, and as such, much too valuable an asset to allow heavy grazing within, grazing that now prevents any re-growth or regeneration.

Many of the fritillaries are woodland glade specialists, and it is no great surprise that the dark green, pearl bordered and small pearl bordered fritillary butterflies have all declined tremendously. Twenty years ago we still had all three of these species using our garden, and probably our buddleia, on quite a regular basis. OK, that's quite a long time ago, and things do change, but in the last 10 years or so l have seen no more than a handful in total, including on my travels around Ceredigion!

It is a sad picture of decline. Habitat loss and a scarcity of larval food plants are only part of the problem faced by these insects. A third major factor has to be the less than predictable weather. It was so cold for such a long period this spring, and between a relieving downpour or two it has been exceptionally dry.

Many butterflies, including the fritillaries, over-winter as caterpillars. A few, such as the sulphur yellow brimstone and the more familiar small tortoiseshell and peacock, hibernate as adult insects, and appear early in the year. Each spring we inevitably have one or two tortoiseshells fluttering at the window, eager to get out of the house on one of the first sunny and warm days and it is always a pleasure to release them.

Unfortunately this year, after a few warm days we then entered that prolonged spell of unseasonably cold weather which I feel sure accounts for a lot of our missing butterflies. Larvae (caterpillars), chrysalis (pupae) and adults, whatever stage they were at, must all have been wondering what was going on. There is no reason why the moths should have fared any better.

Cold, wet and even dry spells, could have equally devastating effects on their numbers, and they are not so easy to monitor.

In mid-July we had a moth trap running for four nights in our garden, and over the period we had a total of 94 moth species identified (not identified by me I might add). If anything moths are more attractive than butterflies, having such a wide range of form and such subtle colouring and complex patterning, with quite a bit of variation in individuals of some species. They also have such fascinating and often descriptive names, such as goldspot, buff arches, white ermine and triple spotted clay amongst many, many others.

One of the commonest and one of the smaller species, that even I could identify, was the rosy footman. I imagine the footman part of the name may be derived from their close relatives the common and scarce footman. These moths appear rather long and narrow when at rest, and the cream and brown of the wings folded over the back does bring to mind those pre-Victorian images of coach footmen and man-servants in long coats. The rosy footman is distinctly pink, holds its wings part spread and is quite unmistakable.

Larger moths such as the drinker (I have no idea where that name comes from) and the buff tip are particularly attractive. At rest the otherwise silvery buff tip looks so like a piece of broken birch twig, it is an amazing piece of camouflage. We also had large numbers of clouded magpie and singles of poplar hawk and lobster moth, the latter being quite the hairiest moth I have ever seen. Possibly most impressive was the garden tiger. One of these turned up on each of three nights of trapping. Anyone who has seen our garden lately will not be surprised we have garden tigers about.

We do all we can to encourage as wide a range of creatures as possible, and this often means letting things go a bit. The vegetation can grow to such an extent that with a bit of imagination we could have real tigers in there!

Garden tigers are large moths, with cream and dark brown on the forewing often covering and hiding the bright red and darkspotted hindwing.

I have not given up on some of the butterflies yet. We have sedums and several varieties of michaelmas daisies, which usually prove attractive to a range of the later-flying butterflies. If not we must look forward to a better season next year, and it could hardly be worse than 2005.

December 2005
Afon Einion

ON ORDNANCE SURVEY Explorer Map OL23, Cadair Idris may be the main attraction but down towards the bottom left hand corner you can find many less well trodden but equally satisfying routes. Here too you will find the Afon Einion, largest of several short-run rivers that flow generally westward through north Ceredigion (Cardiganshire). After rising in the Pumlumon foothills these rivers tumble and fall, quite steeply, a matter of only eight to twelve kilometres before they join the Afon Dyfi in the estuarine, tidal reaches.

Einion was a Welsh prince but the source of the Afon Einion is a rather nondescript mire, hidden deep within a conifer plantation. Here, water oozing out of the peat and into the forestry drainage ditches has barely eight and a half kilometres to travel before it spills into the Dyfi.

Eight and a half kilometres of river that have seen many changes and not a little industrial use, in the past. Less than a century ago, the upper catchment was virtually treeless and large areas of heather were managed as grouse moor by employees of the Gogerddan Estate.

Shortly after the 2nd World war the Forestry Commission purchased a lot of this land quite cheaply and proceeded to plant it with conifers.

No surprise that sitka spruce, was the tree of choice.

At one time I was very familiar with this forested source of the Afon Einion. It often featured as an adventure at the outdoor pursuits/field studies centre where I once worked, following the river down from its source, that is. Passage through thicket sitka spruce and down to civilization could at times be dirty, sometimes quite painful and it was always inevitably wet! City and local children alike, all seemed to love it. Perhaps at times it did get a bit tedious and run-of-the-mill for some of the regular staff but it was always thought to be an achievement to get down the river and out of the forested section without a boot full of icy water. Apart from keeping an eye on the kids it gave us something quite practical to aim for.

There is not a lot of wildlife in thicket spruce and we disturbed relatively little. Certainly these upper, forested reaches of the Einion suffered more as the trees eventually closed canopy and effectively snuffed out what little aquatic life the embryo river might have contained.

Forest policy is now to clear river and streamsides of closely planted conifers wherever practicable. Unfortunately there are so many watercourses (riparian zones) requiring treatment, and so few forest workers able to do the work, that I fear some are going to be waiting a while yet.

Even in its lower reaches the Afon Einion is not overloaded with aquatic, invertebrate life or fish. Several negative effects of large scale afforestation have been identified and having something approaching 6 square kilometres of forested catchment probably does nothing for water quality or flow on the Einion. Conifers are very good at scavenging dry, particulate pollution from the air. This usually arrives and accumulates on the needle leaves during periods of high pressure, when we here in the wetter west experience easterly and dry winds. At the next break in the weather the accumulated pollution will be washed off the trees and through what is already quite an acidic soil. This in turn releases aluminium from the soil and into the watercourses where invertebrates and fish are particularly susceptible to high aluminium levels.

During one torrential downpour, after a particularly dry spell, I watched as the river rose and recorded the pH plummeting. (pH is a measure of acidity, 7.0 being neutral). The pH had fluctuated at around 6.8 for several days during that dry spell. It dropped to a little over 4 (very acid) at the peak of the flood. Not surprisingly, there were dead fish in some of the pools the following morning.

In west Wales the forestry drainage systems are designed to get as much water off the land as quickly as possible, to encourage deeper tree rooting. Hence you can also now get alternating drought/flood conditions on rivers where you would, in the past, have had a much slower and more consistent release of water into the system.

Conifer needle litter also alters the soil chemistry and of course you have the direct effects of shading. Lower light levels, poor and often no plant growth in or on the banks of a watercourse and perhaps more stable but consistently lower water temperatures, all are likely to have a deleterious effect on aquatic organisms, from mayfly larvae to wild brown trout.

That is more than enough of forestry and some of its problems. Having emerged from the forest it is barely a mile downstream to Ystrad Einion mine and the confluence with a major tributary, the Afon Pemprys.

Old mine sites are always interesting, this in its operational time (1880 to 1900) was clearly a considerable venture, although apparently it produced relatively little in the way of lead, zinc and copper ore.

Restoration or more exactly, consolidation of the remaining building was carried out in 1990. Funded by the then Welsh Development Agency and Dyfed County Council the restorers managed to seriously annoy the local archaeologists and mine experts by disturbing and in most cases burying and re-profiling a lot of the more interesting groundworks. Shafts and adits were also barred with substantial metal grills and gates and access to a quite famous, 16 foot diameter, underground water wheel was denied. I have been in there several times and despite considerable dilapidation, it is still very impressive. The local Community Council, many years ago objected to its proposed removal to some West Country mining museum, so here it remains in situ in all its decaying glory, locked deep within a Welsh hillside.

Just below the mine and after the confluence with the Afon Pemprys the Einion enters Dolgoch gorge. The first of several gorge sections as the river flows more forcefully and swiftly now through mainly broadleaved woodland to the Dyfi floodplain. Mosses, liverworts and ferns smother the rocks above high water level in the gorge. A cleft of only some 60 or so metres length, it is nevertheless impressive for its narrowness and the river in such a confined space is a powerful force at all times.

On leaving the gorge the river quietens down considerably and at Pont Tyn y Cwm, where the minor road crosses over, you may even see a few brown trout resting in some of the deeper water.

Sometimes the paucity of trout in Welsh streams and rivers may be traced back to afforestation, sometimes to pollution from the lead mines and mineral workings. Unfortunately it is more often now farm effluent and sheepdips that cause the most serious problems. Here on the Afon Einion it could be a combination of all these causes and their effects.

Certainly we have lost breeding dippers. These very charismatic birds last bred on the Afon Einion 12 years ago and although they successfully raised two young they never attempted a second brood. Few have been seen since and none have attempted breeding. Aquatic invertebrates are their speciality food and they really have no other food source to turn to. If the caddis and other larvae decline or disappear it is almost inevitable that so too will the dippers.

Having handled the occasional dipper for ringing, I would suggest that for its size it is perhaps the most powerful British bird, they really are something of a handful. And perhaps not so surprising when you consider their feeding methods- diving, swimming and walking along the bottom of often fast flowing waters in search of sizeable insect larvae. Bound to build up the muscles!

Dippers come to mind near Tyn y Cwm as two hundred metres downstream the river flows through the dipping pool. Nothing to do with birds, this is sheep associated and west Wales is very sheep orientated.

Often you might find stone built gathering pens where sheep might be corralled beside the river before being driven into the river to wash the fleece. There are no such structures here but it would have been a simple matter to construct some temporary, hurdle type barriers to steer the sheep into the water between some of the large boulders that flank the river here. Several of the farms, from quite a way up the valley, did traditionally bring their sheep down here to make use of the dipping pool.

Now there is ever increasing reliance upon chemicals to prevent and remove parasites from the sheep fleece. But what a problem they often are. There is good evidence that some shepherds and other farm workers have been seriously affected by the neurotoxins in organophosphate based sheep dips. Newer cypermethrin based dips are apparently more user friendly to we humans but their potency on all organisms if they get into watercourses is causing more than a little concern in many quarters and at the moment they are under review. Who would ever choose to be a sheep farmer?

The minor road runs right beside the river here by the dipping pool and as the river runs on, the road takes you slightly away and up through conifers again. Below and hidden from view are the most spectacular waterfalls on the whole length of the river. Craig y Cigfran or Raven Falls are secreted away and best approached from further downstream where there is a public right of way along the north bank of the river, this will take you almost to the foot of the falls. This is where the dippers traditionally and last nested, on the rockface below the second of these twin falls. In flood the falls can be a stupendous sight and extremely noisy as the roar of the river bounces back off high surrounding rock faces and overhangs, where ravens once nested, perhaps before the surrounds became so well wooded as they now are?

The air is always likely to be saturated with mist and spray and it does certainly have an atmosphere! Not easy to find, not many even know of its existence and if you do intend to seek it out, wear boots or wellies as the path is very wet and do beware, it can be slippery.

The sensible access is along the footpath from below Felin y Cwm, a small cottage just above the Afon Einion on the north side. A wide footbridge takes you over the river from the Cwm Einion / Artists Valley road and a stile and smaller footbridge over a stream starts you off back up-river towards the falls. A very indistinct path then leads past a small mill ruin and within a short distance the falls come into view. In spring there is a carpet of wild garlic, just downstream of the falls and look out for the elegant small-leaved limes. Nothing small about these trees, tremendously tall, they are precariously balanced on the richer, riverside soils above a deep pool and beside the garlic.

Downstream of the footbridge below Felin y Cwm the river tumbles over many minor falls and rapids with very little slack water. The Forestry Commission Wales manages much of the south bank but the north bank is RSPB and privately owned.

Much of this north bank is sheep grazed and it is regretful to see that as yet we have no clear strategy to manage or restore these important native woodlands. Sheep grazing allows no natural regeneration of tree species and it also destroys the shrub and most of the field layer communities too. Worse still, with little or no ground cover, steep slopes and a wet climate you inevitably get soil erosion occurring and it is very apparent here on the north side of the Afon Einion. Leaf fall from the mature broadleaves, mainly sessile oak, is virtually all lost as it is blown away on the wind, whereas in the past much of it might have been trapped by a dense shrub and field layer. Little or no leaf litter effectively means little or no recycling of nutrients and a poor micro fauna on the woodland floor. Not a good system, not even for the sheep I would suggest. They are only afforded some meagre shelter and there are very poor pickings from this impoverished forest floor.

Having almost reached the A487, (the main trunk road between Aberystwyth and Machynlleth) the river slows to create a long and deep pool just above Furnace Falls. Together with the water wheel on the mill you have here a real traffic stopper, particularly in the summer holiday season. If I could suggest that any passing motorists use the CADW* car park, just a few metres down the lane across the road from Furnace mill, it will be doing the local residents and the through traffic a favour. Take your time, use the car park and have a good look around this massive and interesting, restored building.

Water to turn the wheel can still be drawn off through a narrow channel from the top of the falls but CADW, for several years now, have locked the wheel as there is no warden or attendant on the site. Nevertheless the wheel that once powered two enormous bellows blasting air into a charcoal furnace for smelting iron (1755 to 1805) is still an impressive sight and it is quite clear from where the village name of Ffwrnais (Furnace) is derived.

Interestingly, just a little way downstream on the south side of the river there is a much smaller and much more recent building. This once housed a turbine that again drew water from the top of the falls. In its time it supplied electricity to most of the houses in the village and before the national grid supply took over. It is no exaggeration to say that many individuals and whole communities in this part of Wales were self-sufficient in electricity, and not so very long ago. Perhaps we are entering another phase when water power will becomes a more practical and economic generator, what with other energy costs rising all the time.

Having passed under the A487 the Afon Einion calms down considerably on its approach to the Dyfi floodplain. Some sections from hereon to the confluence with the Dyfi have been channeled, straightened and otherwise modified. The south bank now forms much of the boundary for the RSPB reserve of Ynys Hir, (long island). Always well worth a visit, the reserve is open throughout the year.

A small group of Scots pine and broadleaves almost at the point of the confluence with the Dyfi marks Domen Las, a motte and bailey fort, and has a heronry in the taller trees. In the evenings an old dead pine also serves as a roost for many of the cormorants that use this part of the estuary. Unfortunately the hide is closed to the public from the end of February until late in the summer as too many visitors at this time would disturb the nesting herons and egrets. Little egrets have only recently begun breeding on the reserve, in 2005 there were at least three pairs of this most elegant of birds nesting here alongside the herons.

Access to all the lower parts of the areas described here are best from the CADW car park near the mill. Otherwise there are several car parking areas along Cwm Einion, up the Artists Valley road. This is a narrow, winding road with a few passing places that might be a problem in summer if you do not like reversing. However, even in the summer, traffic is relatively light since the tearooms at Tyn y Cwm ceased trading. Alternatively you could take the more environmentally friendly and relaxing public transport option. Buses are regular from Aberystwyth and Machynlleth but the nearest railway station is Dyfi Junction, interesting but somewhat isolated and distant, out on the estuary saltmarsh.

*CADW- Welsh Government historic environment service

July 2007
Grey Squirrel

GREY SQUIRRELS seem to be having quite a bad press of late. Some moves are afoot in specific localities to control their numbers in an effort to save the native red squirrel in its few remaining strongholds.

Here in Wales there are few if any strongholds and the red squirrel remains quite a rare species. There can be no doubt that the introduced (north American) grey and the native red do not get on together. Direct competition for food and greater susceptibility to disease in the red has meant that the heavier grey inevitably wins out in the end. Nevertheless, grey squirrels are attractive in some respects and they are perhaps (after rabbits) the most easily recognised and certainly amongst the most conspicuous of our somewhat impoverished mammalian fauna.

During the summer they appeared in almost plague numbers but already I detect something of a decline. The acorn crop this last autumn was minimal and they do seem to rely a lot upon this staple. Given anything like a normal, cold winter I can see grey squirrel numbers plummeting, or is that just wishful thinking?

It will be to little, long term effect I suspect as grey squirrels are very prolific and any survivors may produce up to ten young in two or more litters per year.

Tree rats (they are rodents) with bushy tails is how they are described by most foresters and many woodland owners. Greys have caused untold damage to vast numbers of young plantation trees in the past. They seem to be particularly partial to stripping the bark off young beech trees but will tackle almost any young tree, given half an opportunity.

Back in the 1890s, even the red squirrel was considered something of a pest. Extensive new forests were at that time being planted to replace those previously destroyed for fuel and grazing land. Damage was being caused by a plague of red squirrels and determined control measures had to be used against them. A crash in the population then occurred early in the twentieth century. Possible causes were thought to be epidemic disease allied to the felling of much of the older forest for the 1st World War timber demand.

Red squirrel populations had increased by the 1930s but they were never to approach late 19ᵗʰ century numbers again. Since then, the continuing decline and reduction in range of the red squirrel population has generally reflected a spread and increase in grey squirrels.

During the early part of the 20ᵗʰ century there were widespread and numerous releases of the grey, all with little or no thought to the possible consequences. Now they are virtually everywhere. Cute, but in many respects something of a pest. They can take over at the bird table, eat their way into nestboxes and almost certainly take a toll of eggs and chicks. They also eat all the hazelnuts (before any of them are even ripe) and therefore they must be having at least an indirect effect on our indigenous and endangered dormouse, which is also a hazelnut eater.

I would be quite happy to see a significant decline in the grey squirrel population, perhaps even the eventual extinction of grey squirrels if we could replace some of them with native red squirrels. If it were ever to happen it would be a very long time in the future, but it is perhaps something to look forward to.

September 2013
Wasps

IT IS THAT TIME of year when anyone making jam or pies from this season's bumper crop of fruit might expect some unwelcome visitor to the kitchen table, i.e the common wasp.

Wasps are of the order Hymenoptera, which basically means clear or membrane-winged. There are loads of them, well over 100,000 species worldwide, but here in Wales we might have over 5,000 different Hymenopteran species, of which perhaps 250 are wasps of one sort or another.

Some are solitary, many are parasitic on other insects (think Alien, the movie), and a few are colonial. Amongst the latter and most familiar to many, is the common wasp.

Various bees, including honey and bumble bees, and of course the ants come into the Hymenopteran order as well, though the ants only produce winged males and queens prior to mating flights late in the summer.

All that fruit and activity in the kitchen coincides with a period when worker wasps are on the prowl for some sugary food, so it pays to be aware that when picking blackberries, there may well be a few wasps joining in the feast along with the thrushes and migrant birds such as blackcap, garden warbler and redstart.

Small mammals, and particularly dormice, will also make good use of any blackberry crop as they fatten up for winter hibernation, as will the fox and badger if they can reach them.

Wasps seem to have had a good year with more nests seen, in a variety of locations. You might come across nests in the ground, but most this year seem to have had entrances under slates, giving access to the roof space or have been suspended from the underside of shed roofs or similar.

The queen starts it all off early in the spring when she emerges from hibernation.

A few years ago we were amazed to see our gooseberry bush in flower and smothered in queen wasps. There must have been around a hundred taking nectar from the flowers and thereby doing a great pollinating job when little else (in the insect line) was about.

We usually have a few queens prospecting indoors for nest sites, but we have always managed to keep them out, despite them being very persistent.

This year there is at least one nest in the house wall, one amongst some old coats hanging in the shed and another suspended from a plywood sheet in the wood store. Only the latter has caused some minor inconvenience as I intended filling up that section with firewood, but that can wait until the wasps have finished, which won't be long.

The queen sets about selecting a nest site and builds a hanging paper-mache dome or umbrella shape with a few cells into which she can lay eggs that in a few weeks will produce the first worker wasps (infertile females).

She obviously has to also feed these larvae herself, but after the first workers emerge (four to five weeks) she then has helpers to build further cells, extend the nest and feed subsequent larvae. A very active nest might reach the size of a football by late summer and contain up to two thousand workers.

Don't get alarmed, most nests fail at some earlier stage and those I have seen this year have been nowhere near that size and had nowhere near that number of workers.

During late summer and into September and as the season draws to a close, drone (male) and queen cells are built at the base of the nest.

The queen by this time stops laying in the worker cells and the colony effectively goes into a gradual decline. The new queens and drones emerge and mate, with the new queens moving on to find food and a suitable hibernation site.

The workers and drones are then left with nothing to do but annoy jam makers, fruit growers and others as they see out the season and eventually die. Prior to this, in return for feeding the larvae (usually on chewed-up other insects) the workers are sustained on sugary saliva which they gather from the developing larvae in their cells,

Only the new queens (and relatively few of them) will survive the winter, otherwise we would be plagued with wasps each summer. The queens fix themselves by their jaws to some attachment such as a curtain or perhaps old clothing hanging in the shed, somewhere cool and sheltered.

Here, having folded the wings under the body, they will see out the winter months and hopefully emerge sometime in April or early in May to pollinate our gooseberries and start that new colony.

If you have a wasps nest in or near the house, there is no need to panic, particularly not now, so late in the year. Rarely are they any trouble and they do not use old nests in following years. Having said that, it is not uncommon to find several old nests, (side by side), in favourite locations such as roof spaces.

Anyone hypersensitive to wasp stings is probably well-equipped with suitable medication and, for the rest of us, an antihistamine cream is usually sufficient to quell any irritation a sting might cause.

Enjoy the blackberries if you can, just be a little careful that you don't accidentally give a wasp a squeeze too. Bear with them, they will not be around much longer and they do not sting unprovoked, but it can be a bit of a pain if they do.

November 2013
Local Woodlands

TREES are such prominent features in the landscape, especially so at this time of year. Commonplace and always there, they might sometimes be taken for granted, but they do stand out, even on the dullest, wettest day, demanding to be noticed. And we all know that the vast majority of those colourful leaves will soon have fallen.

Red oak (a North American species), larch and beech have as usual been spectacularly colourful and though none may be native to west Wales they would be sorely missed if they were lost to the landscape. Ash is not such an attractive autumn-colour tree and loses its leaves earlier. Nevertheless the slender, light grey, bare trunks and branches are a welcome contrast to the darker oaks and woodland landscape in general. If ash dieback really does get a grip, the loss of ash, like the previous loss of the elms, will be traumatic. These elegant trees, amongst other things, are home to numerous lichens, some of which just do not prosper on other tree species.

On the south side of the Dyfi Estuary in Cwm Einion, Cwm Cletwr and Cwm Llyfnant, ash trees can be indicators of boundaries in the underlying geology.

They might grow best in the deeper and richer soils near the bottom of slopes and they can even dominate along wet flushes and where the soil is slightly less acid than the average but in these three tributary valleys to the Dyfi there are distinct ash dominated bands that seem to be related to the underlying rock. From vantage points these bands can be seen most clearly in winter due to the lighter bark and branches being exposed.

We also have a problem with larch and phytophthora ramorum. Phytophthoras are fungal-like pathogens responsible for many plant diseases throughout the world and although this particular one has been known in the UK for a good few years it has only relatively recently been recognised as a serious threat to larch. Already large areas of larch have been prematurely felled in the south west, south Wales and elsewhere, including a substantial area at Nant yr Arian in Ceredigion. It remains to be seen whether this may halt its spread but as the spores are obviously airborne, it must be doubtful at best.

It is sometimes quoted that there is now more woodland cover in the UK than at any time in the past 300 years, though we still lag far behind other parts of Europe. In the not too distant past, wood, and charcoal as a by-product, were such important fuels that most of the native woodland in west Wales was felled and the three aforementioned valleys were for long periods virtually bare and devoid of woodland.

There are sketches and paintings (by some famous practitioners) that show Cwm Einion, (Artists Valley) with almost no tree cover. Even allowing for some artistic license for dramatic effect, we can assume there were very few trees present.

Bark for tanning and poles for pit props, timber for ships, barrel making and all manner of other industries have also taken their toll over the past centuries and we have to be grateful to the Forestry Commission and the many private individuals and landowners for re-establishing much woodland cover and getting us back to the state we are now in. The question is, should we be pushing for more?

Much of that tree cover is of course plantation, alien conifer species planted post World War Two and giving rise to various arguments. What cannot be argued is the fact that we continue to consume inordinate amounts of wood and wood products, even in our technological and oil driven age.

The last I heard we were importing well over 80 per cent of timber products consumed in the UK and that ranges from paper to plywood and all manner of products between, some of it very exotic such as the tropical hardwood 'greenheart' that fronts the last defensive wall against the sea at Borth.

How much longer this consumption can continue is debatable but surely we must better look after the trees and woodlands we have and look beyond that to increasing the stock where possible.

That includes managing woods in a sustainable manner by selective felling, coppicing or whatever system is appropriate and it also includes excluding livestock, at least for periods long enough to allow natural regeneration to take place.

Putting up a fence around an existing woodland is often not sufficient. Regeneration will only really take off where the existing canopy is broken, competition is reduced and sufficient light reaches the woodland floor to encourage germination of tree seeds. A combination of measures is often necessary to get a woodland back to anything like good health, and productivity is a part of that equation in the UK.

Last summer I was involved in survey work throughout mid-Wales and in deepest

Montgomeryshire (Sir Drefaldwyn) came across Prosiect Pontbren. The project takes its name from a stream which drains a small catchment of the Afon Hafren (River Severn).

Ten farmers had put their heads together to manage a total of almost 1,000 hectares of land in a more sustainable fashion. Some were fed up with the treadmill of very high stocking rates of less than hardy sheep that had to be brought in ever earlier for lambing and the increasingly heavy inputs of feed and fertilizer and other resources that this entailed.

It is early days yet as the project has barely been up and running ten years. Less than the blink of an eye in landscape transformation terms but I can attest to some vast improvements that are already apparent. Several kilometres of hedge and shelterbelt have been planted as well as more extensive areas of woodland planted around some excavated pools on the poorer land.

The whole project has brought great satisfaction (and a lot of hard work it has to be admitted) for the various landowners. Much of the new fencing around the shelterbelts, existing woodland, watercourses and hedges takes a more sensible line and livestock is thereby excluded from some of the 'more difficult to manage' areas.

Land drainage has been improved and surface run-off is much reduced during downpours, which we all know are getting more severe. Flooding downstream will be reduced and there are obvious benefits to the wildlife in the establishing woodland.

To me, much of the lower hill still looked comparatively bleak but at least this pioneering group of farmers have made a big effort at reversing a trend and they are looking to provide a better future, both for themselves and future generations.

Sometimes it amazes me that we regard wood as just a fuel or a commodity that we can use or abuse at our whim. Occasionally we even burn it for fun, but it is too precious a resource to waste in the profligate and fuel hungry times that we now face. If you ever get the chance, plant a tree (preferably several) and watch it grow, I can assure you it will be a very satisfying experience.

July 2014
Breeding Birds

THE DOLDRUMS are here. For sailors that might be somewhere in the Pacific or Atlantic oceans, but for birdwatchers here in Wales it could also mean we are into July and August. It literally can be the quietest of times as the breeding season for most bird species draws to a close and that dawn chorus diminishes.

In general the season got off to a very good start with most migrants arriving on schedule and in fair numbers. Swallows, house martins and swifts may still be struggling to reach past peaks but other migrants such as the leaf warblers (willow warbler, wood warbler and chiff chaff) seem to have been here in good numbers. At least here in Cwm Einion we have had 10 to 12 wood warbler territories where we usually only have six or seven.

Of the commoner scrub warblers, blackcap and garden warbler have as usual been well represented but the whitethroat seems to me to be on a bit of a downer. The BTO Bird Atlas (2007 to 2011) indicated this quite clearly and in my experience that decline is probably continuing. It could well be related to problems in their winter quarters, south of the Sahara and/or on their migration route but I can say with some assurance that there is an abundance of suitable whitethroat habitat here in Wales, habitat that is under-occupied or not occupied at all. Having said that, we now have a pair or two appearing on Foel Fawr (part of the Ynys Hir reserve) where in the past they have been absent.

How come? Well, the habitat is gradually changing as sheep have been nigh on absent for several years, bramble and trees are taking off and whitethroats like that bit of untidiness, if that is what it is.

Scrubby overgrown roadside verges, entanglements around discarded farm machinery, railway embankments (with nettles and willowherb) and forestry clearfells (after a few years regeneration) are ideal habitats and I expect you may still find whitethroats at such sites but they will probably be in diminished numbers.

Back to a brighter note, redstarts are one of our most striking summer visitors and very good songsters. Arriving from mid-April onwards they have been here in abundance right from the off and they appear to have had a successful breeding season.

Pied flycatchers too seem to have had a good year and we had a pair with young, still in the nestbox, almost into July. Adults and young, once fledged, are very rarely seen again until next spring, so make the most of any pied flys that you might come across.

An equally secretive but no less spectacular bird is the male bullfinch. A year-round resident, the bullfinch has in the past been widely persecuted for its springtime preference for fruit-tree buds. Perhaps as a result of this they tend to be very quiet and elusive in summer and I can't say I have ever heard one singing, though their song is described as quite miserable anyway. They do however have a delightful and distinctively muted contact call which I have been hearing a lot lately.

On one particular site it appeared for a time that there was a bully in every other bush and from that I could only deduce they too have had a good breeding season.

On other survey areas I have been stumbling across numerous skylark and meadow pipit nests, much more than my average but that is more down to the sites allocated this year than any overall increase in the population.

All are in the uplands and it is here that I have also been coming across a lot of whinchat. Another trans-Saharan migrant, the whinchat is undoubtedly in some trouble and has been lost to large areas of the UK over the past few decades. However, I have probably seen more this year than in the past ten years combined, and I even came across a nest, containing six blue eggs dusted with reddish-brown at the larger end. These had hatched and the nest (just about) held six healthy looking chicks near to fledging on a return visit a few weeks later.

Adult and fledgling lapwings are already forming post breeding flocks and it will not be too long before other waders make their way down the coast on passage or to spend the winter with us. And talking of post breeding flocks look out for redstarts, leaf warblers and tree creepers amongst those noisy, combined tit flocks in the woods. They can be a feature of this summer season and possibly all you might expect in the bird line from a walk in the woods.

Here is one for west Wales birdwatchers. Have you ever heard a west Wales tree creeper singing as opposed to the thin, reedy contact calls?

I have, though only very, very rarely. But they do sing quite loudly in other parts of the UK so what is going off here then, in our Land of Song?

May 2015
Life in the Garden

I THINK it is fair to say that spring has been prolonged and somewhat delayed this year. There has been plenty of sun, but often cold nights and some northerly winds have been more than sufficient to cause things to hold back, just a little.

By mid-May, it was still quite chilly and some heavy downpours, whilst being welcome in some respects, again caused temperatures to plummet. Plant growth was suppressed, my runner beans were reluctant to show and even more reluctant to grow. The trees have been slow at coming into leaf and ash has barely got going at all, though by all accounts we should now be in for only a splash.

Has anyone ever seen ash in leaf before oak and then had a soak, I wonder? However, we have seen swathes of spring flowers, they are irrepressible and many have to get on with it before that canopy cover gets too dense.

Blodyn y Gwynt, the wood anemone or windflower has to be amongst quite a few favourites and as usual has put on quite a display.

They might only be in flower for a few short weeks but they are amongst the earliest and most welcome and they do need that spring light.

Many years ago I transplanted a few wood anemone rhizomes, gathered from a nearby plantation where they were surviving but almost none ever flowered. Presumably, the competition from the native oak and birch allied to planted beech trees was just too much?

To cut a short story even shorter, after introducing them into the garden I have kept an annual tally of their flowering. That is, counts of the maximum number of flowers and the date this occurs each spring.

As you can see from the table below both the date and the maximum number of flowers varies a lot, year on year.

Year	Max No	Date
2009	197	7 April
2010	265	16 April
2012	75	29 March
2013	120	19 April
2014	161	2 April
2015	69	11 April

There is a lot more data where that came from, but that is plenty and I might have trouble finding it! What there is does show how important long-term monitoring might be if we are ever to have a true picture of what is going off in the wider environment.

Another notable recent emergence has been the (armadillo-like) larvae of the bloody-nosed beetle. There are some weird and wonderful things in this world and surely this pumped up grub is up there amongst the weirdest of all, though it is only about half an inch long. These beetles have been on the increase for quite some years, so whatever it is the conditions seem to be favouring them.

Butterflies on the other hand, have been scarce, though I have released a couple of small tortoiseshells from within the house where in some dark corner they had been hibernating.

A surprising visitor to the garden has been a hummingbird hawkmoth enjoying the nectar from various flowers on a sunny 16 May. On average, we see perhaps one per year so this was unusually early for us, but they are suspected of breeding in the south west of England and are known to hibernate thereabouts as well, (most hummingbird hawkmoths are later-summer migrants from southern Europe and north Africa).

Their larval food plants are bedstraws and moschatel, a diminutive spring plant and easily overlooked. It has an unusual five-faced flower head and the book says they have also been seen laying eggs on red valerian.

Lots of both can be found in west Wales so perhaps we can look forward to a hummingbird hawkmoth year? It also says that in Italy they are messengers of good tidings!

After the recent General Election, I am looking forward to some of that. Bring on a decent form of proportional representation!

Seasons

March 1995
Tracks in Snow

I HAD COME to accept that this horribly wet weather would merge into spring without any significant snow. March however, came in like a lion and put paid to that idea.

Four inches of snow fell in a little over five or six hours on the 2nd and created a winter wonderland, covering up all that mud, for a day or two at any rate. Marvellous scenes, as with no wind the fall was so gentle that trees, fences and wires were piled high. So much so that many a branch and even a few trees broke under the sheer weight of the stuff.

For a time the snow caused chaos on the roads and it undoubtedly makes the winter more memorable. After all who wants to remember '94/'95 for the rain and wind, now we can recall those amazing snow scenes. And it was also a very unusual event in that there was snow cover right down to sea level. Excellent conditions for tracking and trailing in an attempt to identify what's been out and about.

Surprisingly I couldn't find any fox tracks but I did come across hare tracks quite high on the mountain. In fact two had obviously been travelling at some speed across the bwlch, almost side by side. Each set of y-shaped prints measured almost a metre in length with the stride overall measuring an impressive two metres! I have not seen a hare for almost two years so I was quite pleased to discover that there are still a few about!

I also took the opportunity to call in at an old sett to see if the badgers had been active. Fresh bracken at the entrance and newly dug latrines nearby were sure signs of occupancy. The badger is another shy creature familiar to everyone but seen by relatively few, road casualties apart.

Their normal diet consists of mice, voles, frogs, earthworms and fruit and berries in season. In summer I have seen dried cow pats in the field outside our garden upturned during the night for the worms and larvae to be found underneath, almost certainly the work of badgers or just possibly a fox?

It would appear that badgers in west Wales are doing well, road deaths apart. However there is a continuing threat from the diggers and baiters rumoured to be coming into the area from north and south Wales and from the Midlands. Having all but destroyed their own badger populations, these 'sportsmen' now seek to pursue this despicable activity here in the west.

If you see lights at night near a known sett, men with terriers, spades and otherwise acting suspiciously near a sett, then inform the police. The law now protects badgers and allows for heavy fines and the confiscation of all equipment, including vehicles!

March 2015
Singing Practice

THE DAYS are getting longer, the bulbs are pushing through, snowdrops have been flowering for some time in sheltered spots and even the birds are getting in some singing practice.

Barely a dawn chorus as yet, and a touch of north in the wind can silence what little there is, but there is that feeling of spring being just around the corner.

Great tits are amongst the loudest of these early birds and although their bell-like tones can hardly be termed song, they do carry for some distance. They are also adept at all manner of other much more subtle calls, such that they can cause some ID problems at times, even to practised birders. It is not that they are liable to mimic other bird species, it is just that they have a wide repertoire and come up with some weird sounds at times.

Starlings are probably the best known of British mimics, but occasionally jays too will try it on, though they are the only member of our crow family that will take on that role. Ravens may have the widest range of vocalisations amongst the other corvids/crows but they are all immediately identifiable as raven.

On the few occasions I have realised I have been fooled by a jay it has always been mimicking a buzzard. Not a surprise in west Wales, but recently in Derbyshire I could point out to my brother that it wasn't a buzzard we were hearing, but a jay. And to confirm, we saw it as well.

Buzzards are spreading inexorably eastwards and are now quite frequent in the East Midlands where I never saw a single one in over 30 years before I migrated West. They are progressing ever eastwards with no assistance being required in the way of releases as has been the case with red kite. In contrast buzzards are doing it all by themselves and causing some consternation amongst the pheasant rearing and shooting fraternity.

Although nowhere near true spring, we have also had butterflies emerging from hibernation, one being a rather tattered and battered small tortoiseshell. It was fooled into rousing itself by a bright sunny day and the warmth of the wood-burner in the living room. The butterfly was put out in the shed amongst some hanging material, where with a lot of luck it might survive to emerge on a proper spring day.

Another bird that I have recently heard testing its voice is the song thrush, probably amongst the top three of the British songbird vocalists and certainly in the top 10.

The song thrush is not noted as a mimic but in the not too distant past I have (at several sites) heard bits of curlew amongst its repertoire. Perhaps a strange thing to pick up, but where forest plantations, woodland and overgrown hedges approach moorland, song thrushes clearly can and do, pick up just a few curlew notes. As virtually all the lowland curlew have disappeared, one can only wonder for how long this bit of mimicry might be heard, given that upland curlew are also fast disappearing as a breeding species in Wales.

Another song that will probably not be familiar to many is that of the dipper, which I heard early in January. Sometimes known as the water ouzel, it is a bird most often associated with fast-flowing water and probably doesn't sing all that often. Its song is a little discordant and perhaps not very tuneful compared to the thrushes, but I am always pleased to hear a dipper as it is such a rare experience. No doubt it is doing its best under the trying circumstances of fast flowing, tumbling water and all the background noise that entails.

We can look forward to an ever increasing dawn chorus and it will gradually get ever earlier as well.

Doubtless there will be some respite of a wintry nature, maybe even a long, really cold spell. But if you really want a bit of early morning quiet time and a lie-in without listening to all that racket going on outside, it might be time to find some earplugs.

April 1996
Spring Flowers

THE DAYS HAVE LENGTHENED, Spring is here and the birds certainly know it. We've had sand martins and chiff chaffs about for weeks and soon the swallows should arrive. But to what weather!

March departed roaring like a lion and so it continued over Easter and now well into April, appallingly wet, cold and windy. Surely it must come to an end, and let's hope for a decent summer.

Spring flowers also tell us the season, and more or less on schedule the wood anemone and wood sorrel have reared their dainty heads, defying the weather.

On roadside verges lesser celandine have joined forces with the earliest dandelions and on disturbed ground the beautiful pale yellow flowers of coltsfoot have appeared.

Speedwells and violets represent the blue team and there we just about have it. White, yellow and blue dominate the early wildflower scene. And talking of early, I actually saw a bluebell in full flower on the 30th March which is very early and might be something of a record perhaps?

Fortunately we still have 'bluebell woods' to look forward to each year, a carpet of blue and that wonderful aroma! And talking of aromatics, on a sunny day (yes, we have had one or two) the gorse or furze is one of my favourite plants. With my rather large nose I soon pick up the scent, reminiscent of almonds/coconut and I can never resist a good sniff, despite the spiny leaves.

In the not too distant past gorse was used as feed for livestock, the branches and leaves being crushed and bruised in mangle-like machinery to render it palatable. Now it is looked upon as a weed only good for burning or cutting out, which is something of a pity. It is an attractive shrub, home to linnets and long-tailed tit and a convenient perch for stonechat, whinchat and yellowhammer. The last three are typical birds of heathland or wasteland from which gorse gets its Anglo Saxon name; gorst or waste. We humans now have few uses for gorse; wine or tea may be made from the flowers, otherwise we may prefer just to admire it.

The wine I will give a miss but as a refreshing drink, the tea seems to have possibilities. Two tablespoons-full of freshly picked flowers (wait for a sunny day) in a mug of boiling water and infused for a few minutes. Sweetened with honey and there you have it. Apparently the flowers can also be dried and stored for later use, I will let you know if I find it at all palatable.

February 1994
Ditches and Ponds

VERY FEW of us have never been pond-dipping at some time or other. Whether we were after sticklebacks, newts or perhaps some other more mysterious aquatic life, it has been a pastime enjoyed by many over the years.

Unfortunately ponds have been on the decline for many years now and it is estimated that over 50 per cent of the ponds in Britain have been lost through drainage and infilling over the past 100 years. Others lie so neglected and overgrown that amphibious and aquatic life is seriously threatened. But anyone with more than a postage stamp of a garden can ease the problem by providing a small pond and many farms here in Wales have benefited from schemes to re-establish larger bodies of water as part of farming diversification.

In the garden preformed, moulded-plastic ponds can be difficult to install and unless the 'socket' (to take the shape) is accurately excavated the results may be unsatisfactory. Various grades of plastic liner are available from garden centres and the expert's advice is invaluable when considering a small garden pond. The thicker, black bituminous liners are more 'elastic' and by far the most durable. Well worth the extra expense if you want a pond to last. Excavation is going to be labour intensive but do not skimp on allowing for padding to prevent sharp stones piercing the liner. Sand is advised but a cheaper, readily available and equally effective padding can be had with a thick layer of dampened newspapers (or old carpet) spread over the base and sides of the excavation.

January and early February has been wet and there should be no problem filling the average west Wales pond before the Spring. Be aware, however, of having to top-up with fresh water during any droughts.

Design is important and a range of depths desirable. Have a marshy, shallow end with steps down to the deepest depths, even the smallest pond ought to have over 12 inches depth of water somewhere.

Surround the pond with large, flat stones otherwise it is inevitably going to be muddied and be aware of the attractions of water to children and the inherent safety implications.

Soon our first frogs will be appearing. It is amazing where they come from and how each year they find their way back. They do not hibernate at the bottom, at least I don't think so, so where do they go each winter? High in the forestry plantations I have found them torpid in the peaty mud at the bottom of drainage ditches. There is a whole world of wonder to be found in a pond (or an unspoiled ditch) just waiting to be discovered.

September 2014
Changing Seasons

I HAVE just got hold of the 2013 Ceredigion Bird Report, an annual purchase that keeps me up to date with what the serious birders have been seeing in the county.

Another, very up to date source of information is the Ceredigion Bird Blog, available free for anyone with a computer and internet access.

Just looking through these two sources it is apparent what the advances in technology have allowed in the way of photography. Recent improvements in binoculars and telescopes have been added to with ever more capable digital cameras, digi-scopes and of course the enhancements via computer - all contributing to some impressive photographs.

It is the last report under the editorship of John A Davies, but my hope is that it will go on from strength to strength with local input and support and with more and more people enjoying the activity of bird watching. Other regions in Wales have their individual reports and most will have equivalent blogs.

Back to basics, and as the summer really does comes to an end, it is apparent how quiet it is. Towards the end of August there is little or no birdsong, maybe a short, loud burst from a wren or a few barely audible notes of a willow warbler or chiff chaff before they migrate south.

Swallows are hurrying to get their last young in the air and soon the robin will be taking up its autumnal song, then we will know it is time to think about battening down the hatches. I am guessing it was a good breeding season as, although at times it may have been hot and dry, we at least had that drop of rain when required to keep things ticking over.

Ever pondered why some species have multiple broods/breeding attempts while other species seem to restrict their breeding to just the one effort?

For all species it is obvious that timing has to coincide with food being available to feed the young and multi-brood females have to recover condition to lay further clutches of eggs. In the uplands it was a long season for some species, I was stumbling across my first meadow pipit with eggs early in April and my last in early July, they appeared to be doing fine.

Blackbirds in the garden had three broods, using nest number two for both of the last two attempts. Although during some particularly hot/dry weather I helped out with the occasional, wetted peanut butter sandwich, they for the most part did very well without my help or interference.

A very late pair of pied flycatchers still had young in the nestbox in the middle of July, at least three weeks behind schedule, and it showed, in that only three of the six youngsters managed to fledge.

You would have thought there would have been ample food to raise all six, but I do get a distinct impression that there has not been the usual amount of insects about this year- possibly an effect of the very mild and wet winter?

Spotted flycatchers arrive almost a month later than pied flycatchers and surprise, surprise, they are quite likely to have two broods as opposed to the pied flycatchers' one. Spotted flys just seem to hang around that much longer and they really are flycatcher specialists, catching most, if not all their prey on the wing.

Pied flys are much more reliant upon insect larvae, particularly moth caterpillars that appear in abundance earlier in the season. Once the pied flycatchers have fledged (usually from mid June) they disappear; although a few might be seen on migration or caught by bird ringers.

Most of the bigger birds stick to the one breeding attempt, though wood pigeon and stock dove regularly have two or three broods, (but then they only lay two eggs per clutch). Our tawny owls probably laid more and had large young in the box at the bottom of the garden by late June, but we failed to catch sight of any youngsters as they left.

According to the 2013 bird report, kestrels in Ceredigion were confirmed as breeding at only three sites. You would think there was suitable habitat inland and the cliffs/rough grassland were good nesting sites and feeding areas on the coast, but there has been a steady decline in this species over recent years and no one seems to know why. At least 50 suitable nestboxes have been put up throughout the county by volunteers of the South and West Wales Naturalist Trust and it will be interesting to see if it is a lack of nest sites that is holding them back. Maybe too many barns have been converted and renovated, or too many old trees with holes have been lost? They do like ruins, whether built or grown.

If not kestrels then I am sure stock doves and owls will use some of the boxes and the results should make for some interesting reading in future bird reports.

August 1992
Rain, Hail & High Winds

AS WE APPROACHED a typically wet end to the 'summer', I could not help but feel we had seen this all before. What a wash-out the last bank holiday proved to be. Rain, hail and high winds really put a damper on any late-season holidays with over 70 millimetres (almost three inches) of rain during the last week of August making it the wettest for many years.

The overpowering greenery of late June, July and August I can't wait to be rid of. I look forward to the subtle colour changes that indicate autumn is at hand. And although it may have been wet, bright spells and favourable winds have brought in the clouded yellow and painted lady butterflies.

We also have a fantastic crop of rowan berries, the trees aflame with colour in the bright bursts of sunshine between the showers. Blackberries too have been the best for several years, though the recent downpours may have put paid to the main crop.

The birds are well aware that summer is on the way out. Last, late broods of swallows and house martins should now be out of the nest and it will not be long before they depart on their migration south. The robin long ago changed to its melancholy autumnal song, which absolutely typifies the time of year.

On the beach and estuary things are in full flow. Along the west coast the return migration of waders from northern Europe and Scandinavia is often more interesting than the spring migration. Numbers are obviously swelled by this year's offspring and there is also more chance of a rarity, perhaps a north American vagrant, blown off course by the gales. On the estuary and saltmarsh, greenshank are amongst the noisiest of waders. Pale grey/green with a distinctive white rump and a very loud, piercing call which I will not attempt to describe further. Long, light green legs and a long, slightly upturned bill are also features to look for.

Sanderling are more likely to be seen on the beach and I recently watched a flock of 20, feverishly working the tide-line. Like clockwork toys, almost robotic, they scurry along the tide's edge picking up sandhoppers and other small crustaceans. In amongst flocks of small waders there is always the possibility of a curlew sandpiper or even a little stint. It can be a tedious exercise trying to differentiate between, what at first glance, appear to be very similar species. However if you feel inclined to ignore them, then enjoy the sight and the sound of the surf and watch those autumnal colours, keeping your fingers crossed for a September to rival last year's.

October 1989
Signs of a Hard Winter?

1989 COULD GO DOWN as a year of drought although in Ceredigion it appears well and truly broken now. Alternatively it may be remembered for the abundance of wild fruits. Never can there have been a better crop of rowan berries.

Bright scarlet clusters of berries weighing down the slender branches are now the most striking feature of any walk in the countryside. A few birds are already sampling the rowan fruits and here in north Ceredigion we have a family of chaffinches regularly feeding in the laden rowan outside our front window. They tear off soft flesh from the berries whereas the woodpigeon and thrushes will eat the berries whole.

Blackberries too have been in abundance and many migrants such as the whitethroat, blackcap and garden warbler will have been fattening up on these sweet fruits prior to their return migration to Africa this autumn.

Hazel nuts in abundance have fallen prey to a super abundance of grey squirrels. Given another mild winter it is frightening to think of the possible grey squirrel population by 1990.

Beech mast has been cast down by the squirrels and hereabouts is ground by passing cars into a nourishing mush, the nut fragments attracting chaffinches again. Come the winter the crop of mast may even have been sufficient to attract the occasional brambling which is a rare addition to the large chaffinch flocks in winter. Typically they are found foraging beneath beech trees- look out for the distinctive white upper-tail or rump on the brambling as opposed to the greenish rump of the chaffinch.

Thinking back to the winter of 88/89 when the grass hardly stopped growing, it is somewhat ironic that the grass should have stopped growing when it did, much to the livestock farmer's dismay. At least the lawnmowers have had little use this past summer. I estimate perhaps only 25% of normal usage for the year. Thinking forward for the coming winter, country lore would have it that an abundance of fruits and nuts presages a hard winter. Common sense would indicate a good season of flowering which it undoubtedly was.

However, I have a feeling that this time perhaps country lore will be proved correct. Be prepared always has to be the best policy.

December 1994
A Brief Glimpse of the Sun

SURELY it can only get better, brief glimpses of a wintry sun hardly compensate for more gales, more rain and dull, overcast days.

Well, I have 10 years of weather records to look back upon and as far as December is concerned, I would say 1993 was fairly average, at least up until the 20th.

About 150mm of rain (six inches to you and me) and a lowest, ground temperature of 5-6°C. In '85 and '86 we had over 200mm of rainfall over the month (260mm in 1986). But in 1991, only 56mm, all falling in the second half of the month. Conversely, 190mm fell in 1992, all in the first half of the month! Absolute inconsistency, no wonder the weatherman sometimes gets it wrong, there is certainly no pattern, year on year! November too was fairly average, at least regarding rainfall. 130mm compares favourably with 202mm in 1992 but might seem a little wet when compared to 80mm in 1987 and 90mm in '88.

Temperature-wise, November was certainly cold and the 10.5°C recorded towards the end of the month most unusual. I have to go right back to 1983 to find a comparable cold spell for November.

Unpleasant as they may seem to us, these wet, windy days pose few problems to most birds. Birds of prey might not like the rain, but the buzzard and kite will join in the feast of worms and invertebrates attracting gulls and corvids to flooded fields.

Smaller birds have been coping quite well and recently siskins (small, green and black finches) have been very noticeable around us.

Small flocks (of up to about 20 birds) give away their presence by incessant calling and they are a delight to watch, they seem relatively unafraid of humans. Almost as incomprehensible as the weather! As agile as titmice they hang like Christmas decorations from the slenderest twigs, feeding on birch catkins and helping spread the seed- does it need any help in these high winds?

Over the years, both siskins and redpolls have been popular with cage-bird fanciers and it is easy to see why - robust, easy to feed, breed well in captivity and attractively coloured/marked. It is now illegal to trap wild birds and the old practices of liming branches and netting are hopefully a thing of the past.

Fanciers can now exchange close-ringed (ie captive bred) birds only. Siskin and red poll can roam free and the outlook looks bright for both species as they both prefer conifer forest. In my experience red polls will use spruce plantations from eight to 20 years of age for preference, siskins undoubtedly prefer older conifers, the older the better.

Let's hope the outlook for 1994 is brighter, weatherwise too!

Have a Happy New Year.

January 2017
Stop The World
(Roy's last article written shortly before his death)

"STOP the world I want to get off". I don't know who said it or where it originated but it is something I think about more and more as I get older. Possibly because my brain 'cell' is having trouble coping with the speed of change and the overload of inputs it now has to cope with.

The original Industrial Revolution was almost certainly unsettling, but the information technology revolution and allied industries seems to have come upon us with something of a rush, and it's not over yet by any means. Despite all, we seem to be increasingly Time Poor, despite all the labour saving gadgets and gizmos - perhaps therein lies the problem? Now some laborious and time consuming chores have gone, too much time can be spent busying ourselves earning the money to buy all that stuff that is supposed to save us time.

Well, I am afraid it can't be done, you can't get off, the world that is. Each and every one of us is stuck here. We are all part of the problem and hopefully we can be part of the solution.

Just occasionally I have mused about doing a Tony Hancock and becoming a 'Wild Man of the Woods'. It wouldn't work, as it didn't work for Hancock in that classic comedy sketch of Galton and Simpson. His first attempt at dispensing with society failed quickly and his second more successful attempt was ultimately brought to grief by everyone jumping on the bandwagon and the woods literally disappearing under pubs, shopping precincts and new 'cave developments'. Written in the early to mid fifties it is still extremely funny and occasionally (when I come across my old BBC tape), I listen to it again. Though dated a little, they are still classic performances, quite a relevant subject then and even more so now.

Well, I came to the conclusion that if I took to a cave-dwelling existence or to the woods I might survive a day or two and that would be all. Anyone thinking of getting off the world as we know it to try living such a life is probably in for quite a rough time, unless they have some fallback or 'very cunning plan'. And we all know what happens to Baldrick and his plans.

I liken it to when I was a kid, in short trousers, (probably). The recreation facility or playground always had a rather low roundabout with sections separated by stout iron piping or bars. We called it 'the crown' as that is what in some respects it resembled. Now you could get this rotating at quite a high speed and if the big lads were about and you were on it, the only safe sanctuary was near the centre. Anywhere near the outer edge and centrifugal forces took effect and you could quite easily fly off. As you got older and bolder it was possible to get on and off even at high speed, but there was always a risk you would come a cropper.

That is what is so desperately problematic about our world as it is. If you do want to change anything, or live a different lifestyle, then you have to be prepared to come a cropper.

Competition in world markets and the growth in money supply and consumerism have us all in the western, or First World, within its grip. I don't know how it will all end, but I do know that resources on this world are finite. Even if we do somehow solve the energy crisis there are other consumables that we are using up at an unsustainable, irreplaceable rate.

It has been an amazing journey and some of the great changes have been since the last World War. Some nations may have been left behind, others have been exploited and continue to struggle, but the drive for growth is on in all corners of the world.

Develop and grow or slip into decline seems to be the stark choice. But there is one other option, we could, at least technologically, begin to help raise all nations to approaching developed world levels, while cutting back on our own consumption. Will we do it? Who knows? If we don't then the continued destruction and exploitation of the natural world seems inevitable.

After all, we did it. We have cut down all our natural forests, several times over probably, exploited most of the immediately obvious energy sources and polluted earth, air and water in the process, often without much thought or consideration for tomorrow and future generations.

Do we have to let developing countries go through this destructive phase? Or can we short-cut to a more sustainable world through sensible and truly sustainable development?

Teyrnged
Roy Bamford 1949-2017

Cafodd Roy a'i bedwar brawd a chwaer eu magu yn Heanor yn Swydd Derby.

Roedd Roy yn naturiaethwr brwd o oedran ifanc a threuliodd lawer o'i amser yn gwylio adar ac yn chwilio am nythod, pan nad oedd e'n chwarae pel droed, hyd nes ei fod yn dechrau gweithio yn tua 14 oed.

Roedd pel-droed, fel cerddoriaeth, yn ddihangfa i Roy, a chwaraeodd ym mhob man aeth, cyn i anaf ei orfodi i droi i fod yn ganolwr. Hyfforddodd nifer o dimau ieuenctid.

Gadawodd Roy ei swydd fel peiriannydd a ffitiwr i Rolls Royce yng nghanol ei ugeiniau i gymryd llwybr newydd a chafodd ei arwain gan ei angerdd am natur. Symudodd ef i ucheldiroedd anghysbell yr Alban i ymuno i'r Comisiwn Coedwigaeth. Treuliodd flynyddoedd yn gweithio fel warden gwirfoddol yn yr Alban ac yno cwrddodd i'i wraig a'i bartner bywyd dros 40 mlynedd, tra yn gwirfoddoli gyda'r 'Conservation Corps'.

Bu'n gweithio ar warchodfeydd RSPB yn Lloegr, ac yng Nghymru, yn RSPB Ynys Hir fel cynorthwyydd i Bill Condry. Ymgartrefodd Roy a Vic yma yn 1978, a magu dau fab yng Nghwm Einion. Roedd yn caru'r ardal hon, ac ar gweithio yn y warchodfa, cymerodd swydd fel coedwigwr cadwraeth i'r Comisiwn Coedwigaeth, ac wedyn fel hyfforddwr gweithgareddau awyr agored yng nghanolfan Plas Einion. Doedd fawr o ardaloedd anghysbell a gwyllt o Gymru nad oedd yn eu hadnabod.

Ers 1993 roedd wedi gweithio mewn ystod eang o swyddi cadwraeth gan gynnwys ymchwil cornchwiglen am wyth mlynedd, ac arolwg troellwr mawr ar gyfer Gymru cyfan; ymchwiliodd i'r gylfinir am bedair blynedd a bu hefyd yn gwneud gwaith ar ddyfrgwn, llygod y dwr, pathewod, ystlumod, adar glaswelltir ac adar y goedwig a gwyddau ar y Dyfi ac yn Iwerddon. Roedd hefyd yn warden cynorthwyol (assistant?) yng ngwarchodfa Cwm Cletwr. Bu hefyd yn gweithio i Mencap am nifer o flynyddoedd fel gweithiwr cefnogol rhan-amser.

Bydd pawb yn cofio Roy fel dyn tawel a diymhongar, ond roedd hefyd yn cymryd rhan lawn ym mhob agwedd ar fywyd. Sefydlodd a rhedodd clybiau amrywiol gan gynnwys yr Adaregwyr Ifanc a Thenis Bwrdd, ac roedd hefyd yn rhoi llawer iawn o'i amser a'i egni i gefnogi pobl ifanc i chwarae pel-droed yn y cynghrair ieuenctid Mini Minors yn Aberystwyth. Roedd yn ddyn caredig ac anhunanol.

Treuliodd ei ddyddiau olaf yn gwrando ar gerddoriaeth a gwylio'r adar yn yr ardd. Bu farw yng Nghwm Einion, a chafodd gladdedigaeth werdd yn Nyffryn Dyfi a oedd mor bwysig iddo Fe. Mynychwyd yr angladd gan gyd-chwaraewyr pel-droed o'i ieuenctid, gwylwyr adar a naturiaethwyr lleol, a theulu a ffrindiau o bell ac agos.

Y peth olaf a ysgrifennodd oedd i ddweud wrth ei frawd ieuengaf ei fod yn gallu clywed y ji-bincod yn canu.

Translation: Cathryn Lloyd-Williams

Obituary
Roy Bamford 1949-2017

Roy and his four brothers and sister were out and about over the Derbyshire countryside around Heanor, the boys bird spotting and looking for nests, until they started work or apprenticeships around age 14. They lived in a close knit community largely based on coal mining at a time when young people roamed pretty freely. With pockets of rich countryside round about and the mentorship of his older brothers Roy became a keen naturalist from a young age, and a fascination with the natural world underpinned his life from then on.

Much of his youth seemed to be spent playing football, looking for birds and, as he grew older, listening to music and travelling to gigs to see his favourite bands.

Football, like music, was a favoured place of escapism and he played it everywhere he went, before injury stopped him. Then he refereed and coached numerous youth teams instead.

Roy left his job as a machinist, fitter and inspector at Rolls Royce in his mid twenties taking a complete change in direction guided by his passion for nature. This led him to the remote Scottish Highlands to join the Forestry Commission and 'drop out'. From there the importance of the natural environment to his happiness became obvious and after that he volunteered with the Conservation Corps at Inverpolly National Nature Reserve, where he met his wife and life partner of over 40 years.

He worked on reserves in England (RSPB Leighton Moss, Lancashire, RSPB Church Wood, Buckinghamshire, RSPB Snettisham, Norfolk), and in Wales at RSPB Ynys Hir as assistant to Bill Condry who with his wife Penny, inspired and influenced him from then on. Roy and Vic settled here in west Wales in 1978, and raised two sons in Cwm Einion, (Artists Valley).

He loved this area and after working on the reserve he took up a position as a Forestry Commission Conservation ranger then worked in a wide range of roles at Plas Einion field studies centre. There were few wild and remote areas of Wales that he did not know.

Since 1993 he has worked in a wide range of conservation jobs including lapwing research for eight years and a nightjar survey of the whole of Wales; he did curlew research for four years and worked on otter, water voles, dormice, bats, grassland birds and woodland birds and geese on the Dyfi and in Ireland. He did innumerable voluntary bird surveys and was honorary assistant warden at the Wildlife Trust's Cwm Cletwr reserve. He also worked for Mencap for many years as a part-time support worker. He kept learning all the time, latterly gaining a Diploma in conservation through Aberystwyth University and a certificate in field biology from Birbeck College in the early 1980s, adding to his considerable knowledge in the field.

His belief in the rights of nature ran through his whole life and he tried through his work, volunteering and writing (over 300 articles for the Cambrian News since 1984), to communicate those rights and help as best he could. A self-confessed techno-phobe, he saw great value in the old ways that are more sympathetic to the natural world-learning to lay hedges and coppice woodland among many other skills. The broadleaved woodlands often seemed like his natural habitat.

Though a modest and retiring man in many ways, he still believed in fully engaging with life and the wider world, knowing himself to be a part of it, for better or worse. Setting up and running clubs as diverse as the Young Ornithologists and table tennis, he also put a great deal of his time and energy into giving young people the opportunity to play football in the (then) Mini Minors youth league in Aberystwyth, or teaching them about nature. He was a kind and selfless man who gave a huge amount and asked for little in return.

He spent his last days listening to his record collection and watching the birds at the feeder on his windowsill, many of them ringed by him in the garden. He died in Cwm Einion, where he wanted to be, and had a green burial in his beloved Dyfi valley attended by football team mates from his youth, bird watchers and local naturalists, family and friends from far and near.

The last thing he wrote was to tell his youngest brother he could hear the chaffinches singing.

From a poem written by his friend Jim Marshall,
Dyfi Observatory.

Roy

...As the sward thickens across all tide washed water margins.

Bordered by bunded greening hedgerows.

I hear again the hurried, tumbling song of Willow Warblers

I hear the triumphant, bright descending cadences,

The courting calls of my adopted cousins.

Now so remnant few in numbers.

Return perhaps as sad echoes, again to haunt me

Of a different time, when we called them 'Curlews.'

Over flat, greening meadows lined with soft rush,

Dancing to the gentled springtime breeze.

Across the wayward bends of our beloved Dovey river.

For a short span of time,

No sound of gunshots to defile the tranquil peace of this,

Still amazingly myriad life filled and beautiful,

Contrasting hill and high Raven graced rocky crags.

Atop whispering wooded valleys or flat salted land.

Where Snipe and Redshank and even Skylarks still reign!

Or to offend and assail those others,

With senses made sensitive or stewardship otherwise refined.

Here and at this time;

In warming sunshine ever welcomed,

Even through moving curtains of springtime mizzle.

Another alternative sample of a torch bearing human kind.

Of such quiet and yet imposing, dedicated disposition,

Is seen, carefully striding as a crusader, often solitary.

Across flat meadows, sap greening with renewed urgency.

Then in engaging, earnest intent, on bended knees,

Causing male mewing Lapwing,

On black and white warning wings.

In agitated alarm, to stoop and rise again and again.

Describing urgent weaving aerial circles,

Of his hatched offspring in outraged defence.

While below, his despairing female, feigns her broken wing,

Broken limb, decoying dance of death.

To distract and thus draw away this human intruder.

With strong, long rehears'ed and skill practised hands.

Gently; yet so gently, small rings of many colours,

Are slid onto outstretched limbs of hard won hatchlings,

Near feather flight fledged.

In distinctive, sequential recorded order,

For others of similar habits and protective disposition.

From afar to count with protective anxiety.

Observe and in companionly closeness, to cherish.

In hope: Always in hope.

Willing the survival of another threatened species!

At other similar times and elsewhere,

On high, isolated moorland.

Haunted with memories of courting Curlews.

Golden Plover, in glorious rivalry and in colonies!

Red grouse and swathes of purple heather.

Shivering with the frantic labours of visiting bees.

Their universal presence betrayed,

By the comforting drone of so many restless wings.

In their stead, now reigns a penetrating silence.

Now reduced to barren, sun bleached,

Or rain saturated and wind blasted heaths

And the learn'ed discourse of distant Ravens.

Long exhausting hours and extended near futile days,

Illuminate this same kindly, dedicated and single minded man.

A quiet, unsung hero of our era.

On these desperate times. Despairing more.

Hoped for encounters with our disappearing Curlews.

Are made futile and become forlorn,

By force of reducing circumstance.

Close encounters with rare and illusive pairs

Quickly become a shocking, haunting reality.

With the curse of humankind, universally

Writ large across our suffering planet.

That is, for those who posses the wit and perception

To read and recognize it.

For us: Enraged and oft reduced to tears,

When remembered autumn gathered hosts,

In their exultant thousands. Triumphant Curlews,

Would herald every change of tide.

Their unique, powerful musical voices,

Created overtures of the grandest:

Wildest of all wild chorus.

Often deafening and to enthrall us all

Who dedicated their time to witness it.

Now, in our time, only their persistent lament,

Form despairing echoes from a not so distant past.

This quiet, solitary, dedicated man endeavoured,

Over spring time years and much more.

To halt that terrible decline and loss of whole species.

I who watched him from afar and in detail,

Over decades, now by loss made poignant.

There remains

A legacy of haunting memories, but cherished always.

Remembering old companions

With persistent admiration.

I, unfailingly felt humbled by his endeavour.

Privileged always by his companionly presence.

Go well: In rest and peace

To rejoin your beloved Curlews

And Lapwing hosts, who have travelled onward.

All who patiently await to welcome you

Permanently into their midst.

Copyright © Jim Marshall (1941-2021)
Estuarine Recorder and Honorary Warden MWT and CCW
February 2017

An observation:

We: You; Bill Condry and I,

Exalted in the seasonally massed company of Curlews, Lapwing,

Oystercatchers and hundreds of Redshank on the Dovey Estuary.

Alas; Nearly all have gone.

Welsh Birds List

English vernacular name *Latin name* Welsh name

Black Grouse *Lyrurus tetrix britannicus* Grugiar Ddu

Red Grouse *Lagopus lagopus scotica* Grugiar Goch

Red-legged Partridge *Alectoris rufa rufa* Petrisen Goesgoch

Grey Partridge *Perdix perdix perdix* Petrisen

Quail *Coturnix coturnix* Sofliar

Pheasant *Phasianus colchicus colchicus* Ffesant

Pale-bellied Brent Goose *Branta bernicla hrota* Gŵydd Ddu Canada

Dark-bellied Brent Goose *Branta bernicla bernicla* Gŵydd Ddu Fol-dywyll

Black Brant *Branta bernicla nigricans* Gŵydd Ddu Siberia

Red-breasted Goose *Branta ruficollis* Gŵydd Frongoch

Canada Goose *Branta canadensis canadensis* Gŵydd Canada

Barnacle Goose *Branta leucopsis* Gŵydd Wyran

Greylag Goose *Anser anser anser* Gŵydd Lwyd

Taiga Bean Goose *Anser fabalis* Gŵydd Lafur y Taiga

Pink-footed Goose *Anser brachyrhynchus* Gŵydd Droetbinc

Tundra Bean Goose *Anser serrirostris rossicus* Gŵydd Lafur y Twndra

Greenland White-fronted Goose *Anser albifrons flavirostris* Gŵydd Dalcenwen yr Ynys Las

European White-fronted Goose *Anser albifrons albifrons* Gŵydd Dalcenwen Ewrop

Lesser White-fronted Goose *Anser erythropus* Gŵydd Dalcenwen Fechan

Mute Swan *Cygnus olor* Alarch Dof

Bewick's Swan *Cygnus columbianus bewickii* Alarch Bewick

Whooper swan *Cygnus cygnus* Alarch y Gogledd

Egyptian Goose *Alopochen aegyptiaca* Gŵydd yr Aifft

Shelduck *Tadorna tadorna* Hwyaden yr Eithin

Ruddy Shelduck *Tadorna ferruginea* Hwyaden Goch yr Eithin

Mandarin Duck *Aix galericulata* Hwyaden Mandarin

Garganey *Spatula querquedula* Hwyaden Addfain

Blue-winged Teal *Spatula discors* Corhwyaden Asgell-las

Shoveler *Spatula clypeata* Hwyaden Lydanbig

Gadwall *Mareca strepera* Hwyaden Lwyd

Falcated Duck *Mareca falcata* Hwyaden Grymanblu

Wigeon *Mareca penelope* Chwiwell

American Wigeon *Mareca americana* Chwiwell America

Mallard *Anas platyrhynchos* Hwyaden Wyllt

Black Duck *Anas rubripes* Hwyaden Ddu America

Pintail *Anas acuta* Hwyaden Lostfain

Teal *Anas crecca* Corhwyaden

Green-winged Teal *Anas carolinensis* Corhwyaden Asgellwerdd

Red-crested Pochard *Netta rufina* Hwyaden Gribgoch

Pochard *Aythya ferina* Hwyaden Bengoch

Ferruginous Duck *Aythya nyroca* Hwyaden Lygadwen

Ring-necked Duck *Aythya collaris* Hwyaden Dorchog

Tufted Duck *Aythya fuligula* Hwyaden Gopog

Scaup *Aythya marila marila* Hwyaden Benddu

Lesser Scaup *Aythya affinis* Hwyaden Benddu Fechan

King Eider *Somateria spectabilis* Hwyaden Fwythblu'r Gogledd

Eider   *Somateria mollissima mollissima*   Hwyaden Fwythblu

Surf Scoter   *Melanitta perspicillata*   Môr-hwyaden yr Ewyn

Velvet Scoter   *Melanitta fusca*   Môr-hwyaden y Gogledd

Common Scoter   *Melanitta nigra*   Môr-hwyaden Ddu

Black Scoter   *Melanitta americana*   Môr-hwyaden America

Long-tailed Duck   *Clangula hyemalis*   Hwyaden Gynffonhir

Goldeneye   *Bucephala clangula clangula*   Hwyaden Lygad-aur

Smew   *Mergellus albellus*   Lleian Wen

Hooded Merganser   *Lophodytes cucullatus*   Hwayden Gycyllog

Goosander   *Mergus merganser merganser*   Hwyaden Ddanheddog

Red-breasted Merganser   *Mergus serrator*   Hwyaden Frongoch

Ruddy Duck   *Oxyura jamaicensis*   Hwyaden Goch

Common Nighthawk   *Chordeiles minor minor*   Cudylldroellwr

Nightjar   *Caprimulgus europaeus*   Troellwr Mawr

Chimney Swift   *Chaetura pelagica*   Coblyn Simdde

Alpine Swift   *Tachymarptis melba melba*   Gwennol Ddu'r Alpau

Swift   *Apus apus apus*   Gwennol Ddu

Pallid Swift   *Apus pallidus*   Coblyn Gwelw

Little Swift   *Apus affinis*   Gwennol Ddu Fach

Great Bustard   *Otis tarda tarda*   Ceiliog y Waun

Little Bustard   *Tetrax tetrax*   Ceiliog Gwaun Bychan

Great Spotted Cuckoo   *Clamator glandarius*   Cog Frech

Yellow-billed Cuckoo   *Coccyzus americanus*   Cog Bigfelen

Cuckoo   *Cuculus canorus canorus*   Cog

Pallas's Sandgrouse   *Syrrhaptes paradoxus*   Iâr Diffeithwch

Rock Dove/Feral Pigeon   *Columba livia livia*   Colomen y Graig/Colomen Ddof

Stock Dove   *Columba oenas oenas*   Colomen Wyllt

Woodpigeon   *Columba palumbus palumbus*   Ysguthan

Turtle Dove   *Streptopelia turtur turtur*   Turtur

Collared Dove   *Streptopelia decaocto decaocto*   Turtur Dorchog

Water Rail   *Rallus aquaticus aquaticus*   Rhegen Dŵr

Corncrake   *Crex crex*   Rhegen yr Ŷd

Sora   *Zapornia carolina*   Rhegen Sora

Spotted Crake   *Zapornia porzana*   Rhegen Fraith

Moorhen   *Gallinula chloropus chloropus*   Iâr Ddŵr

Coot   *Fulica atra atra*   Cwtiar

Baillon's Crake   *Porzana pusilla intermedia*   Rhegen Baillon

Little Crake   *Porzana parva*   Rhegen Fach

Crane   *Grus grus*   Garan

Little Grebe   *Tachybaptus ruficollis ruficollis*   Gwyach Fach

Pied-billed Grebe   *Podilymbus podiceps*   Gwyach Ylfinfraith

Red-necked Grebe   *Podiceps grisegena grisegena*   Gwyach Yddfgoch

Great Crested Grebe   *Podiceps cristatus cristatus*   Gwyach Fawr Gopog

Slavonian Grebe   *Podiceps auritus auritus*   Gwyach Gorniog

Black-necked Grebe   *Podiceps nigricollis nigricollis*   Gwyach Yddfddu

Stone-curlew   *Burhinus oedicnemus*   Rhedwr y Moelydd

Oystercatcher   *Haematopus ostralegus*   Pioden Fôr

Black-winged Stilt   *Himantopus himantopus*   Hirgoes Adeinddu

Avocet *Recurvirostra avosetta* Cambig

Lapwing *Vanellus vanellus* Cornchwiglen

Sociable Plover *Vanellus gregarius* Cornchwiglen Heidiol

Golden Plover *Pluvialis apricaria apricaria* Cwtiad Aur

Pacific Golden Plover *Pluvialis fulva* Corgwtiad Aur y Môr Tawel

American Golden Plover *Pluvialis dominica* Corgwtiad Aur America

Grey Plover *Pluvialis squatarola squatarola* Cwtiad Llwyd

Ringed Plover *Charadrius hiaticula hiaticula* Cwtiad Torchog

Icelandic Ringed Plover *Charadrius hiaticula psammodromus* Cwtiad Torchog y Twndra

Little Ringed Plover *Charadrius dubius curonicus* Cwtiad Torchog Bach

Killdeer *Charadrius vociferus vociferus* Cwtiad Torchog Mawr

Kentish Plover *Charadrius alexandrines* Cwtiad Caint

Greater Sand Plover *Charadrius leschenaultii* Cwtiad Tywod Mawr

Dotterel *Charadrius morinellus* Hutan y Mynydd

Upland Sandpiper *Bartramia longicauda* Pibydd Cynffonhir

Whimbrel *Numenius phaeopus phaeopus* Coegylfinir

Hudsonian Whimbrel *Numenius hudsonicus* Coegylfinir yr Hudson

Little Whimbrel *Numenius minutus* Coegylfinir Bach

Curlew *Numenius arquata arquata* Gylfinir

Bar-tailed Godwit *Limosa lapponica lapponica* Rhostog Gynffonfraith

Black-tailed Godwit *Limosa limosa limosa* Rhostog Gynffonddu

Icelandic Black-tailed Godwit *Limosa limosa islandica* Rhostog Gynffonddu Gwlad yr Iâ

Turnstone *Arenaria interpres* Cwtiad Traeth

Knot *Calidris canutus islandica* Pibydd yr Aber

Ruff   *Calidris pugnax*   Pibydd Torchog

Broad-billed Sandpiper   *Calidris falcinellus falcinellus*   Pibydd Llydanbig

Sharp-tailed Sandpiper   *Calidris acuminata*   Pibydd Cynffonfain

Stilt Sandpiper   *Calidris himantopus*   Pibydd Hirgoes

Curlew Sandpiper   *Calidris ferruginea*   Pibydd Cambig

Temminck's Stint   *Calidris temminckii*   Pibydd Temminck

Sanderling   *Calidris alba*   Pibydd y Tywod

Northern Dunlin   *Calidris alpina schinzii*   Pibydd Mawn Gogleddol

Southern Dunlin   *Calidris alpina alpina*   Pibydd Mawn

Greenland Dunlin   *Calidris alpina arctica*   Pibydd Mawn yr Ynys Las

Purple Sandpiper   *Calidris maritima*   Pibydd Du

Baird's Sandpiper   *Calidris bairdii*   Pibydd Baird

Little Stint   *Calidris minuta*   Pibydd Bach

Least Sandpiper   *Calidris minutilla*   Pibydd Bychan

White-rumped Sandpiper   *Calidris fuscicollis*   Pibydd Tinwyn

Buff-breasted Sandpiper   *Calidris subruficollis*   Pibydd Bronllwyd

Pectoral Sandpiper   *Calidris melanotos*   Pibydd Cain

Semipalmated Sandpiper   *Calidris pusilla*   Pibydd Llwyd

Long-billed Dowitcher   *Limnodromus scolopaceus*   Gïach Gylfinhir

Woodcock   *Scolopax rusticola*   Cyffylog

Jack Snipe   *Lymnocryptes minimus*   Gïach Bach

Great Snipe   *Gallinago media*   Gïach Cyffredin

Snipe   *Gallinago gallinago gallinago*   Gïach Mawr

Terek Sandpiper   *Xenus cinereus*   Pibydd Lludlwyd

Wilson's Phalarope *Phalaropus tricolor* Llydandroed Wilson

Red-necked Phalarope *Phalaropus lobatus* Llydandroed Gyddfgoch

Grey Phalarope *Phalaropus fulicarius* Llydandroed Llwyd

Common Sandpiper *Actitis hypoleucos* Pibydd Dorlan

Spotted Sandpiper *Actitis macularius* Pibydd Brych

Green Sandpiper *Tringa ochropus* Pibydd Gwyrdd

Grey-tailed Tattler *Tringa brevipes* Pibydd Cynffonlwyd

Lesser Yellowlegs *Tringa flavipes* Melyngoes Bach

Redshank *Tringa totanus totanus* Pibydd Coesgoch

Icelandic Redshank *Tringa totanus robusta* Pibydd Coesgoch Gwlad yr Iâ

Marsh Sandpiper *Tringa stagnatilis* Pibydd Cors

Wood Sandpiper *Tringa glareola* Pibydd Graean

Spotted Redshank *Tringa erythropus* Pibydd Coesgoch Mannog

Greenshank *Tringa nebularia* Pibydd Coeswyrdd

Greater Yellowlegs *Tringa melanoleuca* Melyngoes Mawr

Cream-coloured Courser *Cursorius cursor cursor* Rhedwr Twyni

Collared Pratincole *Glareola pratincola pratincola* Cwtiad-wennol Dorchog

Black-winged Pratincole *Glareola nordmanni* Cwtiad-wennol Adeinddu

Kittiwake *Rissa tridactyla tridactyla* Gwylan Goesddu

Ivory Gull *Pagophila eburnea* Gwylan Ifori

Sabine's Gull *Xema sabini* Gwylan Sabine

Bonaparte's Gull *Chroicocephalus philadelphia* Gwylan Bonaparte

Black-headed Gull *Chroicocephalus ridibundus* Gwylan Benddu

Little Gull *Hydrocoloeus minutus* Gwylan Fechan

Ross's Gull   *Rhodostethia rosea*   Gwylan Ross

Laughing Gull   *Leucophaeus atricilla*   Gwylan Chwerthinog

Franklin's Gull   *Leucophaeus pipixcan*   Gwylan Franklin

Mediterranean Gull   *Ichthyaetus melanocephalus*   Gwylan Môr y Canoldir

Common Gull   *Larus canus canus*   Gwylan Gweunydd

Ring-billed Gull   *Larus delawarensis*   Gwylan Fodrwybig

Great Black-backed Gull   *Larus marinus*   Gwylan Gefnddu Fawr

Glaucous-winged Gull   *Larus glaucescens*   Gwylan Adeinlas

Glaucous Gull   *Larus hyperboreus hyperboreus*   Gwylan y Gogledd

Iceland Gull   *Larus glaucoides glaucoides*   Gwylan yr Arctig

Kumlien's Gull   *Larus glaucoides kumlieni*   Gwylan Kumlien

Thayer's Gull   *Larus glaucoides thayeri*   Gwylan Thayer

Herring Gull   *Larus argentatus argenteus*   Gwylan Penwaig Brydeinig

Scandinavian Herring Gull   *Larus argentatus argentatus*   Gwylan Penwaig Llychlyn

Caspian Gull   *Larus cachinnans*   Gwylan Bontaidd

Yellow-legged Gull   *Larus michahellis michahellis*   Gwylan Goesfelen

Western Lesser Black-backed Gull   *Larus fuscus graellsii*   Gwylan Gefnddu Fach y Gorllewin

Continental Lesser Black-backed Gull   *Larus fuscus intermedius*   Gwylan Gefnddu Fach y Cyfandir

Gull-billed Tern   *Gelochelidon nilotica nilotica*   Môr-wennol Ylfinbraff

Caspian Tern   *Hydroprogne caspia*   Môr-wennol Gawraidd

American Royal Tern   *Thalasseus maximus*   Môr-wennol Fawr America

Lesser Crested Tern   *Thalasseus bengalensis torresii*   Môr-wennol Gribog Fach

Sandwich Tern   *Thalasseus sandvicensis*   Môr-wennol Bigddu

Elegant Tern   *Thalasseus elegans*   Môr-wennol Gain

Little Tern   *Sternula albifrons albifrons*   Môr-wennol Fach

Bridled Tern   *Onychoprion anaethetus*   Môr-wennol Ffrwynog

Sooty Tern   *Onychoprion fuscatus fuscata*   Môr-wennol Fraith

Roseate Tern   *Sterna dougallii dougallii*   Môr-wennol Wridog

Common Tern   *Sterna hirundo hirundo*   Môr-wennol Gyffredin

Arctic Tern   *Sterna paradisaea*   Môr-wennol y Gogledd

Forster's Tern   *Sterna forsteri*   Môr-wennol Forster

Whiskered Tern   *Chlidonias hybrida hybrida*   Corswennol Farfog

White-winged Black Tern   *Chlidonias leucopterus*   Corswennol Adeinwen

Black Tern   *Chlidonias niger niger*   Corswennol Ddu

Great Skua   *Stercorarius skua*   Sgiwen Fawr

Pomarine Skua   *Stercorarius pomarinus*   Sgiwen Frech

Arctic Skua   *Stercorarius parasiticus*   Sgiwen y Gogledd

Long-tailed Skua   *Stercorarius longicaudus longicaudus*   Sgiwen Lostfain

Little Auk   *Alle alle alle*   Carfil Bach

Northern Guillemot *Uria aalge aalge*   Gwylog y Gogledd

Southern Guillemot   *Uria aalge albionis*   Gwylog y De

Razorbill   *Alca torda islandica*   Llurs

Black Guillemot   *Cepphus grylle arcticus*   Gwylog Ddu

Puffin   *Fratercula arctica*   Pâl

Red-throated Diver   *Gavia stellata*   Trochydd Gyddfgoch

Black-throated Diver   *Gavia arctica*   Trochydd Gyddfddu

Pacifc Diver   *Gavia pacifica*   Trochydd y Môr Tawel

Great Northern Diver   *Gavia immer*   Trochydd Mawr

White-billed Diver *Gavia adamsii* Trochydd Pigwyn

Wilson's Petrel *Oceanites oceanicus* Pedryn Drycin Wilson

Black-browed Albatross *Thalassarche melanophris* Albatros Aelddu

Storm Petrel *Hydrobates pelagicus* Pedryn Drycin

Leach's Petrel *Oceanodroma leucorhoa leucorhoa* Pedryn Drycin Leach

Fulmar *Fulmarus glacialis glacialis* Aderyn Drycin y Graig

Cory's Shearwater *Calonectris borealis borealis* Aderyn Drycin Cory

Sooty Shearwater *Ardenna grisea* Aderyn Drycin Du

Great Shearwater *Ardenna gravis* Aderyn Drycin Mawr

Manx Shearwater *Puffinus puffinus* Aderyn Drycin Manaw

Balearic Shearwater *Puffinus mauretanicus* Aderyn Drycin Balearig

Barolo Shearwater *Puffinus baroli* Aderyn Drycin Barolo

Black Stork *Ciconia nigra* Ciconia Du

White Stork *Ciconia ciconia ciconia* Ciconia Gwyn

Gannet *Morus bassanus* Hugan

Atlantic Cormorant *Phalacrocorax carbo carbo* Mulfran yr Iwerydd

Continental Cormorant *Phalacrocorax carbo sinensis* Mulfran y Cyfandir

Shag *Phalacrocorax aristotelis aristotelis* Mulfran Werdd

Glossy Ibis *Plegadis falcinellus* Ibis Du

Spoonbill *Platalea leucorodia leucorodia* Llwybig

Bittern *Botaurus stellaris stellaris* Aderyn y Bwn

American Bittern *Botaurus lentiginosus* Aderyn Bwn America

Little Bittern *Ixobrychus minutus minutus* Aderyn Bwn Lleiaf

Night-heron *Nycticorax nycticorax nycticorax* Crëyr Nos

Green Heron *Butorides virescens* Crëyr Gwyrdd

Squacco Heron *Ardeola ralloides* Crëyr Melyn

Cattle Egret *Bubulcus ibis* Crëyr Gwartheg

Grey Heron *Ardea cinerea cinerea* Crëyr Glas

Purple Heron *Ardea purpurea purpurea* Crëyr Porffor

Great White Egret *Ardea alba alba* Crëyr Mawr Gwyn

Little Egret *Egretta garzetta garzetta* Crëyr Bach

Osprey *Pandion haliaetus haliaetus* Gwalch Pysgod

Honey-buzzard *Pernis apivorus* Boda Mêl

Golden Eagle *Aquila chrysaetos chrysaetos* Eryr Euraid

Sparrowhawk *Accipiter nisus nisus* Gwalch Glas

Goshawk *Accipiter gentilis gentilis* Gwalch Marth [Gwyddwalch]

Marsh Harrier *Circus aeruginosus aeruginosus* Boda'r Gwerni

Hen Harrier *Circus cyaneus* Boda Tinwyn

Pallid Harrier *Circus macrourus* Boda Llwydwyn

Montagu's Harrier *Circus pygargus* Boda Montagu

Red Kite *Milvus milvus milvus* Barcud Coch

Black Kite *Milvus migrans migrans* Barcud Du

White-tailed Eagle *Haliaeetus albicilla* Eryr Môr

Rough-legged Buzzard *Buteo lagopus lagopus* Boda Bacsiog

Buzzard *Buteo buteo buteo* Bwncath

Barn Owl *Tyto alba alba* Tylluan Wen

Scops Owl *Otus scops scops* Tylluan Sgops

Snowy Owl *Bubo scandiacus* Tylluan yr Eira

Tawny Owl   *Strix aluco sylvatica*   Tylluan Frech

Little Owl   *Athene noctua vidalii*   Tylluan Fach

Long-eared Owl   *Asio otus otus*   Tylluan Gorniog

Short-eared Owl   *Asio flammeus flammeus*   Tylluan Glustiog

Hoopoe   *Upupa epops epops*   Copog

Roller   *Coracias garrulus garrulus*   Rholydd

Kingfisher   *Alcedo atthis ispida*   Glas y Dorlan

Bee-eater   *Merops apiaster*   Gwybedog Gwenyn

Wryneck   *Jynx torquilla torquilla*   Pengam

Lesser Spotted Woodpecker   *Dryobates minor comminutus*   Cnocell Fraith Fach

Great Spotted Woodpecker   *Dendrocopos major anglicus*   Cnocell Fraith Fawr

Green Woodpecker   *Picus viridis viridus*   Cnocell Werdd

Kestrel   *Falco tinnunculus tinnunculus*   Cudyll Coch

Red-footed Falcon   *Falco vespertinus*   Cudyll Troedgoch

Merlin   *Falco columbarius aesalon*   Cudyll Bach

Hobby   *Falco subbuteo subbuteo*   Hebog yr Ehedydd

Gyr Falcon   *Falco rusticolus*   Hebog y Gogledd

Peregrine   *Falco peregrinus peregrinus*   Hebog Tramor

Red-backed Shrike   *Lanius collurio*   Cigydd Cefngoch

Turkestan Shrike   *Lanius phoenicuroides*   Cigydd Tyrcestan

Lesser Grey Shrike   *Lanius minor*   Cigydd Glas

Great Grey Shrike   *Lanius excubitor excubitor*   Cigydd Mawr

Woodchat Shrike   *Lanius senator senator*   Cigydd Pengoch

Red-eyed Vireo   *Vireo olivaceus*   Fireo Llygatgoch

Golden Oriole   *Oriolus oriolus*   Euryn

Jay   *Garrulus glandarius rufitergum*   Sgrech y Coed

Magpie   *Pica pica pica*   Pioden

Nutcracker   *Nucifraga caryocatactes macrorhynchos*   Malwr Cnau

Chough   *Pyrrhocorax pyrrhocorax pyrrhocorax*   Brân Goesgoch

Jackdaw   *Coloeus monedula spermologus*   Jac-y-do

Nordic Jackdaw   *Coloeus monedula monedula*   Jac-y-do Llychlyn

Rook   *Corvus frugilegus frugilegus*   Ydfran

Carrion Crow   *Corvus corone corone*   Brân Dyddyn

Hooded Crow   *Corvus cornix*   Brân Lwyd

Raven   *Corvus corax corax*   Cigfran

Waxwing   *Bombycilla garrulus garrulus*   Cynffon Sidan

Cedar Waxwing   *Bombycilla cedrorum*   Cynffon Sidan y Cedrwydd

Continental Coal Tit   *Periparus ater ater*   Titw Penddu y Cyfandir

Coal Tit   *Periparus ater britannicus*   Titw Penddu

Marsh Tit   *Poecile palustris dresseri*   Titw'r Wern

Willow Tit   *Poecile montanus kleinschmidti*   Titw'r Helyg

Blue Tit   *Cyanistes caeruleus obscurus*   Titw Tomos Las

Great Tit   *Parus major newtoni*   Titw Mawr

Penduline Tit   *Remiz pendulinus pendulinus*   Titw Pendil

Bearded Tit   *Panurus biarmicus biarmicus*   Titw Barfog

Woodlark   *Lullula arborea arborea*   Ehedydd Coed

Skylark   *Alauda arvensis arvensis*   Ehedydd

Crested Lark   *Galerida cristata cristatus*   Ehedydd Copog

Shore Lark   *Eremophila alpestris flava*   Ehedydd Traeth

Short-toed Lark   *Calandrella brachydactyla*   Ehedydd Llwyd

Black Lark   *Melanocorypha yeltoniensis*   Ehedydd Du

Sand Martin   *Riparia riparia riparia*   Gwennol y Glennydd

Swallow   *Hirundo rustica rustica*   Gwennol

Crag Martin   *Ptyonoprogne rupestris*   Gwennol y Clogwyn

House Martin   *Delichon urbicum urbicum*   Gwennol y Bondo

Red-rumped Swallow   *Cecropis daurica rufula*   Gwennol Dingoch

Cetti's Warbler   *Cettia cetti cetti*   Telor Cetti

Long-tailed Tit   *Aegithalos caudatus rosaceus*   Titw Cynffonhir

Wood Warbler   *Phylloscopus sibilatrix*   Telor Coed

Western Bonelli's Warbler   *Phylloscopus bonelli*   Telor Bonelli y Gorllewin

Hume's Warbler   *Phylloscopus humei humei*   Telor Hume

Yellow-browed Warbler   *Phylloscopus inornatus*   Telor Aelfelyn

Pallas's Warbler   *Phylloscopus proregulus*   Telor Pallas

Radde's Warbler   *Phylloscopus schwarzi*   Telor Radde

Dusky Warbler   *Phylloscopus fuscatus fuscatus*   Telor Tywyll

Willow Warbler   *Phylloscopus trochilus trochilus*   Telor Helyg

Chiffchaff   *Phylloscopus collybita collybita*   Siff-siaff

Scandinavian Chiffchaff   *Phylloscopus collybita abietinus*   Siff-siaff Llychlyn

Siberian Chiffchaff   *Phylloscopus collybita tristis*   Siff-siaff Siberia

Iberian Chiffchaff   *Phylloscopus ibericus*   Siff-siaff Iberia

Greenish Warbler   *Phylloscopus trochiloides viridanus*   Telor Gwyrdd

Arctic Warbler   *Phylloscopus borealis*   Telor yr Arctig

Great Reed Warbler *Acrocephalus arundinaceus arundinaceus* Telor Cyrs Mawr

Aquatic Warbler *Acrocephalus paludicola* Telor Dŵr

Sedge Warbler *Acrocephalus schoenobaenus* Telor Hesg

Paddyfield Warbler *Acrocephalus agricola* Telor Padi

Blyth's Reed Warbler *Acrocephalus dumetorum* Telor Cyrs Blyth

Reed Warbler *Acrocephalus scirpaceus scirpaceus* Telor Cyrs

Marsh Warbler *Acrocephalus palustris* Telor Gwerni

Booted Warbler *Iduna caligata* Telor Bacsiog

Melodious Warbler *Hippolais polyglotta* Telor Pêr

Icterine Warbler *Hippolais icterina* Telor Aur

Lanceolated Warbler *Locustella lanceolata* Troellwr Bach Rhesog

River Warbler *Locustella fluviatilis* Telor Afon

Savi's Warbler *Locustella luscinioides luscinioides* Telor Savi

Grasshopper Warbler *Locustella naevia naevia* Troellwr Bach

Blackcap *Sylvia atricapilla atricapilla* Telor Penddu

Garden Warbler *Sylvia borin borin* Telor yr Ardd

Barred Warbler *Curruca nisoria nisoria* Telor Rhesog

Lesser Whitethroat *Curruca curruca curruca* Llwydfron Fach

Siberian Lesser Whitethroat *Curruca curruca blythi* Llwydfron Fach Siberia

Western Orphean Warbler *Curruca hortensis* Telor Llygad Arian y Gorllewin

Rüppell's Warbler *Curruca ruppeli* Telor Rüppell

Sardinian Warbler *Curruca melanocephala melanocephala* Telor Sardinia

Eastern Subalpine Warbler *Curruca cantillans* Telor Brongoch y Dwyrain

Western Subalpine Warbler *Curruca iberiae* Telor Brongoch y Gorllewin

Whitethroat *Curruca communis communis* Llwydfron

Marmora's Warbler *Curruca sarda* Telor Marmora

Dartford Warbler *Curruca undata dartfordiensis* Telor Dartford

Firecrest *Regulus ignicapilla ignicapilla* Dryw Penfflamgoch

Goldcrest *Regulus regulus regulus* Dryw Eurben

Wren *Troglodytes troglodytes indigenus* Dryw

Nuthatch *Sitta europaea caesia* Delor Cnau

Treecreeper *Certhia familiaris britannica* Dringwr Bach

Grey Catbird *Dumetella carolinensis* Cathaderyn Llwyd

Rose-coloured Starling *Pastor roseus* Drudwen Wridog

Starling *Sturnus vulgaris vulgaris* Drudwen

Grey-cheeked Thrush *Catharus minimus* Brych Bochlwyd

Swainson's Thrush *Catharus ustulatus* Brych Swainson

Ring Ouzel *Turdus torquatus torquatus* Mwyalchen y Mynydd

Blackbird *Turdus merula merula* Mwyalchen

Eyebrowed Thrush *Turdus obscurus* Brych Aeliog

Black-throated Thrush *Turdus atrogularis* Brych Gyddfddu

Dusky Thrush *Turdus eunomus* Brych Tywyll Asia

Fieldfare *Turdus pilaris* Socan Eira

Redwing *Turdus iliacus iliacus* Coch Dan Adain

Icelandic Redwing *Turdus iliacus coburni* Coch Dan Adain Gwlad yr Iâ

Song Thrush *Turdus philomelos clarkei* Bronfraith

Continental Song Thrush *Turdus philomelos philomelos* Bronfraith y Cyfandir

Mistle Thrush *Turdus viscivorus viscivorus* Brych Coed

American Robin   *Turdus migratorius migratorius*   Robin America

Spotted Flycatcher   *Muscicapa striata striata*   Gwybedog Mannog

Robin   *Erithacus rubecula melophilus*   Robin Goch

Continental Robin   *Erithacus rubecula rubecula*   Robin Goch y Cyfandir

White-spotted Bluethroat   *Luscinia svecica cyanecula*   Bronlas Smotyn Gwyn

Red-spotted Bluethroat   *Luscinia svecica svecica*   Bronlas Smotyn Coch

Thrush Nightingale   *Luscinia luscinia*   Eos Fraith

Nightingale   *Luscinia megarhynchos megarhynchos*   Eos

White-throated Robin   *Irania gutturalis*   Robin Gyddfwyn

Red-flanked Bluetail   *Tarsiger cyanurus cyanurus*   Cynffonlas Ystlysgoch

Red-breasted Flycatcher   *Ficedula parva*   Gwybedog Brongoch

Pied Flycatcher   *Ficedula hypoleuca hypoleuca*   Gwybedog Brith

Collared Flycatcher   *Ficedula albicollis*   Gwybedog Torchog

Black Redstart   *Phoenicurus ochruros gibraltariensis*   Tingoch Du

Redstart   *Phoenicurus phoenicurus phoenicurus*   Tingoch

Moussier's Redstart   *Phoenicurus moussieri*   Tingoch Moussier

Rock Thrush   *Monticola saxatilis*   Brych Craig Cyffredin

Blue Rock Thrush   *Monticola solitarius*   Brych Craig Glas

Whinchat   *Saxicola rubetra*   Crec yr Eithin

Stonechat   *Saxicola rubicola hibernans*   Clochdar y Cerrig

Wheatear   *Oenanthe oenanthe oenanthe*   Tinwen y Garn

Greenland Wheatear   *Oenanthe oenanthe leucorhoa*   Tinwen y Garn yr Ynys Las

Isabelline Wheatear   *Oenanthe isabellina*   Tinwen Felynllwyd

Desert Wheatear   *Oenanthe deserti*   Tinwen y Diffeithwch

Western Black-eared Wheatear *Oenanthe hispanica* Tinwen Glustddu y Gorllewin

Pied Wheatear *Oenanthe pleschanka* Tinwen Fraith

Dipper *Cinclus cinclus* Bronwen y Dŵr

House Sparrow *Passer domesticus domesticus* Aderyn y Tô

Spanish Sparrow *Passer hispaniolensis hispaniolensis* Golfan Sbaen

Tree Sparrow *Passer montanus montanus* Golfan Mynydd

Alpine Accentor *Prunella collaris collaris* Llwyd Mynydd

Dunnock *Prunella modularis occidentalis* Llwyd y Gwrych

Continental Dunnock *Prunella modularis modularis* Llwyd y Gwrych y Cyfandir

Blue-headed Wagtail *Motacilla flava flava* Siglen Benlas

Western Yellow Wagtail (British) *Motacilla flava flavissima* Siglen Felen y Gorllewin (Brydeinig)

Grey-headed Wagtail *Motacilla flava thunbergi* Siglen Benlwyd

Black-headed Wagtail *Motacilla flava feldegg* Siglen Benddu

Eastern Yellow Wagtail *Motacilla tschutschensis* Siglen Felen y Dwyrain

Citrine Wagtail *Motacilla citreola citreola* Siglen Sitraidd

Grey Wagtail *Motacilla cinerea cinerea* Siglen Lwyd

Pied Wagtail *Motacilla alba yarrellii* Siglen Fraith

White Wagtail *Motacilla alba alba* Siglen Wen

Masked Wagtail *Motacilla alba personata* Siglen Fygydog

Richard's Pipit *Anthus richardi* Corhedydd Richard

Blyth's Pipit *Anthus godlewskii* Corhedydd Blyth

Tawny Pipit *Anthus campestris* Corhedydd Melyn

Meadow Pipit *Anthus pratensis* Corhedydd y Waun

Tree Pipit *Anthus trivialis trivialis* Corhedydd y Coed

Olive-backed Pipit *Anthus hodgsoni yunnanennsis* Corhedydd Cefnwyrdd

Pechora Pipit *Anthus gustavi* Corhedydd y Pechora

Red-throated Pipit *Anthus cervinus* Corhedydd Gyddfgoch

Buff-bellied Pipit *Anthus rubescens* Corhedydd Melynllwyd

Water Pipit *Anthus spinoletta spinoletta* Corhedydd y Dŵr

Rock Pipit *Anthus petrosus petrosus* Corhedydd y Graig

Scandinavian Rock Pipit *Anthus petrosus littoralis* Corhedydd y Graig Llychlyn

Chaffinch - British Chaffinch *Fringilla coelebs gengleri* Ji-binc

Chaffinch - Continental Chaffinch *Fringilla coelebs coelebs* Ji-binc y Cyfandir

Brambling *Fringilla montifringilla* Pinc y Mynydd

Hawfinch *Coccothraustes coccothraustes* Gylfinbraff

Bullfinch *Pyrrhula pyrrhula pileata* Coch y Berllan

Northern Bullfinch *Pyrrhula pyrrhula pyrrhula* Coch y Berllan y Gogledd

Common Rosefinch *Carpodacus erythrinus erythrinus* Llinos Goch

Greenfinch *Chloris chloris chloris* Llinos Werdd

Twite *Linaria flavirostris pipilans* Llinos y Mynydd

Linnet *Linaria cannabina* Llinos

Common Redpoll *Acanthis flammea flammea* Llinos Bengoch

Lesser Redpoll *Acanthis cabaret* Llinos Bengoch Fechan

Coue's (Arctic) Redpoll *Acanthis hornemanni exilipes* Llinos Bengoch Coue

Crossbill *Loxia curvirostra curvirostra* Gylfingroes

Two-barred Crossbill *Loxia leucoptera* Gylfingroes Adeinwyn

Goldfinch *Carduelis carduelis britannica* Nico

Serin *Serinus serinus* Llinos Frech

Siskin *Spinus spinus* Pila Gwyrdd

Lapland Bunting *Calcarius lapponicus lapponicus* Bras y Gogledd

Icelandic Snow Bunting *Plectrophenax nivalis insulae* Bras yr Eira Gwlad yr Iâ

Snow Bunting *Plectrophenax nivalis nivalis* Bras yr Eira

Corn Bunting *Emberiza calandra calandra* Bras yr Ŷd

Yellowhammer *Emberiza citrinella caliginosa* Bras Melyn

Pine Bunting *Emberiza leucocephalos leucocepalos* Bras Pinwydd

Rock Bunting *Emberiza cia cia* Bras y Graig

Ortolan Bunting *Emberiza hortulana* Bras Gerddi

Cretzschmar's Bunting *Emberiza caesia* Bras Cretzschmar

Cirl Bunting *Emberiza cirlus* Bras Ffrainc

Little Bunting *Emberiza pusilla* Bras Bychan

Rustic Bunting *Emberiza rustica* Bras Gwledig

Yellow-breasted Bunting *Emberiza aureola aureola* Bras Bronfelyn

Black-headed Bunting *Emberiza melanocephala* Bras Penddu

Reed Bunting *Emberiza schoeniclus schoeniclus* Bras Cyrs

Dark-eyed Junco *Junco hyemalis hyemalis* Jwnco Penddu

White-throated Sparrow *Zonotrichia albicollis* Bras Gyddfwyn

Song Sparrow *Melospiza melodia* Bras Persain

Bobolink *Dolichonyx oryzivorus* Bobolinc

Baltimore Oriole *Icterus galbula galbula* Euryn y Gogledd

Brown-headed Cowbird *Molothrus ater* Aderyn Gwartheg Penfrown

Black-and-white Warbler *Mniotilta varia* Telor Brith

Common Yellowthroat *Geothlypis trichas* Aderyn Gyddf-felyn Cyffredin

Blackburnian Warbler   *Setophaga fusca*   Telor Blackburn

Yellow Warbler   *Setophaga aestiva aestiva*   Telor Melyn

Blackpoll Warbler   *Setophaga striata*   Telor Penddu America

Myrtle Warbler   *Setophaga coronata coronata*   Telor Tinfelyn

Summer Tanager   *Piranga rubra rubra*   Tanagr Haf

Rose-breasted Grosbeak   *Pheucticus ludovicianus*   Tewbig Brongoch

Indigo Bunting   *Passerina cyanea*   Bras Goleulas

Extract from Roy's CV.

Since 1993 I have worked part time self employed in various conservation areas and capacities outside regular seasonal contracts for the RSPB Research /Reserves Ecology departments and the BTO.

I also work part time (mainly during the winter period) as a support worker with Mencap Cymru and Powys Social Services and on occasional contract for Forestry Commission Wales regarding dormice habitat and monitoring.

Self employment has been based around survey contracts (otter, water vole, dormouse, bats, lapwing, lowland wet grassland birds) and reports for various organizations, including NRW, Countryside Council for Wales (CCW), Forestry Commission Wales (FCW), Environment Agency Wales (EAW), Ceredigion County Council, local Wildlife Trusts, Llandre Heritage and Aberystwyth University/Welsh Institute of Rural Studies.

Also practical coppice woodland management and hedge laying.

Lapwing. Contracts with the RSPB have included senior research asst on the lapwing/ predator project (96 to 2003) and in 2004 assisting with the RSPB/ BTO nightjar survey in Wales. The lapwing work involved detailed data collection, vegetation mapping, liason with various landowners, ringing and radio tracking chicks, compilation and preliminary analysis of results and end of season reports. Lapwing monitoring continued at a lower level in 2004, 2005 and 2006 with work for CCW at Cors Caron NNR and other areas in mid Wales.

Curlew. From 2008 to 2011 I was employed in research re the curlew project at Lake Vyrnwy RSPB reserve. A detailed study of the breeding curlew and factors affecting their breeding success. In the bird breeding season I have most recently (2013 – 2015) been working for the BTO re Glastir evaluation (for the Welsh Assembly Government).

Woodland surveys and management. Contracts with Forestry Commission Wales have included upland oakwood surveys and practical woodland management. I am also involved with FCW in dormouse monitoring and habitat management at a local site.

Water voles. For several years now I have also been involved with a considerable amount of water vole survey work. Mainly for EAW over a large part of Ceredigion, including uplands such as Pumlumon and parts of the Elenydd SSSI and also at Llangors Lake in S Wales. Also water vole work/contracts and reports for Ceredigion County Council and for CCW at Cors Caron, annually from (2005 – 2014). Also for CCW, water vole survey and report (2007) at Laugharne/Pendine SSSI in Carmarthenshire. I have also undertaken water vole and otter survey/monitoring at Cors Fochno, again for CCW, (2011/2012).

During 2005, 06 and 2007 I have also spent a considerable time on ornithological, vegetation and mammalian surveys of potential windfarm sites in upland areas in mid Wales.

Bats. In the past few years I have done several condition assessments related to bats and proposed tree work, mainly for FC Wales but also for Llandre Heritage and in 2009 attended a bat related training course over several days.

Voluntary surveys. I have been involved in numerous other surveys in a voluntary capacity, eg Breeding Bird Survey, otters and waterways, wood warbler, chough and regular Wetland Bird counts. And for several years was a member of the Welsh Kite Committee and took part in red kite fieldwork on an annual basis.

1981 to 1993. Field Studies, outdoor pursuits instructor. Plas Einion. Assist in the development and organisation of courses and activities. Leading groups of mainly secondary school pupils on field trips and expeditions in Wales, Scotland and abroad.

Training. Mountain Leadership Certificate, Cert in Field Biology, Field studies and survey methods relevant to Geography and Environmental Science/biology.

1978 to 1981. Conservation Ranger, mid Wales Forest District, (Forestry Commission). Compiled conservation plans for forests in mid and west Wales involved detailed mapwork and botanical surveys. Also studies of breeding bird populations in a variety of forest types. Reports and articles for internal reference and publication in forestry related and other journals, ie Quarterly Journal of Forestry, Nature in Wales.

1974 to 1978. Voluntary and assistant warden on a number of nature reserves in England, Scotland and Wales. British Trust for Conservation Volunteers, RSPB and local wildlife trusts. Organising volunteers, estate work, wildlife monitoring, Common/Breeding Bird Surveys, dealing with visitors, landowners and managers.

Some details of ornithological survey work:

RSPB lapwing/predator project, 1997 to 2004.
Detailed monitoring of lapwing nesting success, chick survival. Predators and predation effects.

RSPB/ BTO nightjar surveys 2004.
Survey for nightjars throughout much of Wales. Detailed assessment and note taken of woodland type and structure and field layer vegetation.

RSPB, chough surveys, coastal and inland.

RSPB, Curlew Recovery Project. Research on factors affecting breeding success, 2008, 2009, 2010, 2011.

RSPB, WEBS – estuary counts of waders and wildfowl.

BTO Glastir Monitoring and Evaluation Programme. Surveys of breeding birds, random Km squares throughout Wales. 2013, 2014, 2015.

Diploma in Managing Land for Nature Conservation.
Special Study/Report - Intrusive Monitoring Methods and Lapwings. Any effects on breeding success?

Countryside Council for Wales.
Low tide counts of estuary waders and wildfowl.

CCW. Lapwing breeding outcomes on a nearby National Nature Reserve. 2004, 2005 and 2006.

CBC/BB Survey re selected species on National Nature Res. 2004 and 2005.

Lowland wet grass land monitoring transects, Cors Caron, 2010, 2011, 2012.

Forestry Commission
Detailed surveys (Common Bird Census) in a wide range of woodland and plantation types. Nestbox studies (before/after introduction of boxes), pole stage V mature crops, afforestation V restock sites of various ages, 1980s. Published papers in Q Journal of Forestry and Nature in Wales. *

Montgomeryshire Wildlife Trust
Baseline bird surveys and habitat mapping of their upland, Glaslyn reserve, HLF funded. 2002, 2003 and 2004. Mainly using Common Bird Census methodology and transect/Breeding Bird Survey techniques when required.

Wildlife Trust S and W Wales
Regular woodland bird monitoring on a nearby nature reserve.

Upland potential windfarm sites, summer and winter ornithological surveys, 2005/2006.

Upland Breeding Bird surveys for BTO at sites in Shropshire and Glos, 2007.

Breeding Bird surveys for Woodland Trust through Countryside Council for Wales, deciduous woodland in north Ceredigion, 2007.

Greylag goose survey, (Birdwatch Ireland) Rep of Ireland/N Ireland, Winter 2008.

BTO 2012 Woodland structure, deer, bird populations.
Bird surveys of various woodland types in the Welsh Marches and Shropshire. CBC visits (4) to each of the plots and also Rapid Vegetation Assessments of individual plots at the breeding season close.

Additional information

I am involved with the local wildlife trusts and relevant conservation committees. Honorary assistant warden of a nearby Wildlife Trust woodland reserve.

Qualified bird ringer, C licence holder for ca 25 yrs.

Contribute to and occasionally co-edit the Ceredigion Bird Report and write a regular environmental column for the local newspaper.

Involved in various surveys including most recently, water vole, otter, dormouse (Licence No OTH:SA:290:2009), chough, WEBS, and frequently use CBC and other standard techniques for woodland and upland bird survey work.

Most recently some core square surveys for the BTO winter thrush survey.

* Papers: Factors affecting the songbird communities of young conifer plantations. 1979-83, Nature In Wales

* Nestboxes in forest plantations in mid Wales, Nature In Wales

Friday, March 8th 1985

Roy Bamford of Felin Y Cwm, Eglwysfach reflects on the tragedy of the

Diminishing hedgerows

Listening to the ever increasing dawn chorus and the first halting attempts of chaffinch and dunnock to add to it, I was led to reflect on the future of some of the many hedges in the locality. Chaffinches and dunnocks are birds that often nest in hedges but the connecting link is really the still commonly-used mane for the dunnock, ie. Hedge Sparrow.

For many centuries hedges have been a familiar feature of lowland rural landscapes and it is only within the last 50 years or so that neglect and more recently willful obstruction of hedges has taken place. Larger farms, larger fields, increased mechanisation and consequently a much reduced labour force have all contributed to the hedges decline. The final nail in the coffin seems likely to be the widespread use of wire fencing as the average farmers first choice of stock barrier. Farming and Wildlife Advisory Groups acknowledge the wildlife and landscape value of hedges but few farmers in the present circumstances can be expected to maintain what often amounts to a vast length of hedge unless there is a direct benefit to the farm's finances.

Hedges can produce the occasional timber tree and quanti-ties of firewood. They also provide some shelter to stock, particularly when planted atop a bank which is typical of many Welsh hedges.

Hedge laying is the traditional method of hedge maintainance, a the consuming business requiring not a little amount of skill. These days speed is everything and the tractor-mounted flail, with one operator, makes short work of the average hedge. Unfortunately, with repeated flail cutting, hedges develop gaps at the base and will be useless as a stock barrier. Hence wire fencing has to be used as reinforcement and the hedge like as not becomes redundant, eventually to fall still further into disrepair.

If it is expensive in time and hence money, why then should we keep hedges?

Hedges are an integral part of the landscape, without them the whole face of the landscape would be altered. No one would claim that the West Wales landscape could ever become as featureless as parts of East Anglia if hedges disappeared, but without doubt it would be a major loss. Hedges and the banks on which many grow are of great importance to many forms of wildlife.

Most people are familiar with the commoner hedgerow shrubs, hawthorn, hazel, rowan, blackthorn (sloe) to name just a few. Their fruits and nuts provide an invaluable food source for many birds and small mammals during the autumn and winter and with the do. If they did there would be even fewer holly berries to use mind it is clear just how important to some species this food supply is.

This influx of northern European invaders redwing, fieldfares and blackbords, occurs each winter and without the berry bearing trees and shrubs found in the typical hedge their visits would be all too brief. Being truly nomadic during the winter months they move to wherever food is available and the weather permits. By mid-January the berries, although a record crop, finally ran out. The fields were frozen hard, no worms were to be had. Many birds had to resort to picking through the roadside leaf litter for scraps of food, others, as many people know, braved human contact at the bird table. Mercifully the thaw set in just in time.

Redwings and fieldfares are now noticeable by their absence having moved on to strip hedges and woodlands elsewhere. These thrushes are just two of the most conspicuous of the many bird species to directly benefit from hedges. Without a substantial number of berry bearing trees and shrubs these attractive birds would not visit in the numbers that they now do. If they did there would be even fewer holly berries to use for Christmas decoration.

In Spring and Summer hedges also provide nest sites, food and shelter for many more bird species, all that they could ask for. Beneath many a hedge, particularly at roadsides and along ditches there grows a wealth of wild flowers and herbs, many of them useful to the knowledgable country person.

With assistance rather than just encouragement I feel sure many more farmers would be inclined to keep their hedges,

not all farmers and not all the hedges by any means, but poss ibly a significant representativ sample. Perhaps some MSC scheme can be devised whereb it would be available to far mers wishing to maintain o improve their hedges. Howeve it is accomplished, hedges ar worth saving, many are muc older than some of our pre served buildings and deser equal respect and attention they are to continue to be pa of the rural scene.

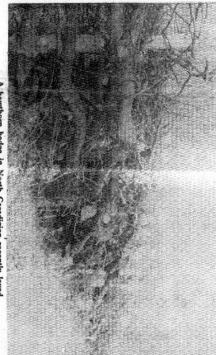

A hawthorn hedge in North Ceredigion recently layed.

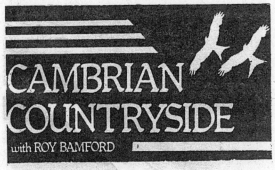

CAMBRIAN COUNTRYSIDE
with ROY BAMFORD

Watch out for a rough winter

1989 could go down as a year of drought although in Ceredigion it appears well and truly broken now.

Alternatively it may be remembered for the abundance of wild fruits.

Never can there have been a better crop of Rowan berries. Bright scarlet clusters of berries weighing down the slender branches are now the most striking feature of any walk in the countryside.

A few birds are already sampling the Rowan fruits and here in N. Ceredigion we have a family of Chaffinches regularly feeding in the laden Rowan outside our front window.

They tear off soft flesh from the berries whereas the Woodpigeon and Thrushes will eat the berries whole.

Blackberries too have been in abundance and many migrants such as the Whitethroat, Blackcap and Garden Warbler will have been fattening up on these sweet fruits prior to their return migration to Africa this Autumn.

Hazel nuts in abundance have fallen prey to a super abundance of Grey Squirrels.

Given another mild winter it is frightening to think of the possible Grey Squirrel population by 1990.

Beech mast has been cast down by the squirrels and hereabouts is ground by passing cars into a nourishing mush, the net fragments attracting Chaffinches again.

Come the winter the crop of mast may even have been sufficient to attract the occasional Brambling which is a rare addition to the large Chaffinch flocks in winter.

Typically they are found foraging beneath Beech trees: look out for the distinctive white upper-tail or rump on the Brambling as opposed to the greenish rump of the Chaffinch.

Thinking back to the winter of 88/89 when the grass hardly stopped growing, it is somewhat ironic that the grass should have stopped growing when it did, much to the livestock farmers' dismay. At least the lawnmowers have had little use this past summer. I estimate perhaps only 25% of normal usage for the year. Thinking forward for the coming winter, country lore would have it that an abundance of fruits and nuts presages a hard winter.

Common sense would indicate a good season at flowering which it undoubtedly was.

However, I have a feeling that this time perhaps country lore will be proved correct. Be prepared always has to be the best policy.

From tiny acorns...voles get many a good feed

OVER THE last few years I have collected and planted (in a small nursery-bed), literally hundreds of acorns. In 1990, over 500 quality acorns failed to produce a single seedling and last year the results were equally disappointing, even though I planted most in pots.

The reason? Voles; once winter sets in they seek out and make a meal of them. If you are thinking of rejuvenating or adding to Ceredigion's woodlands I would suggest you plant in pots *and* out of reach of these ubiquitous little mammals! Another point to bear in mind; from where do you get the seed acorns? I would suggest you pick a tree of 'good form' and most important, a Sessile oak, *Quercus petraea*.

The sessile oak is native to northern and western Britain, it is *the* oak of the Welsh landscape and altogether more able to cope with the rigours of the Welsh climate on poorer quality soils. It can most easily be distinguished from the English (pedunculate) oak, *Quercus robur* by the acorns which form tightly on the twigs. The acorns of the English oak are attached to the twigs by a, more or less, long stalk (peduncle), anything up to 5 cm long.

Felling some *smaller* blocks of conifers and replanting with *native* broadleaves is now being positively encouraged and the long term prospects look good for the landscape and excellent for the wildlife. It is a fact that our native trees support a phenomenal number of insects and the oak is at the centre of an extensive 'food web' helping sustain a wide range of species.

Holm oak, *Quercus ilex* is an unusual 'alien' in that it is evergreen. Its leathery leaves are unlobed and oval. Found only in parks and larger gardens in west Wales, it has been much more widely planted in the drier areas of east Anglia and southern Britain.

Red oak, *Quercus borealis* is a native of north America, planted in reasonable quantity by the Forestry Commission. The

COUNTRY DIARY

ROY BAMFORD

leaf is very distinctive, being *much* larger than either of our native oaks, often reaching 20 cm in length. It gets its common name from the beautiful autumn colours that *can* occur.

Turkey oak, *Quercus cerris* is a rare tree in west Wales. Planted on a few experimental plots, I know it 'survives' in Ystwyth and Rheidol forests.

One of the most inhospitable sites imaginable, for this native of Southern Europe and Asia, is the wide fire-break below Esgair Hir in Rheidol forest, some 400 metres above sea level. Here a 'scrubby' specimen survives, though I very much doubt if it has ever produced an acorn.

However between Bow Street and Clarach there is a small, mixed plantation that does include some Turkey oak. At least, I seem to remember once picking up some of the distinctive, 'scaly' acorn cups here, many years ago.

Squirrels and jays are busy storing their acorns, mice and voles likewise. Me, I'm giving it a break this year, let them get on with it!

Glowing tribute to 'worm'

THE Glow-worm, *Lampyris noctiluca*, is not a worm at all, it is a member of the order *Coleoptera*, - a beetle. The flightless, more strongly luminiferous female is most often seen and about now is the best time to locate them. Rough ground and areas of bracken, grasses or other rank vegetation at the edges of woodland or along roadsides seem to be favourite spots.

Last winter I wrote requesting information as the national Glow-worm Recorder (GWR) as desperate for records from Dyfed and particularly from Ceredigion.

By his reckoning (on past reports), the glow-worm was extinct in Ceredigion, an impression I knew to be false! The glow-worm article generated more correspondence and phone-calls than any other and certainly shed some light on the glow-worm's status within Ceredigion, such that I was able to pass on a considerable amount of information to the GWR.

Country Diary

N. Izon reported sightings from Pontrhydfendigaid over the past five years and earlier records of large numbers of glow-worms beside the track to Faengrach, Devil's Bridge. Another correspondent *from* Devil's Bridge reported seeing several dozen glow-worms in the late sixties along the eastern verge of the roadside. from Bontgoch (Elerch) towards Talybont, above Cefn Gwyn. I wonder if there are more recent records for here? I am also grateful for another up-to-date record from a Mr Wright of Pontrhydygroes who reported up to 20, seen in June/July upon the roadside banks at Grid Ref SN737719, adjacent to the woodland locally known as 'Gelli'. Again in the sixties and seventies, hundreds could be seen (on good nights) amongst the rank grasses beside the old

railway line alongside Cors Caron (Tregaron Bog). Others referred to sightings well into early Autumn, which I take to be September, so there is time yet to see them. A fascinating and worthwhile exercise, thanks for the information, and I trust the GWR has now filled in a few spaces on the glow-worm map, for Ceredigion at least.

If it is past the peak period for sightings bear in mind the early Autumn comment and keep an eye open you insomniacs. Only recently I found them again on Foel Fawr, here in the far north of Ceredigion. Actually, to be honest, It was only one but then I did only cover a 'minute' part of the Foel and where there is one I am positive there are many more! I look forward to a few more warm, balmy nights of glow-worming, hopefully with a little more success.

Roy Bamford

CQ

incorporating Country Quest and Times and Diary

Inside:

Old-time bluegrass at Theatr Mwldan

Trio's artwork on display

Poppies, ox-eye daisy and orange hawkweed

Cowslips alongside the A494 not far from Dolgellau

Nuthatch OCD

So, the nuthatch may be a little obsessive when it comes to its nest, writes ROY BAMFORD, but we humans are just as bad, and our obsession with grass cutting is taking its toll...

IT was several weeks ago, as I was watching a nuthatch busily taking nest material in to a tree hole, that I got to thinking; this is a bird with the avian equivalent of OCD, if ever there was one.

Nuthatches may also appear to be a bit hyperactive when at the bird table, as they attempt to squirrel away as much bird food as quickly as they can.

They stuff sunflower seeds and other large items into cracks and crevices in trees for later, but they take so much I doubt they ever re-find it all.

Their main OCD manifestation, however, comes in the form of a compulsion to plaster up the nest-hole with mud. The actual nest will just be a layer of bark fragments, woodchips and rootlets without any attempt whatsoever to construct a nest cup. The five or six eggs will invariably be buried in this material so be careful if you are lucky enough to have a pair using a nestbox that can be checked. In fact be doubly careful and perhaps leave well alone as a nuthatch will also plaster the inside of the lid with mud, as well as some of the outside and particularly around the entrance hole.

A roadside verge near Machynlleth with lots of lady's smock or cuckoo flower (amongst dandelions and daisies), one of the principal food plants for larvae of the orange tip butterfly, flying now, weather permitting!

Obviously this is something of a deterrent to such as woodpeckers, squirrels and other potential predators, but on a nest box it is rarely necessary or of any practical use as the hole is usually a tight fit for a nuthatch anyway.

This bird, with a slaty blue-grey back and that unique habit of walking head-first down a tree trunk (where does that trick originate?) is less tolerant of disturbance than other nestbox users and the prospect of a lump of dried mud being dislodged while checking a box and falling into the eggs is not a happy thought.

Best leave well alone and observe from a distance if you are fortunate enough to have a few nestboxes to check and notice any mud on the outside! OCD is certainly not uncommon in humans and at its most severe it can be a very debilitating and intrusive trait related to what are usually unwarranted anxieties and perceived threats.

Obsessive, compulsive shopping – quite a few of us must have a mild dose of that. Other more serious manifestations are legion but I suppose excessive cleaning and concerns regarding security and particular numbers come out as some of the most common. Possibly that obsession with air fresheners, especially in cars, ought to be included.

Another widespread manifestation could be our obsession with grass cutting. Already the roundabout near Morrisons in Aberystwyth has had its first cut. Why not let it grow, let us and the insects enjoy a few wild flowers for longer for a change. Is anyone else worried or noticing how few insects there are about? It is supposed to be summer.

Be bold and perhaps sow a wildflower mix that, along with the grass flower-heads, will give a bit of colour and structural variety throughout the season. It will also hide some of that litter, at least for a while, or better still why not educate into not dropping it?

Over the past several years, I have seen some amazingly attractive traffic islands and equally attractive re-profiled verges where wildflower mixes have become well-established.

Recently I had to walk along that part of the busy A494, between Dolgellau and Bala, near where those temporary traffic lights were for so many years. Those lights that I believe once held the record for the length of time that so called 'temporary traffic lights' were in use. Well, the lights have not been there for a good few years and now the verges of the 'new' carriageway have cowslips and primroses in flower and black knapweed amongst many other species this year.

Last year, it was just over the border and into Shropshire where I came across a section of utility-repaired verge awash with the red of field poppy, Papaver rhoeas, ox-eye daisy, orange hawkweed and several vetches amongst the grasses. A stunning example of what some of our verges could look like, although the field poppy has perhaps never been very common over this side, at least not since the demise of cereal crops many moons ago.

West Wales does, however, have its minor roads and by-ways that retain hedges and banks of great floristic diversity. But where we have recent road improvements (Glandyfi, Dolgellau) and verges disturbed for whatever reason, there has to be a case for looking at introducing some variety and colour.

Seeing the season drag itself reluctantly through Spring and into summer, it is quite worrying that there appears to be this dearth of insect life with the birds, including nuthatches, struggling to feed themselves and their young. Things were beginning to pick up towards the end of May but there is still that cold wind and everything is so late and out of sync. At least the oak is out ahead of the ash. Perhaps if the saying is true, we may be in for a splash rather than a soak this year?

While bird surveying up above Dyffryn Ardudwy, overlooking the Llŷn, I came across a few small, flower-rich meadows with a good show of cowslips, loads of violets and many different species of grass, variety in the sward that you very rarely see nowadays.

We owe it to ourselves, not to mention the wider environment, the insects and the plants themselves, to get some considered diversity back wherever we can. Not being too obsessed with tidy, green, tightly mown verges might be a start.

Young Ornithologists Club (YOC)

Dennis p. 211

Moth trap - Felin y Cwm

Lapwings